EARLY AMERICAN PATTERN GLASS

ALICE HULETT METZ

COLLECTOR BOOKS
A Division of Schroeder Publishing Co., Inc.

Front cover: Covered compote Log Cabin, $400.00. Glass provided by Steven Skeim.

Cover design by Beth Summers
Book design by Mary Ann Hudson

Searching For A Publisher?

We are always looking for knowledgeable people considered to be experts within their fields. If you feel that there is a real need for a book on your collectible subject and have a large comprehensive collection, contact Collector Books.

COLLECTOR BOOKS
P.O. Box 3009
Paducah, Kentucky 42002-3009

Copyright© 2000 by Judith Cronin

FOREWORD

The Early American Pattern Glass Society has contributed to this revision of *Early American Pattern Glass*, I and II by forming a committee to revise pricing and pattern information. A committee of eight experienced collectors and dealers from across the United States have contributed their expertise and time to revise and review the content. Because of the incoherent organization, errors, and jumbled pricing structure, some felt this would be a fruitless effort, but a large segment of pattern glass collectors consider Metz's books to be the "bible" of collecting because of the large number of photographs, the reference numbers, and its wide distribution. Mrs. Metz compiled her books in the late 1950s and 1960s when photographic pattern identification books were unknown. Ruth Webb Lee's books were well illustrated with beautiful line drawings, but fewer patterns were included and beginning collectors find it difficult to identify an unknown piece of glass from a drawing. Many collectors have old, tattered copies that need replacing and newer collectors are finding used copies to be very costly in the our-of-print market. Therefore, the revision committee decided to leave the format and Metz's commentary intact. After all, it is a historical document and the author's thoughts should not be altered, but when some statement conflicts with new information, changing collecting habits, or is otherwise erroneous, a note will be included. *(New information, including new pieces, are shown in italic type.)*

Mrs. Metz had strong opinions, to which she was of course entitled, but collectors should not take her pronouncements as literal truth with the pattern glass field as a whole. She despised late imitation cut and Depression era glass; but many of these items are greatly admired and sought after today in their own context. Collectors focus on a specific interest that is personally desirable regardless of any intrinsic worth.

Some of the circumstance that have altered in the last forty years are color desirability and nomenclature: what Metz called yellow or canary is currently called vaseline, an instance of slang over riding reason. Older flint glass is still generally called canary but not consistently. When she called something amethyst or purple she was referring to color added during the manufacturing process, not the tints found in glass exposed to strong sunlight or radiation at a later date. A practice incidentally coveted by some collectors, especially in the west, but abhorred by most serious collectors who see it as damage and prefer glass as close to mint condition as possible. She also generally assigned the same value to yellow as amber glass, but today amber is a poor stepchild and is not especially sought after, while the yellow or vaseline is the more valuable, generally nearly double clear glass with blue somewhat less. Gilding was considered a gaudy embellishment to be removed if possible and today good gold flashing is highly desirable and removal would seriously devalue a piece of glass.

Pattern names have also changed in some cases, with names other than the ones Metz used becoming more common among collectors. Collectors have to be aware of this variation.

The committee hopes that this revision will help inspire and educate another generation of Early American Pattern Glass Collectors.

Phyllis Petcoff
President, Early American Pattern Glass Society
Chair, Metz Committee
September 1999

REFERENCES — ABBREVIATIONS

D. & B.–Daisy and Button.
K.–PATTERN GLASS PITCHERS–Minnie Watson Kamm
L.–EARLY AMERICAN PRESSED GLASS–Ruth Webb Lee
L.V.–VICTORIAN GLASS–above author
M.–GOBLETS–Books 1 and 2–Dr. S. T. Millard
AMERICAN GLASS–George and Helen McKearin

inv.–inverted.	th.–thumbprint.	st.–stippled.
dia.–diamond.	diag.–diagonal.	

ADDITIONAL REFERENCES — 1999

Heacock, William. *Encyclopedia of Victorian Colored Pattern Glass, Volumes 1 – 8*. Marietta, Ohio: Antiques Publications, 1974 – 81.

Husfloen, Kyle. *Collector's Guide to American Pressed Glass, 1825 – 1915*. Radnor, Pennsylvania: Wallace-Homestead Book Company, 1992.

Jenks, Bill, and Jerry Luna. *Early American Pattern Glass, 1850 – 1890*. Radnor, Pennsylvania: Wallace-Homestead Book Company, 1990.

Jenks, Bill, Jerry Luna, and Darryl Riley. *Identifying Pattern Glass Reproductions*. Radnor, Pennsylvania: Wallace-Homestead Book Company, 1993.

Lindsey, Bessie M. *American Historical Glass*. Rutland, Vermont: Charles E. Tuttle, 1980.

McCain, Mollie Helen. *The Collector's Encyclopedia of Pattern Glass*. Paducah, Kentucky: Collector Books, 1982.

McKearin, George and Helen. *American Glass*. New York: Crown, 1941.

Miles, Dori and Robert W. Miller. *Price Guide to Pattern Glass*. Lombard, Illinois: Wallace-Homestead Book Company, 1986.

Mordock, John B. *American and Canadian Early Etched Goblets*. Privately Published, 1985.

Mordock, John B., and Walter L. Adams. *Pattern Glass Mugs*. Marietta, Ohio: The Glass Press, 1995.

Unitt, Doris and Peter. *American and Canadian Goblets, Volumes 1 – 2*. Peterborough, Ontario: Clock House, 1970 – 1794.

Vallier Collection, 50 Favorites: Early American Pressed Glass Goblets. Stevens Point, Wisconsin: University of Wisconsin, 1993.

Welker, John and Elizabeth. *Pressed Glass in America: Encyclopedia of the First Hundred Years, 1825 – 1925*. Ivyland, Pennsylvania: Antique Acres Press, 1985

PLEASE READ. THE MOST IMPORTANT PART OF A BOOK IS THE
PREFACE

This isn't fiction and it isn't biography, only as the story of PATTERN GLASS might be considered as its biography; and it's not a text book. I'm just a student (albeit a rather old one) of pressed glass. This is a manual to help fellow students study. It's like the old laboratory manuals we used in science class. You remember they gave some data, some pictures and then directions for working to prove or disprove listed facts. At rare intervals, a student, sparked by this set of facts, began a line of his own investigation and more was learned. We all build on the work of our predecessors; as we go on we find a minimum of facts and a maximum of questions and the end of a perfect day is some new information or attitude discovered.

In any serious study practically no statement can be positive; and if I seem to be too positive it's because I'm trying to save space and money by omitting the ever-present, "I think." I make no pretense of listing only "the best patterns"; we learn by negation, also, and the unworthiness of poor design frequently is accented by its proximity to that which is good. The we sometimes find that mediocrity can be mitigated by clever use. Hardly a week passes but I find an excellent pattern which has not previously been listed; so do not jump at the conclusion that a pattern or a piece hitherto unlisted is fake. It is a physical impossibility for one person to have seen everything that was made. I MAKE NO SUCH PRETENSE.

Among writers, as among dealers, there are those whose dominating interest is "the quick buck." There is one such who gives as an alibi for his unstudied statements that he puts an error on every page to see if the reader is smart enough to detect it. I hope I don't have an error on each page, but I'll have to confess that in my past six years of writing for the *Antiques Journal* some of my mistakes have come home to roost. I hope they always will and I've appended my address for that purpose. Corrections, added data and news of new reproductions will be continuously published.

Through my years of writing, bits of information, comments and countless questions have poured into me. To answer them all was a physical impossibility. They were not without value, however, for they started me checking one written statement against another; they sent me out searching for answers. It meant growth for me.

Many have offered their collections to be photographed for this book and I'd certainly like to use them all and I have plans for future use of some of them but the cost of cuts is ever present when one is publishing a book. The price of taking the 900 pictures used here would have been prohibitive if I had had to hire a professional photographer, but the late Mr. Kirkland, donated 500 of them. Though an amateur, his work was ranked higher than that of many of the commercial men. His wife, Mrs. Kirkland, has a vast store of glass information, gleaned in collecting her more than 900 goblets. She has been always willing to share her time and information. Mr. Harold Allen, instructor in commercial photography at the Chicago Art Institute, has spent hours with my son, teaching him to photograph glass. Mr. Allen collects pattern glass; his pattern is Egyptian. My neighboring shop, The Aladdin Shop, has donated pieces for pictures. "Thank you," is a feeble phrase for the type of cooperation I've received.

I make no pretense of literary style as I possess none, so do not be surprised if I lapse into the vernacular occasionally or if I resort to listing, outline form or structurally incomplete sentences. I'm saving space. After reading the proof of one of my magazine articles, my son, an exacting young engineer asked me how carefully I had checked it. I replied that it was factually as correct as long years of earnest study, travel, buying and selling quantities of old glass could make it. His reply was, "Mom, I can't speak of the accuracy of the facts, but rhetorically it would do justice to a high school sophomore." So if it's literary quality you seek, turn to Mr. Shakespeare, but if it's information on Early American Pattern Glass read carefully and repeatedly, especially the little topics tucked in here and there under separate headings. Years of thought and experience have gone into their preparation. I've learned much from collectors and I like to hear from them. My only answer will be gratitude and a sharing of the information with other collectors.

Alice Hulett Metz
March, 1958

Dedication

TO ALL THOSE

From the Norsemen, who first touched our shores, to

Our pioneers who struggled in their log cabins to

Our scientists, who put their hearts in their work, kept their heads in the stars and dreamed of flying, to

Our grandmas, who used and treasured these simple things; and to all who have helped keep the Stars and Stripes clean and high, this story of their folk art is gratefully dedicated by just another American,

Alice Hulett Metz

6

FRONTISPIECE AND DEDICATION PAGE PICTURES

There is no field in PATTERN GLASS which needs study more than that of the fine, early, unlisted patterns. Not many of these were made and no catalogs were issued. Many are inclined to follow the path about which the most is known and they pass by splendid specimens simply because they have not been listed by their favorite author. Collectors all over the country should be looking for this type of glass. The beautiful SANDWICH VINE pattern shown as the frontispiece was unlisted until an intelligent collector brought it to my attention. I'd appreciate hearing of more of this worthwhile type of pattern which has hitherto escaped authors' listings. I may not be able to acknowledge all of your communications by anything but subsequent listings but your contribution will earn the gratitude of thoughtful collectors everywhere.

No. 3 – VIKING – L. V. 33 – K Bk. 7-64 calls it BEARDED HEAD. It has been known as OLD MAN OF THE MOUNTAIN and as PROPHET. Clear, non-flint, made in Ohio in *1876*. Two shapes of creamers, one using three heads on base, the other four. Footed sauce, relish $15.00; large footed salt, spooner, open sugar $40.00; bowls, celery $40.00; covered butter, creamer, water pitcher $85.00; platter $75.00; covered sugar $95.00; covered compotes $95.00. I've never seen a true Viking goblet that listed under this name. In Millard on p. 142 is a late imitation cut glass called Panama. This pattern would be an excellent choice for a family of Norse descent to collect. One could use a simple non-flint goblet such as Banded Knives and Forks. *Hobbs originally called it CENTENNIAL, frosted 50%, milk glass, 20% more.*

No. 1 – EARLY HEART – K. Bk. 7-16 calls its HEART. Flint of the 30s in clear and early, thick, opalescent blue. Crude workmanship. Bears a remarkable likeness in shape to the famous Curling Creamer, made in Pittsburgh. Many difficulties were met in first using the pressing machine; the glass lost some of its sheen as a result of contact with the cold mold. Until this difficulty was overcome, the makers frequently covered the surface with a geometric allover to increase light refraction just as was done in this pattern. With more skill in mold making attained, stippling such as we see in Lacy Sandwich was used to accomplish the same end. Clear creamer $125.00; opalescent blue $350.00.

No. 2 – BALLOON – K. Bk. 3-76. Clear, early, flint of the 50s. Very scarce. *Covered sugar $350.00; creamer $250.00; spooner $300.00.*

No. 9 – SANDWICH VINE – Frontispiece. Heretofore unlisted. Clear, brilliant, bell toned flint of the early 40s or late 30s. Has the characteristics of a Sandwich product. Several years ago, a Chicago dealer (not I) found five of these goblets in a family who claimed to have had ancestors who worked in the Sandwich factory; this is one of the five goblets. We have no verification for this story of the family, but here is the goblet, one of the most beautiful I've ever seen, preserved for posterity by a dealer and collector with the right kind of collecting philosophy. If any goblet is worth $5,000.00, this is it. *Recently sold at auction for $10,000.00.*

No. 6 – MAGNET & GRAPE WITH FROSTED LEAF AND AMERICAN SHIELD. Bell toned flint goblet belonging to the early Magnet and Grape family with Frosted Leaf. Rare, goblet $300.00.

No. 5 – SQUARE PANES – M. 104. Has been known as POST. Clear, non-flint made in Ohio in the 80s. A few pieces were made in which the bottom of the base was covered with little diamond points. These are hard to find which may be due to the fact that it was difficult to remove from the mold. The design is so simple that the etched design shown here is more pleasing and hence more in demand. I show it on this page as it is really a thing which "grandma had." Flat sauce $750.00; footed sauce, oblong relish $12.00; spooner $20.00; covered sugar, covered butter, pickle castor with glass cover, creamer $55.00; small (5") covered jelly on high foot $55.00; most attractive when used as a group with a pair of these and a celery $35.00; several larger covered cakestands, covered compotes $65.00; syrup $65.00. Not etched 10% less.

No. 12 – TRIMMED SQUARE PANES – (Not pictured.) Heretofore unlisted. Same as Square Panes above only this has fern spray molded in the panels. Not well known and valued 10% less than for that in which the spray is etched.

No. 4 – LOG CABIN – L. 106. Clear, non-flint of the 70s. A little milk glass bank, which was originally a mustard container, and a covered mustard in the form of a cabin with the word "Tecumseh" are later, and not part of this pattern. Extremely difficult to find in perfect pieces, but the interest of the design makes minor defects unimportant (should be mentioned, however). Flat, rectangular sauce $60.00; spooner $120.00; creamer $110.00; covered butter, covered sugar, water pitcher $300.00; covered compotes $400.00. I've never seen either goblet or tumbler. *Has been reproduced.*

12
Giant Sawtooth

15
Krom

18
Tackle Block

21
Fedora Loop

24
Early Ashburton

27
Way Colonial

30
Giant Thumbprint

33
Pegged Flute

VERY EARLY PATTERNS

This group represents our earliest patterns. In some of them there probably were many more pieces; in fact, as time goes on more and more pieces in these and other patterns are found, I find that most patterns were made in the four piece set, a goblet and a wine. As we go on we find more pieces to the sets and as we come to the late 80s, 90s and early 1900s we find innumerable articles, all sorts of condiment sets, individual as well as standard size four piece sets, many sizes of bowls, some of them divided, banana dishes, jam jars, cracker jars, mugs, etc. We may be able to find so many pieces in the later ware because the factory records and catalogs have been found listing them, so we search for them.

Very little information is at hand on these early designs. Many were probably made in what is termed the Midwest, meaning Pittsburgh or Ohio. An interesting characteristic of this group is the short, thick stem. This probably means that the early workers had difficulty removing glasses from the mold and were more successful with this type. Mold making was a comparatively new process when these were made, being patented in 1829. Even up to the 80s, this difficulty was present and in Classic, a pattern of the later time, the type with little feet had to be changed to collared base because of it.

Later, too, the molded handle supplanted the applied handle on pitchers, tumblers and mugs because when the hot glass handle was applied to the partially cooled pitcher, a heat crack often resulted at the base of the handle where it touched the bowl of the piece. It took a great deal of skill to apply handles to any piece. About twenty years ago, one of the men from a large factory at Wheeling, W. Va. told me that they had only three workers who could apply handles successfully to baskets and cruets and that they could not get apprentices to learn the trade.

No. 12 – GIANT SAWTOOTH – M. Bk. 2-103. Clear flint of the 30s. Very crude workmanship, I've never seen an absolutely perfect specimen. More of this shows up than of some of the others although this may be the earliest; this could be because this one is better known. Goblet $150.00; *lamp $300.00; spill $95.00; tumbler $90.00.*

No. 13 – BULL'S EYE & SAWTOOTH – (Not pictured.) M. Bk. 2-98. Probably followed shortly after Giant Sawtooth. Heavy, thick stemmed flint smaller sawtooths than latter with one row of very large thumbprints around the top. Only goblet $65.00. Scarcer than Giant Sawtooth.

No. 15 – KROM – M. 19. Clear, flint of the 30s. Only goblet $65.00.

No. 18 – TACKLE BLOCK – M. Bk. 2-49. Clear, non-flint of the 40s. Only goblet $40.00. *Could be English, found often there.*

No. 21 – FEDORA LOOP – M. 22. Clear, flint of the 30s. Its crude make would indicate the early date. Only goblet $40.00.

No. 24 – EARLY ASHBURTON – Not listed heretofore. I believe this to be the earliest form of this well-known pattern which was made with slight variations over a period of 30 years. This one is blown, bell toned and the panels are cut which indicate Pittsburgh as source of manufacture. Goblet $45.00.

No. 27 – WAY COLONIAL – M. Bk. 2-132. An early form of this family. Clear, bell toned flint of the 40s. Goblet $75.00.

No. 30 – GIANT THUMBPRINT – M. Bk. 2-103. Clear, flint of the 40s. Goblet $40.00.

No. 33 – PEGGED FLUTE – M. Bk. 2-142. Early form of another well known family. Goblet $35.00.

SIMPLICITY AND FUNCTIONALISM

Simplicity and functionalism are the American way of life. Gilded scrolls, encrusted imitation jewels and sugar-coated cupids do not fit the interior decor of today any more than towers and minaret's of the old castles fit our exteriors. To be of value, ornate decor must be well executed and exquisite in detail. In these days of high labor costs this is costly to manufacture and expensive to maintain. On the other hand, modern design, if not mellowed, can be pretty sterile. One of our daily papers carried an article this week on "The Boom in Antiques" and stated it was caused by folks who found the severity of modern furnishings needed to be softened and humanized. There is nothing that accomplishes this better than a few pieces of old glass.

36
Diamond Thumbprint

39
Sandwich Star

42
Lee

45
Scarab

51
Laminated Petals

48
Loop and Long Petals

57
Ovoid Panels

54
Loop and Petals

No. 36 – DIAMOND THUMBPRINT – L. 3, 25 – M. Frontispiece – McKerin pl. 205-6, pl. 206 1, 2, 3, 10; pl. 209-3. One of the aristocrats of Pattern Glass. Clear, brilliant flint, made at several factories for a period of years, probably from the 1840 – 1850s. Some of the pieces, possibly the earlier ones, are quite crude; most are very rare and in demand, but there is one piece, a low, scalloped edge footed compote, nicely finished and very plentiful worth only about $75.00; sauce dish $15.00; spooner $85.00; tumbler $135.00; creamer, covered sugar, covered butter $150.00–200.00; champagne, wine $275.00; celery $175.00; goblet $700.00; whiskey tumbler $200.00; decanter with original stopper $225.00, minus stopper $175.00; waste bowl $100.00; milk or water pitcher $450.00; wine jug with places for holding glasses $1,200.00–1,400.00. *Goblet rare. Creamer, sugar, goblet, spooner, and tumbler reproduced in non-flint clear and colors marked "S.M."*

No. 39 – SANDWICH STAR – L. 14 – M. 74 – McKerin, pl. 195-No. 2 shows a unique tall covered compote in amethyst which should bring $5,000.00. Another extreme rarity which should bring the same price is the compote with three dolphins forming the stem. In these early flints the pitchers are extremely fine in line and have applied handles. One need not attempt to collect a setting, one piece makes a distinguished decorative note. Large, compote, clear $195.00, covered $425.00; water pitcher, rare $500.00; decanters, no stoppers, quart $95.00, pint $95.00; spooner $75.00; flat relish $100.00; cordial $225.00; wine $275.00; goblet, rare $1,200.00. *Goblet recently sold at an auction for $1,500.00.* These prices are for perfect, brilliant specimens.

No. 42 – LEE – L. V. 24 – M. 143. Early, brilliant flint of the 50s or 60s. Dr. Millard obviously errs in placing this fine flint in the 70s. I'm happy that he chose to name so fine a pattern after Ruth Webb Lee who has done so much to awaken the American people to an appreciation of Pattern Glass, who has so consistently fought for intelligence and honesty in merchandising it and whose monumental work *Early American Pressed Glass* was the trigger which sparked my intensive study of this American folk art when it was published 25 years ago. I only hope that I will arouse an interest in someone who will carry on and find more of the answers to the "I don't knows" and who will correct my mistakes. There's so much more to be done. In quality and design, the pattern Lee equals the finest of continental design and yet it's as American as the person for whom it was named. Tumbler, wine $125.00; decanter $125.00; creamer $145.00; goblet $450.00; lamp $175.00; celery $135.00; champagne $150.00; covered sugar $145.00.

No. 45 – SCARAB – M. 29 – L. V. 55-line 4 – last one. Clear flint of the late 50s or early 60s. Goblet $175.00. Should be other pieces.

No. 51 – LAMINATED PETALS – M. 12 – K. Bk. Clear, fine flint of the 60s. Wine $65.00; goblet $85.00; creamer $95.00; covered sugar $110.00.

No. 48 – LOOP AND LONG PETALS – Hitherto unlisted. This goblet is the only piece of this I've ever seen. Petals are deep amber and the top and base are outlined with the same. McKerin lists this as a silver stain (chemist tells me possibly a silver salt) which has been found rarely on Cable and other early patterns. Although not listed at the time, Mrs. Kirkland took this on the advice of Mr. McKerin; needless to say, she has never regretted it. Goblet $140.00.

No. 57 – OVOID PANELS – M. Bk. 2-26. Clear, medium weight flint of the 60s. Goblet $45.00.

No. 54 – LOOP AND PETAL – M. Bk. 2-1. Clear or clear with frosted petals, a beautiful flint pattern of the 50s. Clear $45.00; with frosted petals $65.00.

FLINT (LEAD) GLASS VS. NON-FLINT (LIME GLASS)

Our earliest glass contained lead which is the element that gives glass its ring. The Civil War used much lead for bullets and as it became scarce, a soda lime formula was used. At times we find patterns which were made over a long period of years and which were produced both ways. When this happens, as in Ashburton, for instance, the non-flint has very much less value. Degrees of tone may differ as the glass contains more or less lead; the better the tone in a flint glass specimen, the more the demand for it. Some patterns were made only in flint and when we find a non-flint we can doubt their authenticity. Occasionally we find a piece in a pattern in flint, when we believed it to be only in lime glass. Flint glass is often more valuable, but it is only one factor. I heard a lecturer talking to a novice audience. "Good glass had lead in it," she said, "tap it and see if it rings. If not, it is not good." She thought only in terms of material, not of design. Jumbo in the goblet, or Squirrel, for instance, is worth more than most lead glass goblets; Frosted American Coin will equal any of them in price. Half truths are as dangerous in this line as in any.

60
Bull's Eye

63
Bull's Eye
with Fleur-de-Lys

66
Bull's Eye
with Diamond Point

69
Comet

72
New England Pineapple

74
Horn of Plenty

77
Lincoln Drape

80
Lincoln Drape with Tassel

No. 60 – BULL'S EYE – L. 48, 49 – M. 87. Type shown has knob near top of stem. On p. 162, Millard shows it with knob near bottom of stem. L. 48 lists this kind as BULL'S EYE WITH PLAINER STEM. As is true of many patterns of this era some specimens were made of a poor quality of discolored glass, and some of the later ones were made of non-flint; while these may have a slight value as specimens, they do not command the price of clear, bell toned glass and it is for this better type that I give valuations. Flint of the 50s. Oval relish $30.00; spooner $45.00; footed sale $60.00; bitter bottle $85.00; egg cup $35.00; wine $75.00; tumbler $125.00; handled mug $125.00; goblet $75.00; decanter with stopper $125.00; lamp $200.00; celery $95.00; champagne $125.00; cologne bottle $130.00; covered egg cup $275.00; water bottle with tumbler $200.00; creamer $120.00; covered sugar $135.00. Milk white or colored pieces are rarities 100% more. *New England Glass, 1860s.*

No. 63 – BULL'S EYE WITH FLEUR-DE-LYS – L. 48 – M 34. Clear, flint of the 50s. Contemporary of above but scarcer; goblet $125.00; covered sugar $135.00; creamer $225.00; water pitcher $600.00; covered butter $100.00; decanter original stopper $195.00; *celery $195.00.*

No. 66 – BULL'S EYE WITH DIAMOND POINT – L. 49 – M. 161. Clear, and another of the fine flint family of the 50s. This one is very scarce and its value is about 50% higher than that of Bull's Eye. Was once known as OWL. *Wine $300.00; goblet $225.00.*

No. 69 – COMET – L. 48 – M. 161. Very scarce, beautiful flint made at the Sandwich factory in the late 40s or early 50s. Goblet $130.00; whiskey tumbler, water tumbler $150.00; water pitcher $800.00. There must be a creamer and other pieces but I've never heard of them. Anything colored in this would be unique and a dealer could about set his own price.

No. 72 – NEW ENGLAND PINEAPPLE – L. 42, 43, 53 – M. 22 – K. Bk. 4-54. Clear flint of the early 60s, made in many forms. Honey dishes, flat sauces $15.00; spooner $50.00; egg cups $35.00; footed salt $60.00; castor bottle $45.00; complete castor set $400.00; either size goblet $95.00; open sugar $40.00; decanter, no stopper $100.00, with patent stopper $250.00; wine, whiskey tumbler $150.00; open compote $95.00; covered compote, scarce flat bowl $190.00; covered sugar $135.00; tumbler with applied handle $375.00; jug and stopper $200.00; 6" plates $110.00; champagnes $200.00; water pitcher $500.00. Goblet and wine now reproduced; they have a little ring but are not bell toned. Any colored piece a rarity. *Reproduced in non-flint clear, amber, pink, medium blue, opaque white.*

No. 74 – HORN OF PLENTY – L. 47, 48 – M. 118 – McKerin Plate 205-No. 1, 2, 7, 10. Another fine clear, flint of the 50s made in many forms. Flat sauce, honey dish $15.00; egg cups $45.00; celery $145.00; round or flat bowls $120.00; oval salt $95.00; plates, open compotes $100.00; goblets $95.00; regular size creamer $175.00; large creamer $135.00; water pitcher $625.00; large all glass lamp $225.00; lamp with marble base $195.00; rectangular covered honey dish $5,000.00; scalloped edge compote, oval $325.00; round butter dish with Washington head finial $1,000.00; regular butter dish $125.00; wine $150.00; champagne $195.00; unique in this pattern are the clarets, 5" tall and flaring; clear pieces edged in color; canary; amber, or blue pieces are extremely rare; the cake plate has been listed at $1,000.00+. The tumbler was one of the first Pattern Glass fakes, there were a few pieces made in old milk white but now the market is flooded with horn of plenty tall fake glass lamps. The fake tumbler is a fine example of a fake pontil — it is stuck on *and non-flint.* *Sandwich, 1860s.*

No. 77 – LINCOLN DRAPE – L. 46 – M. 118. Fine flint of the early 60s. Egg cup $45.00; footed salt $100.00; flat sauce $20.00; spooner $65.00; open sugar $40.00; wine $135.00; syrup $250.00; goblet $135.00; lamp, marble base $135.00; plate $80.00; covered butter $110.00; decanter $200.00; covered sugar $150.00; creamer $125.00; covered compote $175.00; water pitcher $450.00; open compote $65.00. *Sandwich, 1860s.*

No. 80 – LINCOLN DRAPE WITH TASSEL – L. 26, 46 – M. 118. Contemporary of above but slightly scarcer, *goblet $295.00.*

No. 83 – COOLIDGE DRAPE LAMP – Heretofore unlisted. There is a late, non-flint kerosene lamp such as was on the table in the Coolidge farm when their son took the oath as president when Harding died so suddenly. It has since become popular and has been confused with these old flint drapes. It comes in several sizes and has a drape pattern, more like a curtain. Clear $85.00; cobalt blue 125.00. Not pictured.

86
Sandwich Ivy

89	92	95	98
Star and Dart	Star and Circle	Harp	Morning Glory

No. 86 – SANDWICH IVY – Previously unlisted. Fine, brilliant, possibly of the 50s. How can one think that all of the "best glass" has been listed when pieces like these are constantly being brought to light by glass students. I'd appreciate hearing of other pieces. Small creamer $110.00 and I believe the little foot piece $60.00 was for loaf sugar. Shown through the courtesy of Mr. and Mrs. Frank Southern of Crystal Lake, Ill., the owners. *European, not EAPG–dark amethyst, 100% more.*

No. 89 – STAR AND DART – Hitherto unlisted. Fine, heavy brilliant flint of the 50s. Butter dish $65.00.

No. 90 – EARLY MOON AND STAR – K. Bk. 8-72 (Not pictured.) Here is another early, brilliant, heavy flint about which we know little. Rows of huge moons, alternating with stars of the same size, cover the piece, an open sugar. Fragments at Sandwich. There is much more work to be done on these worthwhile patterns which have been neglected, because not listed. I've changed the name from Old Moon and Star to above to avoid confusion. Dates probably from the 50s. Reports of pieces on these will further glass study. Sugar 95.00.

No. 92 – STAR AND CIRCLE – M. Bk. 2-8. L. 45 shows plate with Diamond Point border and center of this pattern and I believe it to be the plate of this pattern which is a fine old, heavy brilliant flint of the 50s. Goblet $95.00; plate $50.00.

No. 95 – HARP – L. 14 – M. 37 – L.V. Clear flint made by Bryce Bros., of Pittsburgh in the 40s or 50s. Finish is frequently crude as can be expected in such an early pattern. Goblet comes with either straight or flared sides. Rare $2,000.00+; honey dish $20.00; spooner, spill holder $60.00; footed salt $75.00; 6" covered dish on low foot $195.00; low, small handled lamp, patent wick $150.00; tall lamp $225.00; *decanter with pewter stopper $350.00.*

No. 98 – MORNING GLORY – M. Bk. 1-Frontispiece – L.V. 1 – K. Bk. 6-3 Flint, though not bell toned, made in the 60s. This is one pattern about which all experts agree in that it was made only at the Sandwich factory. When one sees a piece after seeing the picture, he is apt to be disappointed for many times it is not as brilliant and fine in workmanship as was expected; it's often quite crude. The fakes are brilliant and pretty, though non-flint. Goblet $1,000.00; egg cup $65.00; wine $195.00; open compote $195.00; creamer $195.00. Very much in demand, very scarce and collectors are paying anything to get it. Goblet and wine now reproduced in *non-flint,* clear and color. Generally the pattern detail is not as distinct in the reproduction.

THE REPRODUCTION BUG-A-BOO

I've heard a dealer state, "I don't handle Pattern Glass because of the fakes." If you investigate you would probably find that was not the real reason; we find very little pattern glass in homes, now; dealers handling any quantity are having to pay money for collections, frequently bought from estates. There are more reproductions in other lines than in glass, but there have been people exposing glass fakes for years, writing and lecturing on them. Consider the diamond, of great value, of great variations in value, and probably the most faked article in the world. Would it be possible for the greatest expert on diamonds in the world to write an article which would enable one to judge and value the precious stone? Do we stop wearing them because of the fakes? When we want to invest money in a good stone do we go out in the sticks to hunt for one? Do we try to read and discover how to judge one? Do we go to a little one-horse jewelry shop, even though the owner is an honest man who has been eking out a living possibly selling watches, alarm clocks and costume jewelry for 20 years?

Lately I've seen two articles purporting to tell people how to tell fakes, which, because of ill-informed statements, will aid the fakers. Two of these articles, one in a large New York paper, states that stippling is even in the old. The exact opposite is true; if you get even stippling in many patterns, such as Pleat and Panel, you'll get a fake. Some patterns are listed as fakes, because the writer has found a piece, the measurements of which do not agree with the old one she had, or minor details differ. Nothing is farther from the truth. Different factories, different batches from the same factory differ in detail, color and weight. There are a few fakes in which we can spot a minor infraction of detail; a difference in weight, color or size, but these are few and far between. Makers of reproductions to be sold as old, may not have moral sense, but they are keen and are not going to slip on too obvious details. Know your dealer, know your author; know your show! (See the bibliography for book on reproductions.)

101
Barrel Ashburton

104
Creased Ashburton

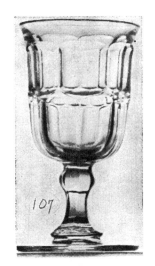

107
Giant Squared Ashburton

110
Squared Ashburton

113
Barrel Excelsior

119
Excelsior
with Double Ring Stem

122
Tall Argus

125
Square Argus

No. 101 – B ARREL ASHBURTON – L. 1, 3 (Ashburton) – M. 6 – K. Bk. 4-99. Clear, generally flint, produced in many factories, in many forms from 1840 almost to the 70s. Cambridge Glass Co. and Bakewell Pears of Pittsburgh were two firms which made it. The later was non-flint and has very little value as compared to the fine early pieces. As is the case when many factories produce a pattern over a long period we find many variations in the pattern; some have top row of ovals connected, while in others it is disconnected. In some of the greatest width of ovals in this row is vertical while in others it is in the horizontal. Stems show varying sizes of knobs appearing in various places on the stems, while in others, such as the one shown here, there is no definite knob but just a gradual enlargement of the stem. One need not try to collect a setting with exactly the same detail; variation adds much interest and charm. Keep to type and never mix flint with non-flint. Mrs. Lee lists over 15 kinds of tumblers, including lemonade glass, Long Tom ale glass, not to mention sarsaparilla and soda tumblers and a rare handle covered toddy glass and plate, valued at $300.00, which is most conservative. (I wonder what posterity will call the glasses in which we serve Old Fashion, Side Cars or Horses' Necks?) Wines, champagnes $45.00–75.00; goblets $40.00; egg cups $25.00; cordials $75.00; tumblers $85.00; footed tumblers, clarets $65.00; decanters, bitters bottles $60.00 – 250.00 depending on the rarity of the type; flat sauces, honey dishes $10.00; celery $125.00; creamers $195.00; covered sugars $110.00; water pitcher $450.00. *Reproduced in non-flint, clear and colors, bowl flares.*

No. 104 – CREASED ASHBURTON – M Bk. 2-156. Another of the family. In this uncommon type the goblet would be worth $45.00.

No. 107 – GIANT SQUARED ASHBURTON – Not heretofore listed. Rare, brilliant member of the family. Goblet in this $40.00.

No. 110 – SQUARED ASHBURTON – Not heretofore listed. At first I thought this to be the lady's size goblet in this pattern but lately I've found the decanter and it too, is small. Goblet $40.00; decanter $95.00.

No. 113 – BARREL EXCELSIOR – M. 19 – L. 4, 7. Another family of clear flint made in the 50s and 60s by many firms including McKee Bros. of Pittsburgh. Candlesticks were introduced in the forms with this pattern. Values are about the same as for Ashburton; candlesticks $200.00–250.00 pair depending on size. Goblet slightly scarcer than most forms of Ashburton, value $55.00.

No. 114 – GIANT EXCELSIOR – (Not pictured) – M. 19 Heavier, with thicker stem, knob near top, undoubtedly an early form, goblet $45.00.

No. 116 – FLARED TOP EXCELSIOR – (Not pictured) – M. 19. Flared top, shorter than Giant, heavy; possibly the earliest form; thick stem with knob at top. Goblet $45.00.

No. 119 – EXCELSIOR WITH DOUBLE RINGED STEM – M. Bk. 2-2 – L.V. calls it EXCELSIOR VARIANT. Goblet $45.00; values of other pieces approximately the same as for Ashburton.

No. 120 – EXCELSIOR WITH MALTESE CROSS – (Not pictured) – M. 162. Contemporary of the pattern with Double Ringed stem which this also has. It is distinguished by a small Maltese cross within the diamond. Rare, goblet $125.00.

No. 121 – TONG – L.V. 25 – K. Bk. 5-24. (Not pictured.) Same as Excelsior, to which family it belongs, only this has a round thumbprint in the diamonds which separate the ovals. Values same as Excelsior. *Footed Pitt, 1856, glass quality varies.*

No. 122 – TALL ARGUS – M. 3. Fine old flint of the 40s and 50s. Varies slightly in proportion, type and position of knob on stem for ARGUS – L. 2, but it is definitely of the same general family. Goblet $45.00; other pieces of Argus about 10% higher than Ashburton.

No. 125 – SQUARE ARGUS – M. Bk. 2-96. Another very early type of the Argus family. Goblet, rare $175.00.

128
York Colonial

131
Colonial with
Diamond Band

134
Washington

137
Waffle

140
Prism and Crescent

143
Mirror

146
Mirror and Loop

149
Loop and Moose Eye

No. 128 – YORK COLONIAL – M. 22 – L. 2 does not differentiate between the types but lists them as COLONIAL. Scarce, clear flint of the 50s, not many pieces found; a few opal and colored fragments found at ruins of Sandwich factory where evidently some of it was made. Differing types would indicate other factories produced it also. Tumbler $55.00; tall, footed ale $55.00; goblet $60.00; celery, covered compote $95.00; creamer $85.00; covered sugar $95.00. Pieces in opalescent, amethyst, or electric blue would be extremely rare and worth 200% more than clear.

No. 129 – HEXAGONAL COLONIAL – M. Bk. 2-110. (Not pictured.) Another similar but scarcer form of the same family. In the goblet, the bowl is angular and the panels form a hexagon at base of bowl. The stem has a huge bulb as the bottom. Goblet of this type $65.00.

No. 130 – COLONIAL WITH GARLAND – M. Bk. 1-11. (Not pictured.) This is a late, non-flint made in the 90s, listed here as it has been confused with earlier form. Around the bottom of the round panels there is a garland of tiny for-get-me-not like flowers. Of course, this is much lighter in weight than the old flints. Wine $25.00; spooner $15.00; goblet $20.00; creamer $15.00; covered butter $25.00; covered sugar $25.00. Forms, other than goblet, uninteresting in shape.

No. 131 – COLONIAL WITH DIAMOND BAND – M. Bk. 2-29. L. 61 calls it BAND. Clear flint of the 50s, made in Pittsburgh. Not as well known as the other form of Colonial, hence the demand is less. Value 20% less than other form with the exception of the goblet, demand for which by goblet collectors increases its value to $55.00.

No. 134 – WASHINGTON – L. 10 – M. 1. Clear, flint of the early 60s. Scarce; made by New England Glass Co. Sauce dish, honey $20.00; egg cups $75.00; footed salt $55.00; spooner $55.00; goblet $150.00; champagne, tumbler, wine $125.00–150.00; bitters bottle $85.00; decanter, no stopper $95.00; cordial $150.00; celery $85.00; open sugar $45.00; covered sugar $125.00; creamer $195.00; decanter, with stopper $150.00; water pitcher $325.00; covered low bowls or compotes or covered tall covered compote $75.00–135.00.

No. 137 – WAFFLE – L. 37, 46. This is the early flint. Waffle, made at the Sandwich factory in the late 40s or early 50s. Some of it is very crude and discolored and other pieces like the handled whiskey shown, which is blown, is brilliant and beautifully finished. Bell toned flint. One should be careful not to confuse this with the numerous cube and waffle variations turned out in the 80s, none of the latter are flint. Prices quoted are for brilliant flint. Flat sauce or honey dish $15.00; egg cup $45.00; goblet $65.00; whiskey or water tumbler $65.00; handled whiskey $85.00; wine, decanter, no stopper $75.00; footed salt $30.00; all glass lamp $175.00; covered salt $75.00; 6" plates, lamp with marble base $95.00; creamer $95.00; covered sugar $110.00; open compote $75.00; covered compote $135.00. Milk white or colored practically 200% more.

Nol. 140 – PRISM & CRESCENT – L. V. 20 – M. 101 calls it PANGYRRIC. Clear, heavy flint made by Sandwich Glass Co. in the 50s. Tumbler $65.00; goblet, handled mug $85.00. Other pieces would have same value as Colonial.

No. 143 – MIRROR – L. 2 – M. 1. Clear, flint made by McKee Bros. of Pittsburgh in the 60s. There should be other pieces but all that has been noted to date is the goblet $35.00. Demand for all of these early flint goblets has risen very sharply lately even in such states as Texas and Illinois.

No. 146 – MIRROR & LOOP – M. Bk. 2-2. Contemporary of Mirror above. Flint, goblet $35.00.

No. 149 – LOOP & MOOSE EYE – Plain stem – M. 108 shows it with knob stem. Goblet $35.00, *champagne $50.00.*

SPECIAL GLASS FOR SPECIAL DAYS

One doesn't need to have all of her glass on display in her home at one time. Keep special pieces away for special days: a little heart shaped relish with red or pink blossoms for anniversaries, Valentine days, announcement parties, showers, etc.; glass with stars or reindeer for Christmas; patriotic motifs for holidays of this kind. Keep motifs simple; do not try to copy the big display in the florist's window or the large shop window. Last Christmas, the florist delivered a poinsettia plant to me. I tore out the ribbon, tinsel bows, silver paper, pine cones (these I used elsewhere), freed its hobbled branches and put plant and container in a simple ironstone tureen. I thought I heard it murmur, "Thank you." Some commercialized decorations give glitter for glow and bulk for beauty. Remember, when the accompanists drown out the soloist, the result is not pleasing.

152
Bigler

155
Grooved Bigler

158
Flare Top
Belted Worchester

164
Ovals with Long Bars

167
Gothic

170
Eugenie

173
Brilliant

176
Eureka

No. 152 – BIGLER – L. 10 – M. 21. Clear flint of the 50s. Goblet seen most frequently. I've never seen the creamer but I believe there was one. Bowls $40.00; double egg cups $50.00; goblet, wine $55.00; water or whiskey tumbler $65.00; champagne, mug with applied handle $75.00; cordial $65.00. The scarcity of the creamer and sugar has probably limited the number of collectors and kept the prices of this fine old pattern lower than they would otherwise be. *Milk pitcher is celery with applied handle 350.00.*

No. 155 – GROOVED BIGLER – Hitherto unlisted. Brilliant, bell toned flint of the early 50s. Have seen only goblet $50.00.

No. 158 – FLARE TOP BELTED WORCHESTER – M. 6. Almost a cousin to Bigler only this pattern does not have vertical lines indented; here they protrude. Flint of the 50s. Goblet, wine $35.00; cordial, handled whiskey $45.00; covered sugar $75.00. Probably other pieces.

No. 159 – STRAIGHT BANDED WORCHESTER – M. 6 (Not pictured.) Very like Flare Top above, only this has the straight sides and has knob at bottom of the stem. I've seen goblet and it is difficult to say which sugar matches the different style of goblet, as the sugars have very minor differences. Goblet $40.00 and values of pieces the same in the different members of this family.

No. 160 – BELTED WORCHESTER – KNOB STEM – M. 11 (Not pictured.) Another member of the Worchester family; this has straight sides and a sharply creased knob at top of stem. Goblet $40.00.

No. 160 – CREASED WORCHESTER – M. 12. (Not pictured.) Slightly different member of the same flint family. Where the other Worchesters have a raised horizontal bar dividing upper and lower panels, this one has a creased indentation. Goblet $40.00.

No. 164 – OVALS WITH LONG BARS – M. Bk. 2-126 calls this BARRED OVALS. Another non-flint pattern is well known by this title so I'm changing it slightly. Brilliant heavy flint of the 50s. Goblet $40.00.

No. 167 – GOTHIC – L. 55 – M. 125. Brilliant flint of the early 60s. Becoming scarce; clear only. Flat sauce $15.00; spooner $45.00; open sugar $40.00; footed salt $50.00; egg cup $50.00; open compote, goblet $75.00; covered butter $155.00; celery, plate $95.00; wine, champagne $145.00; castor bottles of non-flint were probably made later and are plentiful, each $15.00; set of four in original wire holder $65.00; creamer $110.00; covered sugar $100.00.

No. 170 – EUGENIE – L. 5 – M. 125. Clear flint made in the 50s by McKee of Pittsburgh and named by him for the French queen. An American idea of French design it lacks some of the simplicity and directness of its contemporaries. Covered bowls have conventionalized floral finials, but the covered sugar has the most amusing flippant dolphin finial which brings it value to $220.00 because it is so much in demand. Egg cups $35.00; goblet $65.00; tumbler $45.00; cordial $75.00; wine $35.00; champagne, celery $85.00; castor bottles, each $25.00; covered compote $135.00.

No. 173 – BRILLIANT – M. 125 – L. 153 No. 14. Brilliant, bell toned flint of the 50s. Only goblet $55.00. *McKee, 1864.*

No. 176 – EUREKA – L. 6 – M. 147. Clear of the late 60s. Comes in glass which has some lead in it but which is not a bell toned flint. It differs in amount of ring and this affects the value. Not in demand. Made in Pittsburgh. Combines nicely with Sydenham Ironstone china. Pitchers are pleasing in shape with applied handles, covered bowls and covered compotes have pretty bud finials. Flat sauce $10.00; spooner, 6", 7", 8" bowls $35.00; salt $30.00; egg cup $35.00; wine $40.00; open sugar, open compote, footed tumbler $30.00; cordial, covered butter $75.00; creamer $80.00; covered sugar $100.00; covered compotes $85.00; covered bowls $55.00. *McKee, 1866.*

BEAUTY AT A BARGAIN

One source of beauty at a bargain is to be found in the many odd pieces of old flint glass; spooners, spills, open sugars and compotes. Sometimes they are slightly grayed like the mists of morning; sometimes their edges may be rough. Their classic lines and weight make them ideal flower containers. Stems in the water, showing through, make another pattern and are a relief from vases painted by man with gaudy flowers. Simplicity and good taste, not garishness and big price tags, are truly good Americana.

179
Plain Octagon

182
Raised Petal and Loop

185
Inverted Petals
and Fans

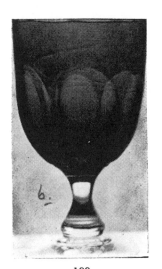

188
Colored **Bowl**

191
Lined Panel

194
Bull's Eye and Bar

197
Waffle and Thumbprint

No. 179 – PLAIN OCTAGON – Heretofore unlisted. Early flint of the 30s or 40s, made in the Midwest. The same contour as the rare octagonal Bellflower, the shape of which was possibly copied from this. There must have been a matching creamer. Value $120.00; rare electric blue one has been reported, would be worth $600.00.

No. 182 – RAISED PETAL & LOOP – L. 4 – line 3 calls this Loop, evidently a typographical error. PETAL & LOOP has been used by Millard for another pattern so I'm adding a descriptive word. In this, the petals seem superimposed on the glass, while in Loop they are outlined in the glass. Flint of the 50s made at Pittsburgh and at Sandwich. Covered sugar, creamer $120.00; covered butter (shown) $75.00; covered compotes $140.00; *candlestick $150.00; open compote $300.00; whale oil lamp $800.00; cologne o/s $200.00; amethyst 300% more.*

No. 185 – INVERTED PETALS & FANS – Heretofore unlisted. Brilliant flint of the late 50s. Only goblet $45.00. Should be other pieces.

No. 188 – COLORED BOWL – Heretofore unlisted. Choice, blown, early Pittsburgh with deep blue bowl and clear stem and base. The blue is deeper than electric but has none of the red overtones of cobalt. On plate 209 – No. 20, McKerin shows tumblers of the same era. Goblet $175.00.

No. 191 – LINED PANEL – Heretofore unlisted. The heaviest flint piece I've ever seen. Of the 40s. Should be other pieces. Celery shown $110.00. *Lyon Co. 1861. Aka Madison.*

No. 194 – BULL'S EYE & BAR – M. Bk. 2-144. L. V. 4 shows covered egg cup in this in opalescent. Flint of the 50s made at Sandwich. Goblet $300.00; egg cup $100.00; rare opalescent egg cup, covered $1,500.00.

No. 197 – WAFFLE AND THUMBPRINT – L. 26 – M. 125. Clear flint of the 50s. Goblet, non-flint $35.00; knob stem goblet $95.00; egg cup $35.00; bar whiskey tumbler $100.00; spooner $55.00; celery $160.00; hand lamp $250.00; claret $190.00; champagne, wine $75.00; water pitcher, rare $450.00; covered sugar $140.00; covered compote $145.00. *Made by several factories. Quality of glass varies. Gray non-flint 50% less.*

No. 198 – WAFFLE AND THUMBPRINT – BULB STEM – M. 80 (Not pictured.) Scarce form of pattern with heavy bulb stem. Goblet $50.00.

No. 199 – WAFFLE AND THUMBPRINT – HEAVY STEMMED – (Not pictured) M. Bk. 2-129. Probably the earliest of the pattern; heaviest and this has a thick stem enlarging where it joins the base. Goblet $40.00.

WHY PATTERN GLASS?

A recent survey of hobbies showed that Early American Pressed Glass is second only to stamps as the object for which collectors search. There are several reasons why this is so. Wars and better communications have resulted in closer contact with the rest of the world and comparisons have deepened our appreciation of our own country and its products and culture. We are now very conscious of Americana, that is, things made by, or for, our forbears. We realize that Raphael was great because he glorified the Italian woman; Millet glorified the French peasant; Rembrandt, too, the Dutch trader as his subject. Greatness in art springs from loyalty to one's own heart. Our homes and furnishings must fit our way of living, our temperament. We study our handicraft of the past to find its good points and to avoid its weaknesses in products of the future. Thus we progress.

Early American Pattern Glass is one of our important folk arts. The first glass made in America was blown by European workmen. While beautiful and valuable, it is continental in design and technique. In 1828, Deming Jarves, working for the Boston and Sandwich Glass Co., invented the first successful pressing machine. Thus came into being the first truly American glass, Pattern Glass. This made it possible for all to have glass for table use; so Pattern Glass played an integral part in American life.

No other country in the world has ever produced a whole series of related table wares such as ours. Ours tells the story of American life, depicts our history, our religious faith, our sense of pattern, our moods, our humor. Where but in America would one find the goblet Ostrich Looking at the Moon?

200
Hairpin

203
Hairpin with
Rayed Base

206
Bakewell Block

209
Block and Thumbprint
Knob Stem

212
Pillar

215
Hercules Pillar

218
Hairpin with
Thumbprint

221
Giant Prism

24

No. 200 – HAIRPIN – M.3 – SANDWICH LOOP – L. V. 31. Clear or milk glass flint, made at the Sandwich factory in the 50s. Pitchers have applied handles, finials are acorns. Flat sauce $15.00; spooner, open sugar $35.00; footed salt $45.00; egg cup $35.00; goblet $50.00; covered sugar, covered compote $90.00; champagne, celery $80.00; creamer $75.00. *Milk glass 40 – 50% more.*

No. 203 – HAIRPIN WITH RAYED BASE – M. Bk. 2-45. Another form of the Hairpin family with the same values.

No. 204 – FLARED TOP HAIRPIN (Not pictured.) M. Bk. 2-45. Another contemporary flint of the Hairpin group. Values the same as for Hairpin.

No. 206 – BAKEWELL BLOCK – L.V. 53. Old flint made by Bakewell Pears of Pittsburgh in the 40s or 50s. Wine, champagne, whiskey tumbler, bar tumbler $110.00; goblet $120.00; whiskey tumbler with applied handle $110.00; spooner $50.00; celery $85.00; decanter $125.00; creamer $140.00; covered sugar $145.00; *covered high compote $195.00.*

No. 209 – BLOCK AND THUMBPRINT – KNOB STEM. L. 101 – M. 117 – K. Bk. 4-21. This early flint was made by Gillinder of Pittsburgh in the 50s and it was made again in non-flint in the 70s; the non-flint of course, is much lighter in weight and valued at 40% of the flint. Goblet, footed tumbler $50.00; celery $55.00; creamer $75.00; covered sugar $85.00; open compote $40.00; covered compote $75.00.

No. 210 – LATER BLOCK AND THUMBPRINT – (Not pictured.) M. 126 – L. 101 – last one on line 4. Made in the 70s, non-flint; plain stem, wider clear band at top and the blocks are almost square. Goblet $30.00; wine 25.00.

No. 211 – FRAMED BLOCKS – M. Bk. 2-126. (Not pictured.) Another member of the Block and Thumbprint family which came in two types, early flint, sometimes crude and blown and later non-flint. Knob stem, sides slant out, sharply upward. One row of large blocks with mitered corners, large bulge in bowl where it narrows for stem. Flint goblet $65.00; wine $50.00. Non-flint 40% of this. *Glass of non-flint often gray in color.*

No. 212 – PILLAR – L. 28 – M. 20. Clear flint made by Bakewell Pears of Pittsburgh in the 50s. Flat sauce $15.00; goblet $60.00; decanter (no stopper) $75.00; ale $85.00; cordial $75.00; should be a creamer and sugar. *A non-flint ale is found $30.00.*

No. 215 – HERCULES PILLAR – M. 3 – L. 28 and McKerin pl. 208 calls this PILLAR VARIANT. I do not agree with the term variant as I believe this to be one of the older members of the family. Double egg cup, goblet $65.00.

No. 214 – PILLAR WITH FACETED KNOB STEM. M. Bk. 2-1 (Not pictured.) Probably the oldest of the Pillars. Same as Pillar but thicker with shorter, heavier stem with knob near the lower part. Goblet $50.00.

No. 218 – HAIRPIN WITH THUMBPRINT – M. 20. Clear, heavy, brilliant flint of the 60s. Only goblet $55.00.

No. 221 – GIANT PRISM – M. Bk. 2-110. On plate 143 the same goblet is listed again as MASTER PRISM. Clear flint of the early 60s. Goblet $100.00; *goblet with applied handle $350.00.*

PATTERN GLASS PREACHES SILENTLY

Four or five generations back, liberty was so young in the lives of the American people that they remembered the pains of its birth and cherished it highly. They expressed their love of the newly found freedom by decorating their articles of every day use with patriotic symbols, the Liberty Bell, reminders of heroes and patriotic events, shields, and devout prayers to the Creator to give them their daily bread. As the nation became prosperous, some "would-be" sophisticates and pedants professed to be disdainful of this naivete. "Victorian sentimentalism," they sniffed as their noses tilted higher. Next, topsy-turvey world conditions jarred their self-sufficient complacency and old-fashioned faith and patriotism regained their rightful place. Men of science affirm what our forbears learned by experience, namely, that repetition of words and symbols creates and strengthens the emotion they represent. Fortunate are we that much of the glass depicting fine sentiments survives. We can use and collect it. The fact that it is a cherished object in the home is a more potent influence on the lives of children and grown-ups than a dozen sermons on patriotism and faith.

224
Panelled Ovals

227
Oval Miter

230
Yoked Loop

233
Pillar and Bull's Eye

236
Frosted Leaf

239
Stippled **Leaf**

242
Hamilton

245
Hamilton with Leaf

No. 224 – PANELLED OVALS – L. V. 30 – M. Bk. 2-6. Clear flint patterns of the 60s; pitchers have applied handles. Spooner, egg cup $50.00; open compote, open sugar $40.00; wine, goblet $50.00; covered butter, covered compote $65.00; covered sugar, creamer $65.00.

No. 227 – OVAL MITER – L. 12 – M. 48. Fine flint made from the late 50s over a period of years. Clear only. Flat sauce $10.00; spooner $30.00; bowls, open sugar, open compotes $25.00; covered sugar, creamer, covered compotes $65.00. McKee, 1864.

No. 230 – YOKED LOOP – M. Bk. 2-54 and he calls the same goblet SCALLOPED LOOP – M. Bk. 2-1. Really not a member of the Loop family. Clear flint of the 60s. Goblet $35.00; open sugar $30.00; covered sugar $75.00. Now that I've seen the sugar I feel confident we'll hear of the other pieces.

No. 233 – PILLAR AND BULL'S EYE – M. 29 – K. Bk. 5-142 – L. 24 shows a goblet with the old trade name of Thistle, a name given to a later pattern. Beautiful heavy brilliant flint made in Pittsburgh in the 50s. Pitchers most unusual and beautiful in form. Wine $65.00; goblet $65.00; tumbler $80.00; water pitcher $225.00.

No. 236 – FROSTED LEAF – L. 94 – M. 114. Scarce, lovely clear flint of the *60s* with the leaves frosted. Sauce dish $25.00; spooner $85.00; salt $65.00; egg cup $125.00; water tumbler $175.00; goblet $125.00; open sugar $65.00; footed tumbler $145.00; decanter, no stopper $125.00; celery $135.00; covered butter $150.00; creamer, covered sugar $140.00; decanter with matching stopper $275.00; water pitcher $450.00; covered compote $260.00. Any colored piece would be unique and a dealer could about set his own price. *Wine reproduced in non-flint, marked "SI." Sandwich, 1860s.*

No. 239 – STIPPLED LEAF – M. Bk. 2-26. Millard lists this as being the same as the Frosted Leaf with the exception of the stippling on the leaves but I've seen it only in non-flint made in the 70s. In non-flint it would be worth only 25% of the flint Frosted Leaf. If there is a flint Stippled Leaf its value would be 40% of the frosted kind. There is a possibility that the molds were reused later and changed slightly. This is not a reproduction, however.

No. 242 – HAMILTON – L. 56 – M. 117 – McKerin 207 No. 6. Clear flint of the early 60s. Flat sauce, honey dish $15.00; spooner $35.00; open sugar, footed salt $40.00; egg cup $50.00; tumbler $80.00; whiskey with handle $125.00; creamer with molded handle $55.00; creamer, applied handle $95.00; celery, tall scalloped edge open compote $85.00; wine $85.00; low open compote $50.00; covered sugar $95.00; hat made from tumbler mold, unique $350.00+. *Cape Cod Glass, 1860s.*

No. 243 – HAMILTON WITH CLEAR BAND – M. Bk. 2-120 (Not pictured.) Same as Hamilton above only in this the center band does not have the little diamonds subdivided, they are left clear. Value less as other Hamilton.

No. 245 – HAMILTON WITH LEAF – L. 57 – M. 117 – K. Bk. 4-18. Clear, flint, contemporary of Hamilton and of some value. M. Bk. 2 – 155 shows what he terms a flare top goblet in this but is really the spooner of the pattern.

No. 245 – HAMILTON WITH LEAF. Flint goblet $75.00.

No. 246 – HAMILTON WITH FROSTED LEAF – M. 147 (Not pictured.) Same as Hamilton with Leaf above, only here the leaf is frosted. Value remains the same.

HAS PATTERN GLASS REACHED ITS PEAK IN VALUE?

Pattern Glass is far from its peak in value. Would you store a piece of glass for ten cents a year? Practically any piece of Pattern Glass is 75 years old. At ten cents a year that would mean $7.50 for storage alone. I just read in the *Chicago Tribune* of a tureen which brought $29,000 this week in the Auction Gallery in New York. Another daily paper carried a story of the tremendous boom in old things and explained it by stating that the high cost of labor has produced so many things which are sterile and uninteresting in design that in order to differentiate the home from store or office folks were having to resort to old pieces.

Internet auctions are now very valuable for putting patterns in the hands of collectors by connecting buyers and sellers across the country.

248
Divided Hearts

251
Honeycomb
with Ovals

254
Elongated
Honeycomb

257
Diamond Point
With Panels

260
Panelled Elipse

263
Fine Rib with
Cut Ovals

266
Large Drop

269
Deep Diamonds in Band

No. 248 – DIVIDED HEARTS – L. V. 21 – M. Bk. 2-68. Clear flint of the early 60s made by the Boston & Sandwich Glass Co. Footed salt $45.00; egg cup $85.00; spooner $60.00; open sugar $45.00; open compote $75.00; lamp with marble base $120.00; covered butter $135.00; goblet $125.00; covered sugar, creamer, covered compote $125.00.

No. 251 – HONEYCOMB WITH OVALS – M. 39. Clear flint of the late 60s. Only goblet $40.00.

No. 252 – LATTICE & OVAL PANELS – M. 81 – L. V. 21 calls it FLAT DIAMONDS AND PANELS. (Not pictured.) Medium heavy brilliant flint made at Sandwich in the 50s in clear, opalescent and the opalescent colors used there. Large goblet, flared top, large rimmed oval panels extending almost the length of the piece are placed in a background of diamond shaped lattice; knob stems near bottom. Goblet $125.00; egg cup $65.00; champagne $125.00; covered egg cups $250.00; creamer $225.00; decanters, patent stopper $125.00; open sugar $55.00; covered sugar $135.00. Opaque white, 200% more; opaque colors are rare, 400% more.

No. 254 – ELONGATED HONEYCOMB – Not previously listed. Flint of the early 60s. Goblet $45.00.

No. 255 – TAPERED HONEYCOMB – M. Bk. 2-43. (Not pictured.) Non-flint of the 80s similar to Elongated Honeycomb, only goblet $20.00.

No. 257 – DIAMOND POINT WITH PANELS – L. V. 20 – M. 7 calls it HINOTO. Clear flint made by Boston & Sandwich Glass Co. in the 50s. Footed salt, spooner $40.00; champagne, wine $65.00; goblet $60.00; creamer $100.00; covered sugar $75.00; celery $65.00.

No. 258 – RIBBED PINEAPPLE – L. V. 23. (Not pictured.) Contemporary of Diamond Point with Panels and very similar, only in this the band of trimming at bottom is more like Sawtooth; groups of three vertical prisms run from this band to the top line. These groups of prisms are separated by plain panels. Some spillholders have been found with the amber (silver stain) trim found in a few other flint pieces of this era. Goblet $65.00; sperm oil lamp $100.00; spooner or spill $50.00. *Aka Prism & Flattened Sawtooth.*

No. 260 – PANELLED ELIPSE – Not heretofore listed. Rare flint of the 50s or possibly earlier. Medium heavy. Goblet shown here is the early electric blue. Clear goblet $50.00; blue $400.00.

No. 263 – FINE RIB WITH CUT OVALS – L. 34 shows this and calls it one of the variants of the Bellflower era which does this pattern an injustice as it is in all probability before the ordinary Bellflower and is more like the Fine Rib with Bellflower Border. It is blown, very fine rib, unusually brilliant bell tone flint and the ovals are cut, which gives the serrated appearance. This may indicate Pittsburgh as place of manufacture. The applied handle is so very skillfully done ending in four little ripples and a finely graduated turned back point. Wine or champagne $250.00; handled whiskey shown $275.00; goblet $400.00.

No. 264 – DOUBLE VINE – Millard Bk. 2 (Not pictured) Frontispiece – L. 34 calls this, again, Ribbed Variant of Bellflower era. It is similar to Fine Rib with Ovals shown above, only in this there is a double vine running horizontally around the goblet with a three leafed grouping of cut leaves, having the serrated appearance, at intervals. Goblet $450.00.

No. 266 – LARGE DROP. Hitherto unlisted. Unlisted flint pattern of the 40s. Master salt, shown. I'd like to hear of other pieces. *Original name "Lotus." McKee, 1868.*

No. 269 – DEEP DIAMOND IN BAND. Hitherto unlisted. Clear flint of the 40s. Egg cup $45.00. Thick, short stem, bell toned flint, and crude.

272
Ribbed Grape

275
Ribbed Ivy

278
Ribbed Palm

281
Inverted Fern

284
Fine Rib with
Bellflower Border

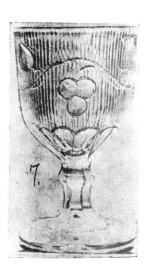

287
Bellflower
with Loops

290
Bellflower
Fine Rib Banded

293
Bellflower
Coarse

No. 272 – RIBBED GRAPE – L. 27, 35, 36 – M. 148. Clear, flint of the 50s. Flat sauce $20.00; spooner $35.00; goblet $55.00; wine $75.00; covered butter $110.00; open sugar $40.00; open compote $55.00; creamer $125.00; covered sugar $125.00; covered 6" jelly compote, a rarity $155.00; milk white 100% more; noted pieces in deep blue or peacock green are unique and worth 200% – 300% of clear.

No. 275 – RIBBED IVY – L. 33, 39 – M. 16. Another beautiful flint of the late 50s. Clear only. Flat sauces, honey dishes $20.00; castor bottles, each, spooner, scalloped edge salt $40.00; whiskey $65.00; bar tumbler $85.00; wine, champagne $110.00; goblet $50.00; open compotes, tall $65.00; extra large one, scalloped edge $110.00; low compote, scalloped edge, rare covered 6" jelly compote $125.00; covered salts, handled whiskey tumblers $125.00; egg cups $35.00; decanters without stoppers $85.00; with stopper $150.00; the two rarities in the pattern are the celery which has been listed at $350.00, and the hat made from tumbler mold $350.00 or more.

No. 278 – RIBBED PALM – L. 33, 38, 38A – M. 3 – K. Bk. 4-55. Clear flint made in Pittsburgh in 1868. Flat sauce $16.00; spooner $35.00; footed salts $40.00; egg cups $35.00; tumblers $95.00; wine $75.00; covered butter $125.00; 6" plate $45.00; champagne, celery $100.00; marble base lamp $125.00; all glass lamp $160.00; covered sugar $145.00; creamer $160.00; water pitcher $240.00; covered 6" jelly compote $125.00; open compotes $95.00. *Goblet reproduced in non-flint.*

No. 281 – INVERTED FERN – L. 33, 36 – M. 66. Clear flint of the 60s. Flat sauce $15.00; spooner $40.00; footed salt $35.00; egg cups $35.00; wine $95.00; compote $75.00; open sugar $40.00; covered sugar $95.00; creamer $195.00; water pitcher $275.00. *Goblet reproduced, marked "Made in France."*

No. 284 – FINE RIB, BELLFLOWER BORDER – McKerin pl. 209 No. 11. Rarest type of goblet of Bellflower group; early flint of the 40s; extremely rare goblet $1,000.00.

No. 287 – BELLFLOWER WITH LOOP – M. Bk. 2 – 40 – McKerin pl. 209 No. 6. Extremely rare form of Bellflower goblet $200.00.

No. 290 – BELLFLOWER, FINE RIB – M. 94 – L. 30 – K. Bk. 4-49. One might write an entire book on Bellflower alone; fine flint produced from the 30s over a long period of years by many companies. There are many qualities and types and this must be considered in valuation. I've listed the two rarest goblets above; the cakestand is a rarity which has been valued at $500.00; and I know an eager collector who paid $700.00 for one which is the only time I've ever seen it. Sometimes it is found with a pontil mark showing that the piece was blown. Made in Single Vine, Double Vine, coarse rib, fine rib, with straight sides and flared sides, design to top and with clear band there, knob stem and plain stem. A few rare pieces in color and milk white have been found. A syrup in electric blue has been reported to me; if perfect, this would be worth $2,500.00+. Little honey dishes and flat sauce $20.00; footed salt, spooner $50.00; 6" plate, tumbler $195.00; compote $125.00; whiskey tumbler $195.00; champagne $195.00; wine $150.00; covered butter $150.00; open sugar, egg cup $35.00; covered sugar, rare octagonal covered sugar $1,500.00; creamer $195.00; rare footed tumbler, celery $165.00; lamp with marble base $135.00; hat, made from tumbler mold $1,000.00; decanter, no stopper $150.00; with stopper $500.00; scarce, whiskey, with applied handle $375.00; water pitcher $350.00; small milk pitcher $600.00. Milk glass 100% – 200% more; electric blue and peacock green, 200% – 400% more. Goblet shown $45.00; *cake stand $2,500.00.*

No. 293 – BELLFLOWER, COARSE RIB – M. 16 shows this with straight sides. (Not pictured.) The straight sided coarse ribbed goblet is worth only about $45.00; coarse ribbed, barrel shaped, shown, is worth $45.00.

No. 294 – BELLFLOWER, FINE RIB, FLARE TOP, KNOB STEM – M. Bk. 2-29. (Not pictured.) Tall, with wide clear flared band. Scarce type $50.00. *A Bellflower milk (quart) pitcher has been reproduced in clear, blue, and canary non-flint thin glass and marked "MMA."*

296
Tulip with Sawtooth

299
Small Flowered Tulip

302
Tulip Band

305
Plain Tulip

308
Bull's Eye & Rosette

311
Chilson

314
Flower and Prism

317
Bull's Eye
and Wishbone

No. 296 – TULIP WITH SAWTOOTH – L. 37, 42, 53, 54 – M. 118 – K. Bk. 3-28. Clear flint of the early 60s and later made in non-flint. This is one of the few patterns which had stoppers which carried the design. Handled decanters in these patterns are especially fine; each with stopper $150.00. Spooner $40.00; footed salt, plain edge $30.00; with petalled edge $35.00; open sugar $40.00; egg cup $45.00; pomade jar, goblet $65.00; covered egg cup $160.00; 6" plate, cruet without stopper, footed tumbler $65.00; flat sauce $12.00; wine $55.00; champagne, mug $85.00; creamer, covered sugar $85.00; covered compote $95.00; covered butter $110.00; open compote $50.00. Non-flint 50% of this. Wine not reproduced. *Bryce McKee.*

No. 299 – SMALL FLOWERED TULIP – M. 78 – L. 50 calls it variant. Produced in the 60s in flint and later in non-flint. Clear. Values the same as for Tulip with Sawtooth. Small flint open compote in this is lovely $40.00; *mug $40.00; cobalt, 300% more.*

No. 300 – TULIP WITH RIBS – M. Bk. 2-52. (Not pictured.) Non-flint of the 70s. Like Small Flowered Tulip only this has ribs below the row of flowers. Goblet $40.00.

No. 302 – TULIP BAND – M. Bk. 2-104. Brilliant, bell toned flint of 50s. I've just found the small 6" compote in this, too, and it's a beauty. Goblet $75.00; small open compote $50.00.

No. 305 – PLAIN TULIP – M. 7. Brilliant, bell toned flint of the 50s. Goblet $50.00; wine, shown $35.00; *covered sugar $75.00.*

No. 306 – DOUBLE PETAL TULIP – M. 10. (Not pictured.) Contemporary of Plain Tulip which it resembles only here the stem is not reeded as it is in the former. Wine $35.00; goblet $55.00.

No. 308 – BULL'S EYE AND ROSETTE – L. V. 29 – M. 126. Clear flint with short thick stem and characteristics of glass of the 40s. Spooner, spill holder $60.00; tumbler $65.00; goblet $100.00; creamer $90.00; covered sugar $110.00.

No. 311 – CHILSON – M. Bk. 2-4. Heavy flint of the 50s. Very similar to Bull's Eye & Rosette, in fact, so very similar that this was one of my booboos several years ago. (Was I called to time.) Very scarce and in demand. Goblet $800.00 should be other pieces which would be as valuable as any flint of its time.

No. 314 – FLOWER AND PRISM – Heretofore unlisted. Clear, flint of the 50s. Another pattern in which only the creamer has been found yet. Only creamer $40.00.

No. 315 – FOUR PETAL – L. 12. (Not pictured.) Although I do not have a picture at hand I could not skip this beautiful flint of the 50s. It has two rows of joined petals as in Flower and Prism above. Sugar and creamer are very bulbous; creamer has applied handle. One sugar has domed lid $65.00; with regular lid $55.00; jam jar $55.00; bowl $33.00; very rare in color. *Creamer $110.00. Dome top covered sugar reproduced in flint for Henry Ford Museum.*

No. 317 – BULL'S EYE AND WISHBONE – M. Bk. 2-Frontispiece. There is really no bull's eye in the pattern, it's the scroll of the wishbone which pictures that way and it's really a fleur-de-lys and not a wishbone, but I'm letting the name stand; sounds nice. Fine, brilliant flint of the 50s. If there are other pieces, and there should be, the value would be comparable to contemporary fine pieces. *Rare goblet $175.00.*

No. 318 – WISHBONE – M. Bk. 2-80. (Not pictured.) Late, non-flint of the 90s. Surface textured with heavy finecut which forms a background for almost full length wishbones. Wine $20.00; goblet $20.00.

DON'T BE A PICTURE READER

Time was that when we bought a book, we read it. Now we have become so used to having our information predigested and presented as amusing or entertaining visual or auditory images via radio and television that we neglect reading. We buy books and magazines, look at the pictures, scan the ads hastily and by-pass the real information. Not all pictures shown here are of worthwhile pieces; some are here because they have been listed though they really have no place in the field of Early American Pattern Glass. Some are here for a basis of comparison. Read!

320
Diamond Point

323
Later Panelled
Diamond Point

326
Knob Stem Sawtooth

329
Later Sawtooth

332
Straight Huber

335
Barrel Huber

338
Crystal

341
Sawtooth Band

34

No. 320 – DIAMOND POINT – L. 42, 43, 44, 45 – M. 123 – K. Bk. 4-134. Clear flint, made in many types and forms over a period of years. Beautiful collared neck pitchers have applied handles. Flat sauce, honey dishes $15.00; spooner $45.00; footed salt, jelly glass $45.00; egg cup $50.00; celery, open compote $35.00; whiskey tumbler $40.00; goblet $50.00; wine $65.00; 6", 7", 8" plates $40.00–55.00; decanter $95.00; handled whiskey $95.00; champagne $95.00; four sizes of pitchers $150.00–250.00; many sizes of open bowls $30.00; covered bowls $75.00; candlesticks $200.00 a pair. Milk white 200% more; any color a rarity, 400% of this. Covered sugar $95.00; covered butter $100.00.

No. 321 – DIAMOND POINT WITH RIBS – M. Bk. 2-64. (Not pictured.) Exactly like above only the section below the diamond points has a design of small transverse ribs. Slightly scarcer, goblet $50.00.

No. 322 – PLAIN DIAMOND POINT – M. 26. (Not pictured.) Non-flint of the 80s. Diamond points cover entire bowl of the goblet and the stem is plain. Wine $15.00; goblet $30.00.

No. 324 – COARSE DIAMOND POINT – M. 153. (Not pictured.) Non-flint of the 80s. Here the points are coarser than usual but they are smaller than Sawtooth. Points cover entire bowl of goblet; stem is plain. Goblet $27.00; wine $15.00.

No. 323 – LATER PANELLED DIAMOND POINT – M. 123. Non-flint of the 80s. Comes in clear, goblet $14.00; canary $35.00; amber $25.00; blue $35.00. *Fostoria reproduced in 1970s – 80s a flint version in clear.*

No. 326 – KNOB STEM SAWTOOTH – L. 40, 42 – M. 123. Brilliant flint made from 50s for several years and in non-flint later. Mrs. Lee mentions sapphire blue in later forms; I've seen the four piece set and footed salt in the early in a blue which is not cobalt but which is deeper than the early electric blue. That color would be rare. I quote prices for brilliant, bell toned flint. Flat sauce $15.00; spooner $40.00; egg cup, wine $45.00; goblet $50.00; covered salt $65.00; celery $55.00 creamer $65.00; covered sugar $75.00; cordial $60.00; open salt, plain edge $20.00; pomade jar with cover $50.00; open compote $50.00; covered butter $80.00; water pitcher $150.00; cakestand, large $95.00.

No. 327 – BULB STEM SAWTOOTH – M. Bk. 2-45. (Not pictured.) Contemporary of the Knob Stem variety. Stem thickens to center and then decreases. Value 10% more than Knob Stem.

No. 328 – UMBILICATED SAWTOOTH – M. Bk. 2-43. (Not pictured.) Flint, just like the Knob Stem, here the sawteeth point inward; they are indented instead of protruding. Value less than Knob Stem $45.00.

No. 330 – NARROW SAWTOOTH – M. Bk. 2-7. (Not pictured.) Same as Knob Stem, only narrower; brilliant flint, Knob is slightly flatter. Value same as Knob Stem.

No. 329 – LATER SAWTOOTH – L. 41 – M. 153. Clear, non-flint of the 70s. The four piece child's set was made for the Philadelphia Centennial Exhibition. Child's covered butter, covered sugar, creamer, each spooner set $175.00. Cruet, open sugar, celery $35.00; covered butter, creamer $40.00; covered sugar $45.00; small cakestand $40.00; large cakestand $50.00; water pitcher $65.00; open compote $35.00; candlesticks, belong to this period, pair $75.00. Oval dishes with lion's head handles (L. 41) have been found in old catalog as belonging to Sawtooth Band pattern. Covers with serrated edges like this pattern, hardly ever fit perfectly; this does not mean they are not originals, on the contrary it's a sign of the work of this period and not of the reproduction makers of today.

No. 332 – HUBER – L. 11 – M. 38 calls this STRAIGHT HUBER. Clear flint of the 60s, made in many forms and used in hotels. Its plainness and good lines fit into our primitive or casual settings, yet its simplicity lends itself to sophisticated surroundings also. Flat sauce $10.00; small salts $15.00; spooner, open sugar, wine, jelly glass $25.00; mugs, tumblers, egg cups $25.00; handled egg cups $40.00; plates, bowls, goblets $35.00; celery, cordial $45.00; creamer, covered sugar $65.00; small covered dishes $45.00; decanter, no stopper $55.00; covered compotes, decanter with stopper $95.00.

No. 335 – BARREL HUBER – M. 21. Same as Straight Huber, only sides flare slightly more. Same value as Huber.

No. 338 – CRYSTAL – L. 2, 9, 9A. – M. 22. Beautiful, simple, versatile flint made by McKee Bros. of Pittsburgh from 1859 for several years in many forms. Bowls, wine, egg cup, spooner $25.00; goblet, celery $35.00; tumbler $35.00; ale glass, open compote $40.00; cracker dish which is tall compote with hinged metal cover $65.00; covered compotes, covered sugar, covered bowls $55.00–65.00; decanter, champagne $50.00; egg cup with applied handle, covered butter $65.00; creamer $55.00; water pitcher $95.00.

(Continued on Page 37)

344
Roman Key

347
Frosted Roman Key
with Flutes

350
Roman Key with Loops

351
Clear Roman Key

354
Stippled Roman Key

357
Wedding Ring

360
Single Wedding Ring

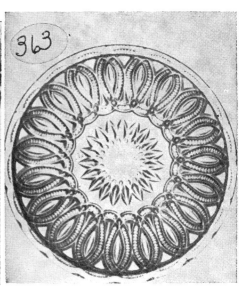

363
Scroll with Star

No. 344 – ROMAN KEY – L. 94 – M. 72 calls this one FROSTED ROMAN KEY WITH RIBS. Flint of the 60s. Sauce $20.00; egg cup, relish, low open compote $45.00; goblet $55.00; tumbler $75.00; berry bowl $45.00; wine, celery $65.00; covered butter $95.00; plate $60.00; covered sugar $85.00; decanter with stopper $165.00; creamer $110.00; water pitcher $250.00; spooner $45.00; footed salt $50.00; open compotes $55.00; covered compote, 3 piece castor set $125.00–150.00.

No. 347 – FROSTED ROMAN KEY WITH FLUTES – M. 143. Flint, contemporary of above; same values.

No. 352 – CLEAR BANDED ROMAN KEY – M. 11. (Not pictured.) Flint, same as Roman Key with Flutes but there is no frosting. All clear; value 30% less than frosted.

No. 350 – ROMAN KEY WITH LOOPS – M. 103. Non-flint of the late 70s. Goblet $35.00.

No. 351 – CLEAR ROMAN KEY – M. 17. Non-flint of the 70s. Pitchers have applied handles. Sauce dish $9.00; spooner $25.00; celery $30.00; creamer $35.00; covered sugar $40.00; open sugar $30.00; open compote $35.00; covered butter $50.00; covered compote, water pitcher $65.00.

No. 354 – STIPPLED ROMAN KEY – M. 17. Non-flint, clear stippled pattern of the 80s. Only goblet, scarce $30.00.

No. 355 – DOUBLE GREEK KEY – L.V. 38. (Not pictured.) Rather awkward, non-flint, made in Ohio (western part) or Indiana in the 80s. Found in clear blue and a blue opalescent. Tumblers, etc., have two rows of the keys with an interlaced band of circles, separated by small, plain strips between them. Creamer, spooner, and sugar have two rows of keys on the body of the piece with circles between them and a row of keys on the collared base. Molded handles. Sauce dish $9.00; spooner, tumbler $15.00; creamer $25.00; open sugar $18.00; covered butter $45.00; covered sugar $35.00; water pitcher $50.00. Opalescent 150% of this, blue opalescent (attractive color) 250% of this.

NOTE: The Greek or Roman key motif has been a favorite in classical design for centuries right down to the present day. It of itself adds no value; it's how it's used and on what it is used. I've seen horrible squat glass sugars and creamers in the dime store for the last 15 years and now occasionally some dealer hears the term applied to a pattern and some of these late nightmares find their way into shops. Patterns should be checked accurately with known text.

No. 357 – WEDDING RING – L. V. 19 – M. 2 calls it DOUBLE WEDDING RING and on plate 113 shows the same in slightly heavier form and calls it DOUBLE WEDDING RING – HEAVY. Heavy, clear, brilliant flint of the 60s. Goblet $65.00; wine $90.00; decanter $125.00; creamer $75.00; tumbler, champagne $85.00. *Goblet reproduced in non-flint, clear and colors.*

No. 360 – SINGLE WEDDING RING – M. 2. Clear, non-flint of the 70s. Only goblet $25.00. Should be other pieces.

No. 363 – SCROLL WITH STAR – L.V. 28 – M. Bk. 2-6 calls it Wycliff. The only place the star appears in the pattern is in the center of flat pieces such as the saucer or the plate. Clear, non-flint of the early 90s. Sauce, saucer, bowls $8.00; cup, spooner $15.00; cup and saucer $18.00; 6" plate, goblet $20.00; 10" plate $25.00; creamer $20.00; covered butter $45.00; covered sugar $25.00. Tall pieces mediocre in form.

No. 364 – YOKE AND CIRCLE – M. Bk. 2-124. (Not pictured.) Around the top of the goblet is a curved line beneath which is a horizontal band of interlaced circles as in Scroll and Star; beneath this are fan-like arrangements of prisms. Non-flint of the 90s. Only goblet $25.00.

(Continued from page 35)
No. 341 – SAWTOOTH BAND – M. 46 – L.V. 42 calls it AMAZON as does K. Bk. 3-10. The oval dish with clear top, sawtooth base and lion head handles and finial shown in L. 41 with Sawtooth, has been found in an old catalog as belonging to this, the Sawtooth Band, pattern. Clear, non-flint, made by Bryce Brothers in Pittsburgh, in the late 70s and early 80s. Individual salt dip, flat sauce $15.00; footed sauce $10.00; salt shaker $35.00; handled olive dish, spooner, open sugar, flat relish, tumbler, vase $20.00–30.00; wine, tall celery, bowls, goblet $30.00; small cakestand, oval lion handled dish, champagne, claret $50.00; water pitcher, syrup, medium cakestand, creamer, covered butter $55.00; covered sugar, large cakestand, covered compote $50.00. *Sometimes found ruby-flashed.*

366
Seneca Loop

369
Yuma Loop

372
Loop with Knob Stem

375
Loop and Honeycomb

378
Short Loops

381
Belcher Loop

384
Loop and Argus

387
Blucher

No. 366 – SENECA LOOP – M. 13 – L. 1 calls all LOOP and L. 154 No. 19. Clear flint made in the late 50s or 60s and continued in non-flint over several years. It's classic in simplicity and its fine appearance is more apparent when seen in a group. The fact that it comes in flint as well as non-flint allows one to get a fine pattern in any price range. Prices quoted are for flint; non-flint 50% of these. Footed salt $25.00; tumbler, egg cup, wine, goblet, champagne $30.00; spooner, open sugar $25.00; small open compotes $25.00; covered butter, large open compotes $60.00; extra large, scalloped edge compotes $55.00; covered sugar, covered compotes, creamer $70.00; water pitcher, cakestand $95.00.

No. 369 – YUMA LOOP – M. 161 – L. 154 No. 20. Contemporary of above. Same values.

No. 372 – LOOP WITH KNOB STEM – M. 2 – 105. Non-flint of the 80s. Only goblet $18.00.

No. 373 – MIDGET LOOP – M. Bk. 2-105. (Not pictured.) Lady's size of goblet above. Goblet $18.00.

No. 375 – LOOP AND HONEYCOMB – M. Bk. 2-2. Flint loop of the 60s. Only goblet $22.00.

No. 378 – SHORT LOOPS – M. Bk. 2-154. Non-flint of the late 80s. Only goblet $15.00.

No. 381 – BELCHER LOOP – M. 156. Flint loop of the 60s. Only goblet $25.00.

No. 384 – LOOP AND ARGUS – M. 56. Made in flint in the late 60s and in non-flint in the later years. Goblet, flint $35.00; non-flint $20.00. I just saw an open sugar in this and I believe we will eventually find that most of these goblets were made in sets with other pieces.

No. 387 – BLUCHER – M. 150. Non-flint of the late 80s. Only goblet $15.00.

SHOWS

For the past few years the number of shows has been mushrooming. It bespeaks a fine interest and has been an aid to innumerable good causes but has been the instrument of fooling many people who have parted with good money for reproductions or poor merchandise. People feel that because the articles are seen at a show which is advertised as an antique show that the things displayed are of that caliber. A show should have a professional manager and by that I mean not a self-styled one, but a person who has been or is a dealer. Otherwise it should not be put on as an antique show — it could be called "Nice Old Pieces," or "We're Having a Sale...There May Be Some Antiques There." There is a definite moral question involved and these good people should realize it. Even in the best of shows a weak spot will suddenly appear. Generally the right kind of manager notes it and asks the dealer, who may simply be uninformed, to remove the questioned pieces from display. Collectors who definitely know weak spots, should help protect novice collectors by informing the management of misrepresentation. Care must be taken to speak from some knowledge and not from Sairey Gamp type of information.

If you saw the truck loads of pieces which dealers buy at shows, you would realize they are some of the best places to buy. There is a true adage among dealers that, "There is a bargain in every shop." Think what possibilities there are in a show full of shops.

390
New England Flute

393
Bessimer Flute

396
Sexton Flute

399
Reed Stem Flute

402
Sandwich Flute

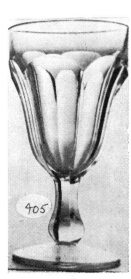

405
Long Panelled Flute

408
Square Flute

411
Dutchess Loop

No. 390 – NEW ENGLAND FLUTE – M. Bk. 2-142 – L. 1 and 13 does not name the different types of the family. Clear flint, made from the 50s through the 60s. Beautiful sets of goblets may be combined using similar types; one could use a set of tall, thin ones or a set of small squatty ones. It is much more effective than trying to get an exactly matching set. Many pieces were made in many forms and they are all outstanding in design and are as fitting to primitive and casual settings as they are to the most sophisticated surroundings. Not fully appreciated now, hence they are a real bargain in flint glass. Flat sauces, honeys $15.00; egg cups $20.00; footed salts $35.00; tumblers $20.00–25.00; wines $25.00; champagnes, ale glass $40.00; bitters bottles $55.00; candlesticks, pair $95.00; decanter $65.00; goblets listed below. Goblet of this type $25.00–30.00.

No. 391 – BANDED FLUTE – M. Bk. 2-111. (Not pictured.) Same as New England Flute only knob is larger and the top of panels are gently curved instead of being highly arched. Flint goblet $25.00.

No. 393 – BESSIMER FLUTE – M. 4. Squat, early type. Goblet $25.00.

No. 394 – PYRAMID FLUTE – M. Bk. 2-158. (Not pictured.) Like Bessimer Flute only this has a wider, clear band at the top. Bulb stem is slightly more angular or less round. Flint goblet $25.00.

No. 395 – BROOKLYN FLUTE – M. 4. (Not pictured.) Another one of the early squatty flutes, very like Bessimer only here the panels are highly arched and the goblet is about ½" taller. Flint goblet $25.00.

No. 396 – SEXTON FLUTE – M. 8. Flint goblet $25.00.

No. 399 – REED STEM FLUTE – Hitherto unlisted. Flint goblet $25.00. Note that here the panels narrow and continue, uninterrupted to extend down to form a reeded stem.

Nol. 400 – CONNECTICUT FLUTE – M. 8. (Not pictured.) Narrower than Reeded Stem and panels form stem but come to definite end as they form the little platform on the base of the goblet. Flint goblet $25.00.

No. 402 – SANDWICH FLUTE – Heretofore unlisted. This is a very brilliant flint, blown goblet. This type $25.00.

No. 405 – LONG PANELLED FLUTE – Heretofore unlisted. Note how panels continue to stem in one line. Flint goblet $25.00.

No. 406 – HEXAGON FLUTE – M. 134. (Not pictured.) Non-flint of the 80s which resembles Long Panelled above only here panels do not run onto stem, clear band at top is wider and the foot is a hexagon. Put here for comparison. Non-flint goblet $15.00.

No. 408 – SQUARE FLUTE – M. 8. Flint goblet $25.00.

No. 409 – ELEGANT – M. Bk. 2-4. (Not pictured.) Really a square flute, the panels are not arched but end in horizontal line across the top. Brilliant flint goblet $25.00.

NO. 411 – DUCHESS LOOP – Really another flute. M. Bk. 2-1. Brilliant flint goblet $25.00–30.00.

No. 412 – PITTSBURGH FLUTE – M. Bk. 2-126. (Not pictured.) Just like Dutchess Loop only this has rounded knob stem and arch of panels is slightly less curved. Flint goblet $25.00 – 30.00.

No. 413 – GIANT FLUTE – M. Bk. 2-132. (Not pictured.) A beauty; angular bowl similar to Dutchess Loop, but taller and more flared, tall stem with huge round knob at top. Scarce $25.00.

No. 414 – RED FLUTE – M. Bk. 2-21. (Not pictured.) Not flute and NOT OLD. Orange red, belonging to dime store set found in tumblers, pitchers, etc., about 25 years ago. Old glass was not made in this color. This is squat, panels run to hexagon base. No value as far as old glass is concerned.

No. 415 – TAPERING FLUTE – M. Bk. 2-81. (Not pictured.) Very slender MODERN crystal goblet in which there is no separation between goblet bowl and stem; the panels, after an inch plain band, run to base; very tall and thin. No value as far as Early American Pressed Glass is concerned.

417
Pitt Honeycomb

420
Bumble Bee Honeycomb

423
Late Barrel Honeycomb

426
Banded
Vernon Honeycomb

429
Lyston Honeycomb

432
Laredo Honeycomb

435
New York Honeycomb

438
Frosted
Top Honeycomb

No. 417 – PITT HONEYCOMB – L. 24. Flint of the 60s; comes in medium weight and a heavy type. Honeycomb was made over a long period of years with the later being non-flint and worth 40% of the flint. Prices quoted are for flint. Again a combination of related types is more interesting than all of one type. Early pitchers have applied handles, are bulbous and classic in line. Egg cup $20.00; handled whiskey $100.00; celery design to top $45.00; tumbler $35.00; creamer $50.00; water pitcher $125.00; covered sugar $75.00. The price of this old flint glass is soaring at present as its usefulness and beauty are being recognized. Pitt goblet shown $35.00 *OMN Pitt, Diamond, Bakewell and Pears mug, applied handle $110.00.*

No. 418 – GIANT HONEYCOMB – M. 9. (Not pictured.) Very rare type of flint honeycomb; with honeycombs going from top edge of goblet all the way down the stem. Goblet $50.00.

No. 419 – MASTER HONEYCOMB – M. Bk. 2-149. (Not pictured.) Very scarce type similar to Bumble Bee Honeycomb, below; in this early form, the stem is slightly shorter, the narrower bowl flares slightly and the base is rayed. Goblet $35.00.

No. 420 – BUMBLE BEE HONEYCOMB – M. 9. Flint Honeycomb of the 60s. Goblet $35.00.

No. 423 – LATE BARREL HONEYCOMB – Heretofore unlisted. Non-flint of the 70s. Goblet $15.00–20.00.

No. 424 – BARREL HONEYCOMB – M. Bk. 2-129. (Not pictured.) Flint of the 50s slightly more rounded than Late Barrel, above, and this has large ball knob at base of stem. Goblet $25.00–30.00.

No. 426 – BANDED VERNON HONEYCOMB – M. 9. Non-flint of the 80s. Clear $25.00; canary $45.00; amber $30.00; blue $35.00.

No. 429 – LYSTON HONEYCOMB – M. 10. Non-flint of the 80s. Clear $15.00; canary $30.00; amber $20.00; blue $25.00.

No. 430 – OPAQUE WHITE HONEYCOMB – (Not pictured.) M. 65 is Lyston in milk glass. Value $35.00.

No. 432 – LAREDO HONEYCOMB – M. 10 – L. 24 shows it on original catalog page as NEW YORK HONEYCOMB. Made in flint. Goblet $25.00, in non-flint $15.00; wine, flint $25.00, non-flint $15.00; goblet, canary $35.00; amber $30.00; blue $35.00.

No. 435 – ENGRAVED NEW YORK HONEYCOMB – or Laredo – M. 10 – L. 24. In this, which is non-flint, engraving adds to value. Goblet $30.00.

No. 438 – FROSTED TOP HONEYCOMB WITH MEDALLION. Not heretofore listed. Here is a truly unique form of honeycomb, flint with molded medallion in the frosted top. Grapes are engraved in the medallion. Only goblet $35.00. I believe it to be a Pittsburgh version of the pattern.

COLOR TERMINOLOGY

CRYSTAL means simply clear glass. The commercial use of it to denote a glass which rings is a misnomer. If you stop to think, you will realize that serving pieces are not cut from pieces of crystal; glass which rings is simply glass with high lead content.

Vaseline[1] is a blown Sandwich product, made in candlesticks, bottles, inkwells, etc. The similar color in table wares is termed YELLOW or CANARY. In light blue we use the term SAPPHIRE; a medium dark blue, cold in tone with no red overtones, we call ELECTRIC BLUE; deep blue, with red over-tones is termed COBALT BLUE; in pale green, we have the similar APPLE GREEN[2] or LIME; in amber we have the pale shade known as PALE AMBER; a medium shade called GOLDEN AMBER; and a deep shade with coppery overtones, we call BLOOD AMBER; a light smoky shade is known as SMOKY AMBER; the glass with red in the glass is the beloved CRANBERRY; the glass in which the red is flashed over the glass is RUBY; the glass made from red with a touch of gold in it is AMBERINO which at times shades to a fine deep Fuchsia color; the glass which starts with the greenish yellow and goes to cranberry is RUBINO; PIGEON BLOOD is hard to describe – red with vivid overtones of a color which approximates sunlight; there is a LIGHT and a DARK AMETHYST; and a DIRTY MUDDY AMETHYST which is FOUND ONLY IN REPRODUCTIONS.

EDITORS NOTE: While Metz felt amber and canary were equal in value, nearly 40 years later, canary or vaseline is far more valuable and amber has fallen from fashion.

[1]Currently Vaseline refers to a yellow color glass that will fluoresce under black light.
[2]Apple Green will also fluoresce under black light.

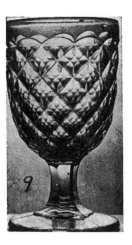

441
Smocking

444
Almond Thumbprint

447
Barrel Thumbprint

450
Three Row
Baby Thumbprint

453
Wide Band
Baby Thumbprint

456
Challinor Thumbprint

459
Thumbprint and Hobnail

462
Crystal with Honeycom

No. 441 – SMOCKING – L.V. 25 – McKerin pl. 207 No. 3 – M. 2 calls it Plain Smocking. Fine old flint of the 50s; pitchers are stunning with big flare top and beautifully applied handles. Goblets $65.00; creamer $95.00; sugar $75.00. Should be other pieces, a water pitcher shaped like the creamer would bring $200.00.

No. 442 – LINED SMOCKING – M. 2. (Not pictured.) Same as above in shape, but this has transverse lines through the bottom of the units. Value same as for Plain Smocking.

No. 444 – ALMOND THUMBPRINT – L. 154 – No. 14 and M. 156 show later type than the very early flint shown here. Has been known as Pointed Thumbprint. Prices for flint are quoted; non-flint 50% of this. Wine, $35.00; egg cup $35.00; goblet $40.00; tumbler $35.00; spooner, bowls $30.00; creamer $55.00; covered sugar, water pitcher $70.00.

No. 447 – BARREL THUMBPRINT – M. 1. Brilliant, early flint; goblet $35.00; wine $30.00. Clear only.

No. 448 – HOTEL THUMBPRINT – M. 1. (Not pictured.) Contemporary of the Barrel type. Does not curve quite as much on sides and is slightly heavier. Goblets $30.00; wine $25.00. Clear only.

No. 450 – THREE ROW BABY THUMBPRINT – M. Bk. 2-2. Non-flint of the late 80s. Wine $15.00; goblet $20.00–25.00.

No. 453 – WIDE BAND BABY THUMBPRINT – M. Bk. 2-11 calls this Baby Thumbprint – Three Rows, a name which he has used for another pattern. Non-flint of late 80s. Goblet $25.00. Same as below.

No. 453 – FOUR ROW BABY THUMBPRINT – M. 156. Here is the same non-flint as is called Three Row in Bk. 2-11. It's a question as to whether one counts the partial row at bottom of goblet bowl as a row. It's unimportant as is the goblet $25.00. *Reproduced in color.*

No. 456 – CHALLINOR THUMBPRINT – L.V. 58 – M. 2-40 calls it TALL BABY THUMBPRINT. Clear, non-flint of the 80s. Flat sauce $7.50; spooner, tumbler, flat relish $20.00; salt shaker $15.00 each, pair $25.00; bowls, open sugar, water bottle $25.00; goblet $30.00; creamer, covered butter $40.00; covered sugar $45.00.

No. 459 – THUMBPRINT AND HOBNAIL – Heretofore unlisted. Early flint of the late 50s. Brilliant and beautiful. Another argument for the continued search for fine unlisted patterns. Should be other pieces. Goblet $55.00.

Nol. 460 – GIANT BABY THUMBPRINT – M. Bk. 2-40. (Not pictured.) Belongs to same family as above. Brilliant flint, shallow, wide bowl goblet with long bulb stem. Four rows of thumbprints. Goblet $65.00.

No. 462 – CRYSTAL WITH HONEYCOMB – M. Bk. 2-138. Clear, non-flint of the 80s. Only goblet $25.00.

INTERESTING COLLECTIBLES

Goblets with unusual stems — Wines with unusual stems.

Goblets with berries — "Granmother's berry patch."

Ribbed goblets — either all flint or all lime glass — do not combine flint and non-flint.

Animal goblets — these are very scarce only on the etched but these are beautiful.

A set of etched goblets; these were made in the late 60s and early 70s. They have not been reproduced. Due to the fact that they are difficult to photograph, they have not been stressed. There are lovely scenes, dogs, birds and flowers.

It is much more interesting to have a set of related goblets or wines than all of one kind.

A few patriotic pieces for special days. One patriotic piece should be in every American home. It will do its own talking.

465
Knives and Forks

468
Banded
Knife and Fork

471
Block and Honeycomb

474
Prisms with Loops

477
Flaring Eight Panel

480
Cayuga

483
Plain Mioton

486
Tick-Tack-Toe

No. 465 – KNIVES AND FORKS – M. 158. Flint of the 60s and made later in non-flint. Flint goblet $30.00; non-flint goblet $15.00.

No. 466 – LIPPED KNIFE AND FORK. (Not pictured.) M. Bk. 2-127 calls this KNIVES AND FORKS but I'm adding a word to distinguish it. Non-flint of the 80s. Divided into panels, one wide panel, representing knife blade, and a panel with prisms representing fork tines, alternating around the bowl. The bottom of goblet bowl is lipped where it joins the stem which has a ring at the top and at the bottom. Goblet $15.00.

No. 468 – BANDED KNIFE AND FORK – M. Bk. 2-137. Lightweight, non-flint of the late 80s. Not of the same family as the flint Knives and Forks above. Lately, at a small show I found this labeled, "Knives & Forks – flint" and it had a flint price. I wanted it to picture here and called the dealer's attention to the mistake; it had absolutely no resonance but his reply was that he heard Knives and Forks was a flint pattern. One can see why I'm trying to correct some of these listing and how important it is for the student to check the pattern name carefully. Wine $12.00; champagne $15.00; goblet $15.00. *This is a Depression era pattern, not Early American Pattern Glass. Aka "Colonial" from Hocking Glass, 1934 – 36.*

No. 471 – BLOCK AND HONEYCOMB – Heretofore unlisted non-flint pattern of the 80s. Only goblet $17.00.

No. 474 – PRISMS WITH LOOPS – M. 63. Non-flint of the 80s. Only goblet $15.00.

NO. 477 – FLARING EIGHT PANEL – Non-flint of the 80s, found in clear and colored. Clear $15.00; green, pictured $25.00; amber $20.00.

No. 480 – CAYUGA – M. Bk. 2-142. Clear flint of the 60s with most interesting stem. Goblet $25.00.

No. 483 – PLAIN MIOTON – RED TOP. Lightweight non-flint of the late 80s, comes plain and with red top. Plain $15.00; with red $30.00.

No. 486 – TICK-TACK-TOE – M. 63. Clear, non-flint of the late 80s. Only goblet $15.00.

IS PATTERN GLASS ANTIQUE?

Yes, if you use the term correctly. The word *antique* is relative. A piece of furniture made in 1880 would not be classified as antique as the making of furniture was mostly mechanized as we emerged into the mechanical way of manufacturing in the time of the industrial revolution, the 1830s. There was very little difference in the techniques in manufacturing furniture or china from the 1830s – 1890s. That is why 1830 is generally considered the dividing line between the antique and the modern. In Pattern Glass we have a technique of manufacturing, namely pressing, which was not in use prior to the invention of a practical pressing machine in the late 1820s. Pressed glass made in 1880 is old in comparison to the age of the form of manufacture. To be true Pattern Glass, the design must be of the type used in the product in its a better specimens, designs which expressed the history, moods or tastes of its time. When Pressed Glass aped the cut glass of the 90s it lost its value and became just pressed glass and not Early American Pattern Glass. That the word *antique* is really relative can be understood when I say I just heard an archeologist from our Oriental Institute pass on a brass vase. "It's 500 years old, no doubt," he said, "but that with us is not old." The term will ever be relative, but it should not be carelessly used.

489
Big Ball Honeycomb

492
Master Argus

495
Iconoclast

502
Prism and
Block Band

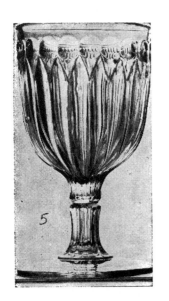

505
Brooklyr

508
Giant Prism with
Thumbprint band

511
Prism

514
Fine Prism

No. 489 – BIG BALL HONEYCOMB – Hitherto unlisted. Very early flint, possibly the earliest form of Honeycomb. Clear of the 40s. Rare, only goblet $50.00.

No. 492 – MASTER ARGUS – M. Bk. 2-142. Very early form of this family. Brilliant flint of the 40s. Only goblet $55.00.

No. 495 – ICONOCLAST – M. 20. Clear flint of the 60s. Only goblet $50.00.

No. 502 – PRISM AND BLOCK BAND – M. Bk. 2-34. Clear, non-flint of the late 80s. Goblet, clear $30.00; with red top $40.00.

No. 503 – CROWN JEWEL – L.V. 68 – M. 163 calls it CHANDELIER. (Not pictured.) Just about like Prism & Block Band above, only in this, below the band of the blocks is a row of elongated jewels. These same jewels form the stem. Flat sauce $15.00; finger bowl, bowls, spooner, open sugar $30.00; goblet, wine $75.00; open compote $75.00; water pitcher $95.00; celery $40.00; salt shaker $30.00; tray for water set $45.00; creamer $45.00; covered butter $75.00; covered sugar, round covered compote, square covered compote $65.00; footed salt $35.00.

No. 505 – BROOKLYN – M. 131 – K. Bk. 7-3. Flint of the late 60s. Goblet $65.00; creamer $75.00. The rare punch bowl listed by McKerin is not Brooklyn but a much rarer pattern listed below.

No. 508 – GIANT PRISM WITH THUMBPRINT BAND – M. Bk. 2-99. Unique bell toned flint of the 40s. On plate 213 No. 9 of McKerin, look at the foot of the punch bowl and then at the stem of this goblet and you will see the punch bowl belongs to this pattern. Goblet $85.00; punch bowl $400.00; *wine $75.00; champagne $95.00.*

No. 511 – PRISM – M. 75 lists this with the base rayed to the edge. Flint of the 60s. L. 13, 27. Heavy clear flint which should not be confused with later non-flint Prism and Flute, the trade name of which was Prism. Egg cup $20.00; decanter $75.00; footed salt $30.00; champagne, wine $35.00; creamer $40.00; water pitcher $75.00; open compotes, goblet $35.00. These prices are for the type which is rayed to edge; type pictured 20% less.

No. 514 – FINE PRISM – M. Bk. 2-157. Another of the flint Prism family, made in the 60s. Values 20% less than Prism rayed to edge.

COLLECTORS' ITEM

Time was, a generation or so ago, when connoisseurs used the term objets d'art frequently. Then the term was appropriated by those seeking to add prestige to inferior wares. A gilded sign, a fawning "Continental" manner and a high-brow atmosphere were their stock in trade. It may have impressed the "Get culture quick class," but no one else. I remember Mr. G. W. Eggers, former head of our Art Institute, asking us students how much art we had ever spotted in such a place. This term lost much of its appeal but is succeeded by the overworked "collectors' items." Literally, of course, the old keys, bits of string, etc., which make up the contents of the pockets of a 12-year old are collectors' items. However it is the usage, among discriminating antique dealers and collectors to reserve the term for the fine, the unusual, the rare. Lately, I've seen modern novelty salt shakers, common butter pats and carnival glass listed as collectors' items. Did it ever occur to the unwary purchaser that these motley assortments are foisted on the public by people whose sole interest is to have something easily attainable with little outlay of cash and for which a mass market can be developed. Buying and selling is necessary to life and is not evil in itself, but crass commercialism cannot be the dominant motif in merchandising any form of art.

517
Fine Rib

520
Fine Rib—Plain Band

523
Later Prisms with
Diamond Point

526
Banded Prisms

529
Plain Paling

533
Transverse Ribs

536
Celtic Cross

539
Triple Band Mioton

No. 517 – FINE RIB – L. 36 – M. 148 calls it FINE RIB TO TOP. Mrs. Watkins in *Cambridge Glass* states it was made by New England Glass Co. in the 60s. Clear, brilliant, flint and later, made in non-flint. This pattern is of the early ribbed families such as Bellflower, Ribbed Pal, etc. Many open compotes on high and low standards $60.00 – 70.00; decanter with stopper $85.00; lamp with applied handles $145.00; pitcher $250.00; celery $75.00; covered butter $95.00; handled mugs $65.00 bitters bottles $70.00; covered, footed salt $100.00; covered colored egg cups $750.00+; covered sugar, creamer $75.00; wines $65.00; champagnes $125.00; goblets $75.00; 6", 7" plates $75.00.

No. 520 – FINE RIB, PLAIN BAND – M. 75. Made in flint in the 60s and non-flint later. Prices same as for Fine Rib above.

No. 523 – LATER PRISM WITH DIAMOND POINT – M. 73 – K. Bk. 3-28. Non-flint, later form of the pattern listed below. Made in the late 70s; pitchers have applied handles. Footed salt $15.00; egg cup $22.00; spooner $20.00; celery $20.00; covered butter $50.00; open sugar $20.00; creamer $30.00; covered sugar $40.00; covered compote $50.00.

No. 524 – PRISM WITH DIAMOND POINT – L. 96 – M. 73. (Not pictured.) Early flint form of this pattern, heavier in weight than above and pieces have knob stems. Footed salts $35.00; spooner $40.00; egg cup $35.00; double egg cup, tumbler $50.00; bowls, open compotes $35.00; covered butter $50.00; celery, covered jelly $40.00; goblet, wine $45.00; creamer $70.00; covered sugar $75.00.

No. 526 – BANDED PRISM – M. Bk. 2-148. Non-flint of the early 80s. Clear; only goblet $25.00.

No. 529 – PLAIN PALING – M. Bk. 2-14 shows this as BANDED plain stem. The banded type is more angular, too, bowl of goblet is not rounded. Non-flint of the 80s, clear. Goblet $20.00; open sugar, spooner $20.00; celery $30.00; open compote $25.00; small cakestand $35.00; covered butter $50.00; creamer $30.00; covered sugar, large cakestand $50.00.

No. 533 – TRANSVERSE RIBS – M. Bk. 2-42. Large, heavy, non-flint of the 80s. This is a side view, base is square; front and back views are entirely covered with meeting ribs. Goblet $35.00.

No. 536 – CELTIC CROSS – K. Bk. 2-111. Made by Duncan, Miller Glass Co. in Pittsburgh in the late 80s. Much better when not etched; it is entirely "too busy" to have more trimming. Bowl of goblet resembles Square Panes from this view but in this the goblet is rounded while in the former the pillars form the corners. Goblet $27.00; creamer $25.00; covered butter $40.00; covered sugar $35.00.

No. 539 – TRIPLE BAND MIOTON – Not heretofore listed. Non flint of the 80s. Only goblet $20.00.

WHAT GLASS DATA IS IMPORTANT?

In education of bygone days, we memorized heaps of facts, names, initials, exact dates, etc., till most folks hated school. Modern education stresses live, pleasurable reaction, ties the past with the present, and gleans information for the future from it. It is no longer a question of locating events within a few miles, a few months, a few identifiable, but unimportant persons. Now it is: How did it happen? How did it affect the lives of people of the past? Was it important? What can I do with it? What can I learn from it? It isn't a question of whether Jonathan Ordinary working at a factory at Tompkin's Creek, Pa., from Sept. 7, 1869 – Feb. 6, 1871, produced 2,469 pieces falling into 30 classifications or whether the questioned pieces were made by him and not by Simpson Nobody, who worked ten miles from there two or three years later. If Jonathan were Paul Revere or Chippendale, it might be different. We no longer consider walking encyclopedias, people of brains, culture or "nice to be near to." Today we take the things made previously, learn the characteristics of the decades, learn their possibilities and uses in our daily lives. That's the glass data we want.

542
Stedman

545
Manting

548
Banded Icicle

551
Belted Icicle

554
Icicle with Diamond Bowl

557
Low Fluted Icicle

560
Mioton—Pleat Band

563
Saxon

No. 541 – BLAZE – L. 13 – M. 76. (Not pictured.) Clear flint, made by New England Glass Co. in the 60s. Sauce dish $10.00; spooner, open bowls $40.00; rectangular salt, egg cup $35.00; wine, champagne, tumbler $75.00; goblet, cordial $55.00; handled egg cup, celery, lemonade glass, open compote $50.00; 6", 7" plate $30.00; with cheese dish cover $75.00; creamer $55.00; covered sugar covered compote, tall $75.00; low covered bowls and compotes $65.00. Like Stedman, only all prisms are thin.

No. 542 – STEDMAN – L. 13 – M. 88. On plate 13 Millard lists Stedman with plain base, on plate 76 shows it with sides slightly more rounded and calls it Stedman – Barrel shape. Clear flint of the 60s. Made in many forms, values same as for Blaze, a contemporary.

No. 545 – MANTING – M. 148. Clear flint of the late 60s. Only goblet $35.00.

No. 546 – ICICLE – L. 19, 22. (Not pictured.) Non-flint of the 70s, much like Flute Icicle only in this the icicles climb more sharply and go all the way to bottom of body of the dish. Flat sauce $10.00; footed salt, spooner, oval relish, open sugar $25.00; oval bowls, open compotes, goblet $35.00; flat butter $45.00; footed covered butter, creamer, covered sugar $50.00; water pitcher $75.00. In milk glass 100% more.

No. 548 – BANDED ICICLE – M. Bk. 2-137. Non-flint of the 70s. Goblet $25.00.

No. 549 – ICICLE WITH BULB STEM – M. Bk. 2-42. (Not pictured.) Same as Banded Icicle above, only it has three icicles spaced at equal intervals which reach almost to top of goblet. Goblet, non-flint $30.00.

No. 550 – ICICLE WITH CHAIN BAND – M. Bk. 2-52. (Not pictured.) Same as Banded Icicle only this has a band formed of diamonds and lines above the icicles and has a long stem which grows into a bulb at the bottom. This I've found in brilliant flint $45.00.

No. 556 – DOUBLE ICICLE – M. Bk. 2-74. (Not pictured.) Non-flint of the 80s. This has an angular shaped goblet bowl and a second row of icicles extends down from the top to almost meet the row of icicles coming from the bottom. Only goblet $25.00.

No. 554 – ICICLE WITH DIAMOND BOWL – M. Bk. 2-87. Millard says this is Diamond base but I'm sure that is a typographical error as the diamonds are in the bowl of the goblet, not in the base. Flint of the late 60s. Goblet $50.00; may be found in lime glass $22.00.

No. 555 – ICICLE WITH LOOPS – M. Bk. 2-137. (Not pictured.) Same as Icicle with Diamond Bowl only this has loops where above has diamonds; design and loops are slightly lower on the bowl. Flint goblet $50.00.

No. 551 – BELTED ICICLE – M. 102 calls it BANDED ICICLE and K. Bk. 3-66 calls it LATE ICICLE. Non-flint of the 80s. Spooner, open sugar $25.00; covered butter $75.00; creamer $35.00; cakestand $50.00; covered sugar $35.00; goblet $30.00. *Fostoria, 1889.*

No. 557 – LOW FLUTED ICICLE – Heretofore unlisted. Clear, flint of the late 60s. Only goblet $30.00.

No. 560 – MIOTON, PLEAT BAND – M. Bk. 2-131. Clear flint late 60s. Only goblet $28.00.

No. 563 – SAXON – L. 20, 21 – M. Bk. 2-12. Clear, non-flint of the early 70s but another pattern that carries the characteristics of the old flints in appearance. Flat sauce, individual salt $10.00; spooner, open sugar, relish dish, oval platter, oval bowls $20.00; open compote, goblet $35.00; 6" plate, tumbler, egg cup $30.00; covered butter $45.00; creamer $25.00; covered sugar, covered compote $35.00. It seems strange that there is very little demand for this pleasing, early pattern.

566
Cabbage Rose

569
Open Rose

572
Rose-in-Snow

575
Rose of Sharon

578
Rose Sprig

581
Hundred Leaved Rose

584
Primrose

587
Clematis

No. 566 – CABBAGE ROSE – L. 122 – M. 52 – K. Bk. 3-40 and Bk. 7-66. Beautiful, clear, non-flint, made in Wheeling, W. Va., in the 70s and shown in catalogs as late as 1881. Pitchers have applied handles, finials are a pointed rose bud. Roses are very tightly curled. Six sizes in flat sauces from 4" – 7" range from $10.00 – 12.00; spooner $25.00; open sugar, footed salt, oval relish dish $25.00; egg cup, open compotes $45.00 two smaller sizes of cakestands $95.00; goblet $45.00; wine $45.00; tumbler, celery, creamer $45.00; two larger cakestands $95.00; creamer $45.00; covered sugar $55.00; covered compote $65.00; water pitcher $125.00. Goblet now copiously reproduced.

No. 569 – OPEN ROSE – L. 122, 123 – M. 52. Another, beautiful, non-flint pattern of the 70s made only in clear. Pitchers have applied handles; finials are interesting geometric. Patterns of this type are much more attractive on a shelf where light passes through them and seems to make them alive, than most of the late, garish, hard colored specimens which some folk seem to crave. Made in two types, normal impression and heavy, which Millard lists M. 52. In the latter, the roses seem to stand out from the body of glass an eighth of an inch. Prices given are for the regular type; extremely heavy, which is difficult to find, is worth 20% more. Flat sauce $10.00; spooner $35.00; oval relish $20.00; open sugar, oval vegetables $25.00; egg cup $30.00; tumblers $50.00; compotes $50.00; goblets $35.00; covered butter $75.00; covered sugar, creamer $50.00; covered compotes $80.00; water pitcher $185.00. *Spooner reproduced in cobalt, pink, amber, clear.*

No. 572 – ROSE IN SNOW – L. 120, 73, 122 – L.V. 8 – M. 17 – K. Bk. 4-43. Non-flint of the 70s, comes in two types, round and square. Goblets and pieces with exception of the four piece set are common to both kinds. Molded handles, geometric finial; large round plate is handled, smaller plates are not. SQUARE TYPE: covered butter $65.00; covered sugar $50.00; creamer $35.00; open bowl, spooner $35.00; low covered compote $65.00. ROUND TYPE: Flat sauces $10.00; footed sauce $15.00; oval relish $25.00; water pitcher $125.00; 6", 7" plates $25.00; "In Remembrance" mug $30.00; large mugs, applied handles $42.00; 5" plates $35.00; goblet $35.00; 10" plate $25.00; rare oval platter, rare double pickle with rose handles and roses on the sides $100.00; 5" covered jelly $55.00; rare covered toddy jar, complete with plate $100.00. Color in old are scarce; amber, canary 25% more, blue 50% more. Goblet, "In Remembrance" mugs, 10" plate, *goblets, square sugar bowl* now reproduced in clear and colors. *Rare cake stand $100.00.*

No. 575 – ROSE OF SHARON – M. 116. Clear, non-flint of the late 80s. In shape and quality of glass, this is like Sugar Pear. Both probably were made for commercial jelly containers. Only goblet $25.00.

No. 576 – CLOVER AND DAISY – M. 116. (Not pictured.) Another non-flint contemporary of Rose of Sharon. Spray of clover on one side of goblet and a daisy on the other. These three patterns, though not the sparkling, sophisticated type, which so many like, have a charm of their own which one discovers if she studies them; it's the relaxing charm of dusk after the sharp sunshine of a busy day; ideal in primitive settings. Only goblet $25.00.

No. 578 – ROSE SPRIG – L. 86, 124, 125 – M. 77 – K. Bk. 3-42. Non-flint, late 80s, made in clear, yellow, amber, blue. Footed sauce $15.00; oval pickle, spooner, $25.00; open sugar, 6" square handled nappy, boat shaped relish $25.00; sleigh salt $35.00; with patent date 1888 $50.00; tumbler $35.00; handled tumbler $45.00; celery $20.00; 8" plate, water tray, water pitcher $25.00; goblet, creamer $40.00; covered sugar $55.00; cakestand $85.00; low covered compote $75.00. Yellow, 50% more, amber 25% more, blue, 30% more.

No. 581 – HUNDRED LEAVED ROSE – K. Bk. 2-28. Interesting, non-flint of the late 80s, in clear. Flat sauce $10.00; spooner, bowl, open sugar $20.00; covered butter $65.00; creamer $30.00; covered sugar $40.00.

No. 584 – PRIMROSE – L. 136, 114 – M. 138 – K. Bk. 3-119. Non-flint of the late 80s, made in clear, yellow, amber and blue and a few pieces of light green. Flat sauce $10.00; spooner $25.00; toddy plate, footed sauce $15.00; egg cup, 6", 7" plate, waste bowl $30.00; plain stemmed goblet $25.00; knob stem goblet $30.00; handled cake plate, creamer $35.00; covered butter $45.00; covered sugar, water tray $40.00; water pitcher $75.00; cakestand $65.00; covered compote $55.00. Amber 25% more, yellow 50% more, blue or green 50% more. What is called the toddy plate in this pattern is not really the toddy plate of the old flint pattern but a little plate which came in a wire frame and was used at times for calling cards.

No. 587 – CLEMATIS – L. 75 – M. 31 – K. Bk. 3-25. Non-flint of the late 70s made in clear only. Pitchers have applied handles. Flat sauce $10.00; spooner $25.00; goblet $35.00; creamer $35.00; covered butter $55.00; covered sugar $45.00.

590
Panelled Forget-me-not

593
Barred Forget-me-not

596
Stippled Forget-me not

599
Ribbed Forget-me-not

602
Forget-me-not in Scroll

605
Corcoran

608
Dewdrops
With Flowers

611
Double Band Forget-me-not

No. 590 – PANELLED FORGET-ME-NOT – L. 79, 130, 133 – M. 122 – K. Bk. 3-43. Non-flint of the 70s, made in clear, blue, amber, apple green and a very few pieces in amethyst by Bryce Bros. of Pittsburgh. Flat sauce $10.00 – 12.00; footed sauce, oval pickle or relish $15.00; spooner $30.00; open sugar $25.00; open compote, goblet $40.00; platter $35.00; celery $35.00; creamer $35.00; covered butter $55.00; covered sugar $45.00; covered compote $55.00; water pitcher $65.00. Amber 30% more, blue, green 60% more, amethyst 150% more. *Colors rare. Wine $90.00.*

No. 593 – BARRED FORGET-ME-NOT – L. 132, 131 – M. 140 – K. Bk. 4-34. Non-flint, made in Ohio in the 80s in yellow, amber, blue, green. Flat sauce $10.00; handled relish dish, spooner $25.00; open sugar $20.00; open compote, wine $35.00; goblet $30.00; covered butter $45.00; cakestand $65.00; creamer $35.00; covered sugar, covered compote $50.00; celery $30.00; water pitcher $65.00. Amber 25% more, yellow 50% more, blue 40% more, apple green 50% more.

No. 596 – STIPPLED FORGET-ME-NOT – L. 74, 128, 129, 130, 138 – M. 93 – K. Bk. 4-126. Non-flint, made in Pittsburgh 1880s and in the early 90s in Ohio. A few very rare pieces found in milk glass. Interesting plates with varied centers; 7" plate, star center $30.00; 9" plate, kitten or star center $55.00; large tray for water set, has water scene with aquatic birds and life $65.00; flat sauce $10.00; footed sauce $15.00; spooner, oval relish, open sugar, mug with collared base $25.00; large oval salt $35.00; tumbler, celery, cup and saucer, creamer $35.00; small cakestand $40.00; goblet, wine $40.00; large cakestand $75.00; covered sugar $45.00; syrup, covered compote, covered butter $65.00; open compote $30.00; toothpick, shaped like a hat $125.00. Amber 30% more, milk white 100% more.

No. 599 – RIBBED FORGET-ME-NOT – L. 137 – K. Bk. 1-67. Clear, non-flint of the late 70s, made in small sized table set and cup only. Fine for bridge table or breakfast tray. Spooner $20.00; covered mustard (use for jam) $30.00; covered butter $45.00; creamer, covered sugar $35.00; cup $15.00. *OMN Pert.*

No. 602 – FORGET-ME-NOT IN SCROLL – L. 77 – M. 86. Non-flint of the 70s, made in clear. Pitchers have applied handles. Flat sauce $8.00; spooner $18.00; open sugar $18.00; covered butter $35.00; covered sugar, creamer $30.00; goblet $25.00.

No. 605 – CORCORAN – M. 81 – K. Bk. 2-45 calls it WHEEL IN BAND. Non-flint of the late 70s. Made in clear. Wine $20.00; goblet $25.00; water pitcher $45.00; just found the covered jam jar $35.00 and it is very pretty. It has a cover which is made of two steps and carries the little flowers; the finial is a rectangular prism supported by scrolls. So thoughtfully has it been designed that even the inside of the base carries the pattern. Another example of why we should continue to hunt the unlisted and report them. *Flat sauce $8.00; footed sauce $10.00; berry bowl $20.00.*

NO. 608 – DEWDROPS WITH FLOWERS – K. Bk. 1-50 – M. 171 calls it QUANTICO. Non-flint of the 80s, made in clear. Goblet $30.00; wine $25.00; water or milk pitcher $35.00; covered butter $35.00; creamer $25.00; spooner $20.00; open compote, open sugar $25.00; covered compote, covered sugar $40.00.

No. 606 – FORGET-ME-NOT FESTOONS – M. Bk. 2-147 (Not pictured.) Non-flint of the 80s, made in clear. Shaped like Dewdrops with Flowers, has a band of flowers similar to that in Fans with Baby Breath Band and from this are draped the festoons of flowers. Only goblet $25.00.

No. 611 – DOUBLE BAND FORGET-ME-NOT – M. Bk. 2-47. Non-flint of the 80s, clear only. Goblet $25.00; covered jelly compote, shown $35.00.

FUN WITH OLD GLASS

When your garden is in bloom, use your glass; if a city apartment dweller, you can find treasurers along the roadside. Put forget-me-nots in a pink milk glass salt shaker, nasturtiums in finger bowls or butter bases, verbenas or pansies in shallow large sauces or relish dishes; repeat on the colors found in the flowers, in the candles, place in clear glass candlesticks, close by. Invert a cakestand with hollow stem; use lemons, limes, concord or wild grapes, tomatoes, radishes, etc., on the low, flat surface; in the vase part above any vines, purple nightshade, wandering jew with its tiny bits of bright blue, a spray of ivy, long branches of petunias, wild wayside weeds or grasses. Old glass, nature and imagination, spell fun, good design and good living.

614
Sprig Spray

617
Sprig

620
Panelled Sagebrush

623
Panelled Flowers

626
Panelled Julep

629
Bleeding Heart

632
Lily of the Valley

635
Scroll with Flowers

No. 614 – SPRIG SPRAY – M. Bk. 2-113 calls this Panelled Sprig but the well known Sprig is sometimes called that and this has no panels. Non-flint of the late 70s, clear only. Goblet $20.00.

No. 615 – TREE OF LIFE WITH SPRIG – K. Bk. 2-27. (Not pictured.) Non-flint of the 90s and like many of this era, too busy. Pitcher has panelled bowl with spray of sprig and then where it narrows has lower part of tree-of-life allover. From this extends a large and a small disc with no meaning or connection with the design. Creamer $30.00.

No. 616 – PANELLED HONEYCOMB – K. Bk. 3-56. (Not pictured.) Another late creamer, probably the 90s, of wretched design. Metal cover, long panels of fancy honeycomb on either side with spray of tiny flowers extending full length of the panel. Top is not pewter but later metal. I neglected to mention it has scalloped handle, fluted spout, another type of base paneling, etc., etc., ala worst of the Victorian. Pitcher $30.00 and not worth it.

No. 617 – SPRIG – L. 78 – M. 126 – K. Bk. 3 – 14 and Bk. 8-3. Non-flint, made by Bryce Higbee & Co. in the mid 80s; clear only. Has been called Indian Tree and Panelled Sprig. Sugar bowl is handled, very large and clumsy but goblets and wines are most pleasing. Flat sauce $10.00; footed sauce $12.00; spooner, oval relish, open sugar $25.00; round or deep oval bowls $25.00; open compote, goblet, wine, celery $40.00; covered butter $45.00; covered sugar $40.00; oval platter $25.00; water pitcher $50.00; covered compote $60.00. *Rare pieces in blue.*

No. 620 – PANELLED SAGEBRUSH – M. Bk. 2-13. Non-flint of the 80s. Clear; only goblet $30.00.

No. 623 – PANELLED FLOWERS – M. 43. Non-flint of the late 80s. Only goblet $25.00.

No. 626 – PANELLED JULEP – M. Bk. 2-74. Another flower pattern of this era. Clear only, goblet $25.00.

No. 629 – BLEEDING HEART – L. 123, 128 – M. 43 – M. Bk. 2-91 and Bk. 1-11. The goblet M. Bk 2-92 is an extremely heavy impression and has a fluted stem which is wider at the top and again at the bottom. Comes with plain stem, much of which is grayed and of poor impression (jelly container type), and knob stem, the knob being at the bottom of the stem. Finials of covered pieces are pretty blossoms; L. 128 shows creamer with molded handle; it comes with lovely applied handle on bulbous type creamer. Flat sauce $15.00; oval flat sauce $25.00; thin, plain, jelly container goblet $15.00; plain stem, goblet, good quality $35.00; knob stem goblet $40.00; open sugar $30.00; straight sided egg cup, oval vegetable dish, handled mug, open compote $40.00; wine $165.00; creamer $40.00; large cakestand $100.00; creamer with applied handle $80.00; low footed covered compote $75.00; tall covered compote $90.00; low oval covered compote, oval platter $70.00; plate $50.00; water pitcher, applied handle $195.00; divided relish $65.00; rare covered egg server, has compartments for eggs $425.00, *price for good impression of flowers and leaves.*

No. 632 – LILY-OF-THE-VALLEY – L. 123, 126 – M. 43 – K. Bk. 4-4. Very desirable, non-flint of the 70s. The four piece set and the salt come in two forms, one of which has three tall legs and one which has plain stem. The legged type is worth 25% more than the plain footed type with exception of the creamer. The plain type has applied handle, the legged type, molded handle. Goblets, wines, etc., all have plain stem. Flat sauce $12.00; spooner $35.00; oval relish $15.00; plain open sugar, footed salt, oval vegetable dish $40.00; covered master salt $75.00; cruet, original high stopper $100.00; wine $50.00; egg cup $50.00; open compote $50.00; large cakestand $110.00; either creamer $60.00; legged covered sugar, legged covered footed salt $85.00; plain covered sugar, covered butter $125.00; tall covered compote $85.00; goblet $55.00.

No. 635 – SCROLL WITH FLOWERS – L. 118, 140 – M. 61 – K. Bk. 1-65. Non-flint of the late 70s. Principally clear but a few pieces have been found in apple green, amber and blue. Spooner, footed salt, handled oval pickle $20.00; quaint double handled egg cups, goblet $25.00; wine $30.00; open sugar $20.00; water pitcher, small covered mustard pot, open compote $45.00; cordial $35.00; creamer, covered butter $40.00; handled cake plate $35.00; covered sugar, covered compote $45.00. Amber 30% more, blue or green 50% more. *Rare syrup pitcher with applied handle $150.00.*

638
Curled Leaf

641
Panelled
Potted Flower

644
Panelled Nightshade

647
Jardiniere

650
Panelled
Apple Blossoms

653
Panelled Sunflower

656
Sunflower

No. 638 – CURLED LEAF – K. Bk. 3-21. M. Bk. 2-145 lists a goblet as VINE BAND which seems to be the same. One of the very pretty florals of the 70s which should be better known. Pitchers have applied handles. Flat sauce $15.00; handled mug (not applied) $35.00; spooner, open sugar $30.00; covered sugar $45.00; creamer $40.00; egg cup $30.00; goblet $40.00. *Cobalt, vaseline, amethyst, King Glass logo more.*

No. 641 – PANELLED POTTED FLOWER – M. Bk. 2-22. Non-flint of the 80s; only clear; goblet $45.00. *Bellaire, 1890s.*

No. 642 – FLOWER POT – L. 133, 136 – K. Bk. 1-86. (Not pictured.) In this the flower pot with flowers is placed among a stippled medallion. There should be a goblet or a tumbler, but I've never heard of one. Handled square flat sauce $8.00; footed sauce $12.00; spooner, open sugar $27.00; covered compote $50.00; covered butter $55.00; creamer $35.00; bread tray $55.00; In God We Trust covered sugar $45.00; cakestand $50.00; water pitcher $60.00; goblet $35.00. *Aka "Potted Plant" forms squared.*

No. 644 – PANELLED NIGHTSHADE – M. 177. Non-flint of the late 70s, made in clear, amber and blue. Goblet $45.00; wine $50.00; tiny cordial, scarce $55.00. If one had little space, a collection of these cordials would make charming decor. Amber 50% more, blue 100% more. *Bellaire goblet, 1890s.*

No. 647 – JARDINIERE – K. Bk. 3-42. Non-flint of the late 80s. Clear only. Creamer $40.00.

No. 650 – PANELLED APPLE BLOSSOM – L. 164 No. 16 – M. 157. Non-flint of the *1900s*; clear only. Goblet $30.00. *D. C. Jenkins mug with "Baby" or "Darling," $30.00.*

No. 653 – PANELLED SUNFLOWER – M. Bk. 2-25. Clear, non-flint of the 80s. Goblet $20.00; *syrup $35.00; berry set $45.00.*

No. 651 – SUNFLOWER CONTAINER – K. Bk. 8-29. (Not pictured.) This is a creamer with narrow neck that resembles a syrup more than a creamer. It originally had a cover and was probably used as a commercial jelly container. The bowl of it is panelled and a large sunflower is surrounded by leaves. Would be pleasing used with Sunflower for sauces or salad dressing. Clear $45.00.

No. 656 – SUNFLOWER – L. 108 – K. 1 – 55. Non-flint of the 80s; comes in clear, amber and scarce milk white. No goblet nor tumbler has been seen. One could used Panelled Sunflower with it. Spooner $30.00; open sugar $30.00; creamer $45.00; covered butter $60.00; covered sugar $55.00. Amber 50% more; milk white 100% more; *slag 150% more. Also found in purple slag glass aka LILY.*

BUYING PATTERN GLASS BY MAIL

It is ideal to buy Pattern Glass by mail because you have the protection of Uncle Sam if you order carefully. Specify in your order and if you do not know the dealer, write it with a carbon copy, that the glass must be old, authentic and in proof condition. Do not expect replies in 24 hours and cut correspondence to the minimum. Our big business firms figure that each letter which goes out, costs them almost a dollar to write. If a dealer does not have your article in stock, it is silly to reply to that effect. The letter is filed and you can be notified when it comes into stock. In this business, the owner is frequently away at shows, or on buying trips; his brevity is not because the dealer is unfriendly or unsociable but if he has a large clientele, his correspondence is huge; you have no idea how many people in the big country are interested in old things. Our big department stores are now operating warehouse salesrooms where you get just merchandise, not too much service, for your money. Don't forget that the customer pays the overhead. Mail can miscarry; several years ago I had a letter from an irate customer who had received no recognition of her order. The day after I received her complaint, her first letter came to me from the post-office stamped, "Delayed, found in second-class mail."

NOTE: There is confusion between open sugar and buttermilk goblet. The latter is now (1999) considered a misnomer. What has been called a "buttermilk" is in fact a sugar bowl and an "open sugar" was once a covered sugar now missing the lid. Very few patters had a true "open sugar," but still have value as a lid-less sugar.

662
Willow Oak

665
Wildflower

668
Windflower

671
Panelled Daisy

677
Sunk Daisy

680
Stippled Daisy

683
Big Daisy

No. 662 – WILLOW OAK – L. 45, 129, 159 – M. 53 – K. Bk. 1-37. Non-flint of the 80s made by Bryce Bros. of Pittsburgh, in clear, amber, blue vaseline. Flat sauce $15.00; footed sauce $20.00; open sugar $20.00; spooner $35.00; finger or other bowls $20.00; open compotes $35.00; tumbler $30.00; 7" plate (scarce), 9" plate $30.00; celery $40.00; pair of salt and pepper shakers $50.00; goblet $35.00; creamer $35.00; covered butter, cakestand $50.00; milk or water pitcher $55.00; covered sugar, covered compote $45.00. Amber 30% more, blue, *canary, vaseline 100% more.*

No. 665 – WILDFLOWER – L. 123, 126 – L.V. 6 – M. 53 – K. Bk. 1-37. Non-flint of the 70s made in clear, two shades of amber, yellow, blue and apple green. It's popularity brought forth a flood of reproductions in many of the pieces; when points of variance between old and new were published, these were corrected and other new batches made. In some of the old, worn molds were used and the resulting impression is faint, this should be considered in valuing the individual piece. Some of the fakes have been made with poor impressions, too. Quoted prices are for excellent impressions. Flat sauce $15.00; footed sauces, small flat and footed bowls of many sizes $15.00 – 20.00; flat relish, spooner $20.00; tumbler $30.00; creamer $40.00; goblet $30.00; celery $40.00; square plate, open compote $30.00; flat covered butter $40.00; wine, champagne $30.00; footed covered butter $50.00; pair salt and pepper shakers $45.00; covered sugar $35.00; syrup $70.00; cakestand $65.00; turtle salt $35.00; large oval tray $40.00; tall cake basket with metal handle $160.00; water pitcher $50.00. Canary 100% more, light amber 20% more, deep amber 60% more, blue or green goblet $80.00; other blue or green pieces 100% more. Reproduced in colors and clear. *Adams & Co. 1880s. Ocassionaly found in amethyst, 150% more. Goblet $500.00+. Wildflower reproductions are heavier in weight. Not all forms were reproduced, be wary of goblets especially.*

No. 668 – WINDFLOWER – L. 120 – M. 25 – K. Bk. 5-5. Frequently, when readers see this in print they read it as Wildflower. Non-flint of the late 70s. Goblets, celery $40.00; covered butter $50.00; flat pickle $20.00; tumbler, spooner, open sugar $35.00; egg cups $40.00; wines $50.00; cordial $80.00; water pitcher $70.00; creamer $40.00; flat sauce $15.00; open compote $35.00; tall covered compote $80.00.

No. 671 – *Mckee* PANELLED DAISY – L. 95, 134-136 – M. 25 – K. Bk. 3-65 but the drawing does not look like the pattern. Non-flint made by Bryce Bros. of Pittsburgh in the *late 1880s.* Clear with an occasional piece in amber being found. Pitchers have molded handles. Flat sauce $8.00; bowls $15.00 – 20.00; footed sauces $15.00; flat pickle $20.00; spooner $30.00; tall celery $45.00; covered butter, 7" round plate $25.00; large mug $35.00; tumbler $30.00; sugar shaker $55.00; syrup, pair salt and pepper shakers, 8" or 9" cakestand $45.00; water pitcher $55.00; covered sugar $45.00; footed covered butter $70.00; tray for water set $50.00; square 9" plate $35.00; 10" or 11" cakestand $60.00; covered compote $70.00; goblet and tumbler now reproduced *as is 6" covered compote.*

No. 672 – PANELLED WILD DAISY – M. 106. (Not pictured.) Thin, non-flint goblet of the 90s. Has telltale line around the top and looks like another commercial jelly container. Single, rather small, lonesome daisy repeated four times around the goblet. Only goblet $20.00.

No. 677 – SUNK DAISY – K. Bk. 3-89 – M. Bk. 2-138 calls it Kirkland for Mrs. J. L. Kirkland who loaned so many goblets to picture in his books. I'm sorry that a pattern which would be more representative of the quality of her collection does not carry the name. This is non-flint of the late 80s, made in clear and green. Flat sauce $8.00; goblet $25.00; wine $22.00; creamer $25.00; covered butter $35.00; covered sugar $35.00. Green 50% more. *Cooperative Flint Glass, 1896.*

No. 680 – STIPPLED DAISY – L. 101 – K. Bk. 3-85. Clear and stippled non-flint of the 80s. Rarely seen in Illinois, Iowa region; probably a Pennsylvania product. No goblet has been listed. Flat sauce $8.00; spooner $20.00; oval or rectangular relish $15.00; open sugar $20.00; trumbler $15.00; open compote $20.00; creamer $30.00; covered sugar $30.00.

No. 683 – BIG DAISY, *INTAGLIO DAISY, U. S. Glass 1911.* Heretofore unlisted. Non-flint of the 90s. In this pattern the four piece set is uninteresting and of little value but the goblet has charm, especially in casual surroundings. It is carefully made, there is even a daisy beneath the base. It is improved by removal of the gilt on the edge. Goblet $30.00; tumbler $20.00; *butter $40.00; bowl $15.00 – 35.00; pitcher $40.00.*

686
Dahlia

689
Stippled Star Flower

692
Mountain Laurel

695
Dahlia with Petal

698
Beaded Tulip

701
Water Lily

704
Frosted Magnolia

707
Frosted
Flower Band

No. 686 – DAHLIA – L. 105, 126, 129, 130, 138 – M. 18 – K Bk. 1-73. Sometimes called STIPPLED DAHLIA. Non-flint of the 80s, comes in clear, yellow, amber, blue and apple green. Well known; colors extremely scarce as are some of the clear pieces such as goblets, wines, champagnes, cordials and round plates. This is a pattern of wide diversity in the values of the pieces, due to number found. I've been told that water pitchers were baking powder premiums, that sugars and creamers were given as prizes for Sunday school attendance and that merchants stocked other pieces. Possibly the venture was not too successful, as pieces not given as premiums are difficult to find. Be that true or not, we find water pitchers everywhere and $50.00 – 60.00 is a fair value for them; creamers, plentiful $30.00; open sugar $20.00; flat sauce $12.00; footed sauce $15.00; mug $40.00; footed salt $20.00; handled plate $20.00; egg cups $30.00 small cakestand $40.00; large cakestand $50.00; wine $40.00; handled mug $40.00; champagne $55.00; goblet $45.00; egg cup with naturalistic vine, not the one with vine in plain horizontal line $50.00; 7" plate $25.00; covered sugar $45.00; cordial $45.00; platter $35.00. Blue 50% more, green 70% more, yellow 100% more, amber 30% more. *Bryce Higbee & Canadian Companies.*

No. 689 – BANDED STIPPLED STAR FLOWER – L. 153 No. 2 – M. 64 – K. Bk. 8-70 calls it STIPPLED FLOWER BAND. Non-flint of the late 80s, clear only. Goblet $25.00.

No. 690 – STIPPLED STAR FLOWER – (Not pictured.) M. 139 calls this STAR FLOWER BAND but it is exactly the same as above without the band. Goblet $30.00.

No. 692 – MOUNTAIN LAUREL – M. 64. Non-flint of the 80s, made one in clear. Goblet $30.00. *Central Glass.*

No. 695 – DAHLIA WITH PETAL – M. Bk. 2-165. Non-flint of the late 80s, made in clear with leaves painted green and flowers in red; also comes in all dark green. Clear, wine $25.00; goblet $30.00; dark green, wine $45.00; goblet $40.00. 25% more for good paint. *Aka Double Dahlia & Lens. U.S. Glass, 1905.*

No. 696 – DAHLIA WITH FESTOON – M. 138. (Not pictured.) This is a modern goblet; the whole background of the bowl is stippled, a large dahlia rests in the center and scrolled festoons go to bottom of the body of the goblet. Stem is short, has knob of globules. This pattern has been made for the last 25 years in many pieces, including large plates, wines, tiered metal server made with plates of graduated sizes. Has no place with old glass, many pieces in resale shops now. *Sandwich Pattern of the Depression era.*

No. 698 – BEADED TULIP – L. 44, 116-124 – K. Bk. 3-127. Has been found in the catalog of McKee Bros. of Pittsburgh dated 1894. Non-flint, comes with some minor differences of design. Some pieces have clear leaves, others have stippled. Bowls, one water tray and the butter have serrated edges following the flower form; frequently these have minor chips which are not noticeable and detract little from the value. Possibly some of this happened in removing piece from the mold; this should be mentioned when selling, however. Oblong bowls $25.00; spooner $35.00; oval pickle $20.00; flat sauce $6.00; footed sauce $12.00; covered butter dish, cakestand $55.00; water pitcher or milk pitchers $50.00; goblet $40.00; wine $35.00; large water tray $55.00. I've seen water tray in blue $110.00. *Aka Andes. Emerald green 150% more.*

No. 701 – WATER LILY – M. 152 – K. Bk. 2-116 calls it ROSE POINT BAND. Non-flint of the early 1900s. Other pieces are so poor in design they have no value. Goblet $25.00. *Aka Rose Point Band, Indiana Glass, 1913. Butter $45.00; creamer, sugar $25.00; berry bowl $20.00; sauce $10.00.*

No. 704 – FROSTED MAGNOLIA – M. 99 – K. Bk. 4-136 calls it WATER LILY and mentions that the pattern is similar to frosted Magnolia but that there is no seaweed in the picture shown by Millard. In Frosted Magnolia there is no seaweed on the goblet but there is on other pieces such as the syrup shown here. This is a highly prized pattern among collectors though it is a non-flint of the late 90s. I wonder why writers have not previously stressed it. I've seen goblets sell readily for $20.00; large deep flat sauce $55.00; covered sugar $170.00; creamer $160.00; syrup $300.00; cakestand, large $200.00; covered butter $200.00. *Dalzell Gilmore and Leighton Co., 1890s.*

No. 707 – FROSTED FLOWER BAND – M. 74 – K. Bk. 4-47 – L. 107, 109 calls it FLOWER BAND. Beautiful, non-flint, clear and clear and frosted of the 70s. Has oak leaf motif on bases and oak leaves above and below border on sauces, compotes, etc. Sugar and celery and spooner are handled. Handles are molded; finials are, on some pieces, love birds. Footed sauce $25.00; spooner $20.00; open sugar $40.00; celery $90.00; creamer $100.00; covered compote $150.00; covered sugar $120.00; covered butter $180.00; goblet $110.00. Prices quoted are for frosted band, all clear 30% less. *Reproduced in pink and blue (goblet).*

No. 708 – FROSTED OAK BAND – M. Bk. 2-41. (Not pictured.) Contemporary of Flower Band but much scarcer. Bowl of goblet is same as above only the band is made of acorns and oak leaves. Stem is a truncated one. Flower Band has the oak leaf incorporated in part of its design which shows the relationship is close. Only goblet $150.00.

710
Stippled Fuchsia

713
Marsh Pink

716
Fans with
Baby Breath Band

719
Aster Band

722
D. & B. with
Narcissus

725
Bouquet

728
Panelled Diamonds
and Flowers

731
Stippled Panelled Flower

No. 710 – STIPPLED FUCHSIA – M. 33 – L.V. 33. Clear and stippled non-flint, some of it made at the Sandwich factory in the 70s. Pitchers have applied handles and finials are nutlike. Flat sauce $10.00; spooner $35.00; relish $20.00; open sugar $25.00; open compote $20.00; covered butter $60.00; creamer $45.00; covered sugar $48.00; covered compote $65.00.

No. 711 – CLEAR FUCHSIA – M. 15 – K. Bk. 8-5. (Not pictured.) Same as the stippled form above only this has clear background, no stippling. Values 10% less than stippled.

No. 713 – MARSH PINK – K. Bk. 2-30 – L.V. 23 calls it SQUARE FUCHSIA but is definitely not a fuchsia and as Mrs. Kamm knew her botany I prefer her title. Non-flint made in Ohio in the 80s. Clear, but a few, rare pieces in amber have been reported. There are covers for the little square sauces and bowls which make these into charming little candy dishes. Flat sauces $15.00; bowls $20.00 with covers $20.00 – 30.00; spooner $30.00; open sugar $25.00; covered jam jar $50.00; water pitcher $80.00; large square plate $40.00; pair salt and pepper shakers $50.00; creamer $35.00; covered butter $50.00; small cakestand $45.00; covered sugar $40.00; covered compote $55.00. *Amber 100% more.*

No. 716 – FANS WITH BABY BREATH BAND – M. 177. Clear, non-flint of the 70s. Only goblet $40.00.

No. 719 – ASTER BAND – M. 49. Clear, non-flint of the late 70s. Only goblet $30.00 – 35.00.

No. 720 – GEDDES – M. 49. (Not pictured.) Non-flint of the 70s, like Aster Band above only in this the trimming band is made of diamonds. In the center of each is a single daisy like flower. Only goblet $25.00. Item comes to small bulb at base.

No. 721 – CANTILEVER BAND – M. 174. (Not pictured.) Like Aster Band only this has trimming band of row of one small and one large diamond, alternating; each diamond has small daisy in the center; plain stem. Only goblet $25.00. Of late 70s.

No. 722 – DAISY AND BUTTON WITH NARCISSUS – L.V. 34, 73A – K. Bk. 4-139 – M. 152 calls it DAISY AND BUTTON WITH CLEAR LILY. Clear, non-flint of the late 90s. Comes with flowers and leaves painted green and red and gilt edges. Removal of all color with paint remover improves. *Metz often recommended removing color or gold to improve the design. Today, this is not recommended as it devalues the piece.* Quality of glass is generally only fair. Oval relish $15.00; creamer $30.00; deep sauces $10.00; wines $25.00; pair salt and pepper shakers $40.00; decanter $45.00; plain edged tray $30.00; covered butter $55.00; water pitcher $50.00; open compotes $30.00; covered sugar $40.00; tray with serrated edges $35.00; spooner, open sugar $25.00; goblet $30.00. Wine now reproduced in clear and peculiar shade of medium green. *Color flashed 30% more. Indiana Glass.*

No. 725 – BOUQUET – M. 62 – L. 153 No. 8. Contemporary of above. Large plate in either $30.00. *Aka Narcissus Spray. Indiana Glass. Values 20% less above.*

No. 726 – PANELLED HEATHER – M. 152. (Not pictured.) Same shape as its contemporary, Bouquet, above, only this has plain stem which is formed by continuation of panels into which bowl of goblet is divided. In each panel, extending its full length, is a spray of heather. Same values as Bouquet. *Glass quality varies.*

No. 727 – HORSEMINT – M. Bk. 2-22. (Not pictured.) Another non-flint of this late family. Shaped same as Daisy and Button with narcissus; same type of stem and fancy base; the trim consists of an inch band of blocks and diamonds below which are the sprays of horsemint. *Indiana Glass. Values 25% less. D & B with Narcissus.*

No. 728 – PANELLED DIAMONDS AND FLOWERS – M. 87 – L. 164 No. 7. Non-flint made in clear in the 70s. Only goblet $35.00. *Central Glass.*

No. 731 – STIPPLED PANELLED FLOWER – L. 77 – L.V. 52 – K. Bk. 4-86 calls it MAINE. Clear, sometimes found with enameled trim and emerald green; non-flint, made in Pittsburgh in the 90s. Flat sauce $15.00; spooner $75.00; relish $25.00; open sugar $20.00; toothpick $125.00; 8" relish dish $25.00; bowls $30.00; handled mug $45.00; tumbler $45.00; creamer $65.00; covered sugar $125.00; goblet $225.00; Green 100% more. *MAINE now preferred name. All "States" patterns very desirable. U. S. Glass, 1899.*

734
Ivy-in-Snow

734
Ivy-in-Snow Red Leaves

737
Budded Ivy

740
Ivy Band

746
Panelled Thistle

749
Thistle

753
Teasel

755
Thistle Shield

No. 734 – IVY-IN-SNOW – L. 103, 119, 145 – M. 146 – K. Bk. 3-97. Non-flint pattern of the late 90s made in Pennsylvania. Sugar and creamer are flat and small; the handles are molded; the finials are conventionals. Comes in clear and stippled and also with leaves in red or in green. This pattern is later than most of the ivy patterns which have applied handles and ivy leaves for finials. Flat sauce $15.00; 6" plate $20.00; spooner $40.00; open sugar $25.00; open compote $35.00; goblet, wine, celery $35.00; small cakestand $50.00; creamer $35.00; 10" plate, covered sugar, covered jam jar, large cakestand $60.00; water pitcher $60.00; covered compotes $50.00. Reproduced continually in clear and milk white over a long period of years. *Cooperative Flint, 1894.*

No. 734 – IVY-IN-SNOW, RED LEAVES. This is the rare form of pattern above and has not been reproduced. Value, 200% of all clear. Goblet $175.00.

No. 737 – BUDDED IVY – L. 119 – M. 47 – K. Bk. 8-6. Non-flint of the early 70s. Clear only; pitchers have applied handles; finials are ivy leaves. Flat sauce $10.00; spooner $30.00; footed salt $35.00; open compote $40.00; goblet $40.00; egg cup $35.00; flat covered butter $60.00; syrup $100.00; pitcher $90.00; low covered compote $65.00; covered sugar $60.00; creamer $50.00; tall covered compote $95.00.

No. 738 – STIPPLED IVY – L. 119, 146 – M. 47. (Not pictured.) Same as its contemporary, Budded Ivy, above, only this has no buds and the stippling is slightly finer which seems to make the leaves stand out more. Values the same as for the Budded.

No. 740 – IVY BAND – M. Bk. 2-45. Non-flint of the early 80s. Clear only; creamers have applied handles. Spooner $40.00; goblet $50.00; covered sugar $50.00; creamer $45.00; covered butter $50.00. There are probably other pieces. *Iowa City 1881.*

No. 741 – SPIRALLED IVY – L. 147 – K. Bk. 6-23. (Not pictured.) Non-flint of the mid 80s. Easily identified; bands of clear ribs alternate with rows of ivy leaves diagonally around the pieces in continuous line. Pitchers are flat, molded handles; finials are conventional knobs. Sauce dish $8.00; tumbler $25.00; spooner, open sugar $35.00; covered butter $50.00; water pitcher $55.00; creamer $40.00; covered sugar $45.00. No goblet has been found.

No. 742 – SOUTHERN IVY – L. 166 – K. Bk. 3-123. (Not pictured.) Non-flint, clear of the mid 80s. Ribbed background, not like early flint ones, on which rather awkward ivy sprays upward at slight angle. We see little of it, possibly because the demand is light. No goblet. Pitchers, sugars, etc., flat and uninteresting in line. Sauce dish $5.00; bowls $15.00;

spooner, open sugar $25.00; tumbler $20.00; creamer $25.00; covered butter $50.00; covered sugar $35.00; mug $25.00.

No. 743 – PANELED IVY – M. 112. (Not pictured.) Same as Paneled Forget-Me-Not only this has sprays of ivy in the panels. Non-flint of the 90s; clear only. Rather scarce goblet $30.00. *Doyle/U. S. Glass.*

No. 744 – ROYAL IVY – K. Bk. 5-87. (Not pictured.) Non-flint, made by Northwood Glass Co. of Ohio in 1889 and 1890. Very popular today but is used for decor and condiments rather than a setting. Upper part of pieces tinged with cranberry which fades as it goes down. Body of pieces are swirled diagonally and on this swirling runs sprays of ivy. Pieces are squat and creamers and sugars have wide collar atop the bulbous bowl. Toothpick $150.00; finger bowl $80.00; creamer $180.00; covered sugar $220.00; covered marmalade jar $300.00; covered butter $190.00; pair salt and pepper shaker $120.00; syrup $320.00. *Rubina/clear 40% less, clear/frosted, 80% less.*

No. 745 – ROYAL OAK – K. Bk. 3-86. (Not pictured.) Companion set of Royal Ivy. The same, only here oak branches and acorns replace ivy. Value the same as for the ivy.

No. 746 – PANELLED THISTLE – L. 114, 141 – M. 163 – K. Bk. 1-82. Non-flint of the early 1900s, made in clear. Made in Pittsburgh, Pa. Although made at a time when pattern glass was losing much of its merit because it started to ape cut glass, the sparkle of this design appeals and demand has been very heavy. Made in an endless number of pieces, some flat, some footed and some with little knobs for feet. There is one kind which has the small outline of a bee in the base; it is a trademark and so small that close inspection is needed to locate it. It is only about ½". Individual salts $20.00; flat honey dishes $15.00; flat relish dishes, small bowls $20.00; wines $35.00; sherbet cups $10.00; large bowls $35.00; cruets with original stoppers $60.00; open compotes, small cakestands, goblets, pair salt and pepper shakers $50.00; square plates $25.00; covered butter $70.00; covered sugar $50.00 round plates $20.00; covered compotes, square covered honey-dish $75.00; water pitcher $75.00; milk pitcher $165.00. Pieces bearing bee 20% more. Reproduced. *Color rare. Higbee, 1908. Amber square plate $80.00. OMN: Delta.*

No. 747 – LATE THISTLE – L. 187. (Not pictured.) Contemporary of above, no panelling, large, slightly conventionalized thistle covers glass of same weight as above. Not many forms. Sherbet cup $30.00; large round plate $35.00; *tumbler $40.00; pitcher $80.00. Found in emerald green, with and without gilt. 80% more. Cambridge, 1908. Reproduced.*

(Continued on Page 71)

758
Garden Fern

761
Fern Frond

764
Crossed Ferns with Ball and Claw

767
Panelled Fern

773
Marsh Fern

770
Cat Tails and Ferns

776
Stippled Maiden
Hair Fern

No. 758 – GARDEN FERN – M. 44. Non-flint of the 70s. Only goblet $30.00.

No. 759 – WILD FERN – M. 44. (Not pictured.) Very like Garden Fern only in this the narrow notched strip dividing panels is absent. Fern fronds are slightly less curved. Only goblet $30.00.

No. 760 – FERN WITH LILY-OF-THE-VALLEY – M. Bk. 2-68. (Not pictured.) Has same notched bar dividing panels as does Garden Fern, but here the panel is filled with large lily-of-the-valley leaves and blossoms and fern leaves. Non-flint of the 70s; clear only. Goblet $40.00; scarce.

No. 761 – FERN FROND – Hitherto unlisted. Non-flint of crude workmanship of the 70s. The entire piece is made of a frosty, grayed glass, sometimes called "clam broth." Only pitcher $35.00. I'd like to hear of other pieces.

No. 764 – CROSSED FERNS WITH BALL AND CLAW – Belknap-Opaque Glass-209 – K. Bk. 3 calls it simply Crossed Ferns, a name belonging to another similar pattern. In this type the finials are the lovely fiddle heads of ferns. Found more frequently in milk glass and opalescent blue. Opalescent blue prices given. Spooner $55.00; covered butter $95.00; creamer $65.00; covered sugar $75.00. Clear glass 40% of this. *Milk glass 75% less. Atterbury Glass, 1876.*

No. 765 – CROSS FERN – L. 190 line 1 No. 2. (Not pictured.) In this the fern part is the same but there is collared base instead of claw feet and creamer and sugar are taller and narrower in shape. Footed sauce $10.00; spooner $30.00; creamer $35.00; covered butter $45.00; covered sugar $45.00; covered compote $60.00; 6", 7" collared bowls $40.00. New Martinsville, 1903.

No. 767 – PANELLED FERN – M. 2-124. Non-flint of the late 80s. The round panel is occupied solely by fern fronds, the curved lines are reflections; note honeycomb stem. Only goblet $40.00.

No. 770 – CAT TAILS AND FERNS – M. 141. Most pleasing, non-flint of the 80s. Only goblet $30.00. *Richards and Hartley/U.S. Glass, 1890.*

No. 773 – MARSH FERNS – M. Bk. 2-24. Clear, non-flint late 80s. Goblet is angular, trim and pleasing with design around base of bowl; finials trimmed with nice frond detail. Goblet $45.00; spooner $40.00; bowls $30.00; creamer, tankard type $45.00; covered butter $55.00; covered sugar $40.00; *covered compote $75.00; water pitcher $90.00; sauce $10.00. Riverside #327, 1889.*

No. 776 – STIPPLED MAIDENHAIR FERN – M. 157. Non-flint of the late 80s. Slightly grayed glass, was cataloged with tin tops available for jelly containers. Only goblet $25.00. *Maiden Fern, Specialty Glass, 1892.*

No. 777 – FERN SPRIG – M. Bk. 2-163. (Not pictured.) Three fern fronds meet on one stem and form the unit on each side of the goblet. It is a large sprig reaching nearly from top to bottom of goblet. Non-flint of the 90s. Goblet $35.00; covered butter $55.00; creamer $35.00; covered sugar $40.00. *Bellaire goblet.*

(Continued from Page 69)

No. 749 – THISTLE – L. 140 – M. 132. Non-flint and flint of the early 70s. Beautifully designed pitchers with applied handles. Clear only. Flat sauce $15.00; oval relish $25.00; spooner $40.00; open compote, bowls, egg cup $40.00; wine $60.00; goblet $55.00; tumbler $65.00; cordial $70.00; milk pitcher $150.00; water pitcher $120.00; creamer $70.00; covered sugar $75.00; large cakestand $100.00; covered compote $100.00; *syrup $150.00. Bryce Walker.*

No. 753 – TEASEL – L. 96 – M. 92 calls this SHORT TEASEL. Made by Bryce Bros. of Pittsburgh in the 70s. Round flat sauce $10.00; square footed sauce $15.00; cruet $45.00; open compote $40.00; square 7" plate $35.00; goblet $35.00; celery $40.00; creamer $35.00; cakestand $50.00; covered butter $55.00; covered sugar $45.00. *Similarities with Millard pattern.*

No. 753 – LONG LEAFED TEASEL – M. 124. (Not pictured.) Later than other form of Teasel, comes with gilt edge. Same, only goblet flares and leaves extend closer to top. Goblet of this type $35.00. Aside from goblet values are the same; the pieces combine well. *New Martinsville #702, 1906.*

No. 755 – THISTLE SHIELD – M. 124. Non-flint of the 80s. Only goblet, clear $65.00; blue $95.00. Should be other colors.

782
Acorn

785
Panelled Acorn Band

791
Oak Leaf

794
Beaded Acorn Medallion

797
Pressed Leaf

803
Maple Leaf Band

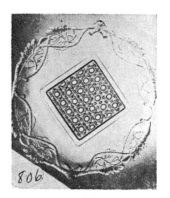

806
Square Maple Leaf

809
Long Maple Leaf

No. 782 – ACORN – L. 125 – M. 114. Non-flint and flint of the 70s, made in clear only. Pitchers have applied handles; finials are acorns. Flat sauce $16.00; footed sauce $15.00; spooner $35.00; footed salt $30.00; egg cup $25.00; open sugar $20.00; open compote $60.00; celery $40.00; covered butter $50.00; goblet $35.00; creamer $40.00; covered sugar $45.00; covered compote, water pitcher $85.00. Goblet now reproduced. *Flint 100% more.*

No. 785 – PANELLED ACORN BAND – M . Bk. 2-46 – L. 125 row 4-1 listed as variant. Contemporary of Acorn; same values.

No. 786 – ACORN BAND – M. 46 – L. 125 row 4-1 listed as variant. (Not pictured.) Same as contemporary Panelled Acorn Band only this does not have the leaves which divide the panels. Values same as Acorn.

No. 787 – ACORN BAND WITH LOOPS – M. Bk. 2-43. (Not pictured.) This has conventionalized acorn band around top and loops which rise from the bottom of goblet bowl almost to band. Non-flint, clear, of the 70s. Only goblet $40.00.

N0o. 788 – CHESTNUT OAK – K. Bk. 6-4. (Not pictured.) Same as Acorn, and another contemporary of it. This has a bracketed border above and below the leaves. Not quite as well known, value 10% less than Acorn.

No. 789 – LATE CHESTNUT OAK – K. Bk. 2-86. (Not pictured.) Pattern very much like Acorn put on late, non-flint, flat creamer with squarish molded handle. Of the 90s. Creamer $35.00.

No. 790 – WHITE OAK – K. BK. 2-65. (Not pictured.) Another pitcher of the 90s in which the oak and acorns are put on late, flat, creamer with bark like surface and tree branch handle. Poor lines. These last two do nothing but add numbers to a collection. Creamer $30.00.

No. 791 – OAK LEAF – M. 164. Non-flint of the late 70s or early 80s. Clear only, goblet $40.00.

No. 794 – BEADED ACORN MEDALLION – L. 65, 124 – M. 85. Non-flint of the late 60s and early 70s. Pitchers have applied handles; finials are acorns. Flat sauce $15.00; spooner $35.00; flat relish $25.00; footed salt $30.00; egg cup $30.00; covered butter $70.00; goblet $35.00; covered sugar $45.00; covered compote $75.00; water pitcher $80.00; creamer $45.00. *Also found in flint, 100% more. Boston Silver.*

No. 795 – BEADED ACORN WITH LEAF BAND – M. Bk. 2-10. (Not pictured.) Again we have the same convention-alized oak leaf and acorn band around the top of the goblet but below it is a stippled bowl on each side of which is a scalloped medallion enclosing the acorn unit. Clear, non-flint of the 70s. Scarce $45.00.

No. 797 – PRESSED LEAF – L. 29A, 125 – M. 44 – K. Bk. 3-20. Non-flint, clear, made by McKee of Pittsburgh in 1868 under the name New Pressed Leaf. It has been known for years as Pressed Leaf and as there is nothing new about it, it would be wiser to continue calling it Pressed Leaf. Handles are applied and finials are acorns. Flat sauce $10.00; spooner $35.00; footed salt $20.00; egg cups $30.00; champagnes $45.00; goblets $40.00; covered butter $50.00; covered compotes $70.00; creamer $45.00; covered sugar $50.00; water pitcher $70.00. *Also found in flint, 70% more.*

No. 798 – PRESSED LEAF WITH CHAIN – L. 153, No. 16 – M. Bk. 2-10. (Not pictured.) Like Pressed Leaf but above the leaves is a band of large chain set in band of stippling. Non-flint, clear, of the 70s. Goblet $45.00.

No. 799 – CROSSED LEAF – M. 164. (Not pictured.) Millard calls this CROSSED PRESSED LEAF but as the leaf is a birch leaf I'm changing it. In this, vertical leaves rising from base of bowl are met at points by horizontal leaves which encircle the bowl. Non-flint, of the 70s. Only goblet $40.00.

No. 800 – BIRCH LEAF – (Not pictured.) M. 44 calls this PRESSED LEAF, but as that name has been taken and this resembles the leaf of the birch, it would be better to continue what most collectors have done and use this terminology. In M. Bk. 2-65 Millard shows this goblet with the narrow leaf and calls it BIRCH LEAF. It is about half as wide as the leaf in Pressed Leaf. Goblet $40.00; *egg cup $30.00. Also found in flint and milk glass, 40% more.*

No. 803 – MAPLE LEAF BAND GOBLET – M. 56 calls this MAPLE LEAF but there is another by that name. This is the best goblet to use with any of the maple leaf patterns because this is not reproduced. Goblet $50.00.

No. 804 – MAPLE LEAF – L.V. 73A. (Not pictured.) Easily identified and almost impossible to get in the old which has a tree trunk with three branches which hold goblet bowl which is covered with large stippled maple leaves standing upright. Non-flint, comes in yellow goblet $90.00; amber $50.00; blue goblet $110.00. Woods is full of fakes in clear and colors. Goblets copiously reproduced. See the one above. There are many other interesting pieces in Maple Leaf which are old and not too difficult to find.

(Continued on Page 75)

812
Holly

818
Holly Leaves

821
Rose Leaves

824
Palm Stub

827
Florida Palm

830
Block and Palm

833
Palm Leaf Fan

836
Panelled Stippled
Scroll

No. 812 – HOLLY – L. 116 – M. 83 – K. Bk. 8-5. Very desirable non-flint made in the 70s at the Sandwich factory. Finials are acorns, handles are applied. Flat sauce $25.00; spooner $65.00; open sugar $60.00; egg cup $70.00; open compote $50.00; goblet $135.00; tumbler $125.00; covered butter $165.00; creamer, celery $120.00; covered sugar $135.00; covered compote $170.00; water pitcher $250.00; *large cake stand $200.00.*

No. 813 – HOLLY BAND – K. Bk. 6-64. (Not pictured.) In this the holly is a conventionalized band of single leaf, stem, curved, and three berries between bands of cord. Non-flint of the 70s; applied handles. Creamer $50.00; water pitcher $95.00; *goblet $35.00.*

No. 814 – PANELLED HOLLY, *HOLLY CLEAR* – K. Bk. 5-81. (Not pictured.) This clear is the "poor relation" form of the famous Holly Amber. Non-flint made at Greentown, Indiana, in 1903; clear. Beaded convex bands at top and bottom enclose naturalistic band of holly. Molded handles. Sauce $75.00; spooner $185.00; tumbler $185.00; creamer $225.00; open sugar, covered butter $280.00; covered sugar $275.00; pair salt and pepper shakers $300.00; toothpick $150.00. *Indiana Tumbler and Goblet, 1903.* Compare this with its aristocratic sister below:

No. 815 – HOLLY AMBER – (Not pictured.) Same pattern as above in opalescent amber, made at Greentown, Indiana, in 1903. The finest product this factory ever made. Berry bowl $700.00; covered butter $2,100.00; creamer $850.00; large covered compote $2,750.00; water pitcher $3,000.00 or more; tumbler $850.00; spooner $800.00; syrup pitcher $1,500.00; toothpick $725.00; vase, 6" high $850.00; sauce dish $300.00, very rare and in demand. Toothpick, tumbler, and 3½" sauce reproduced. *No goblet made, Indiana Tumbler and Goblet, 1903. Aka Golden Agate.*

No. 818 – HOLLY LEAVES – M. 116. Clear, non-flint of the 80s. Only goblet $35.00. *Gillinder & Sons #22.*

No. 821 – ROSE LEAVES – M. 60. Clear, non-flint of the 70s. Only goblet $30.00. A collection of goblets in these varied naturalistic leaves is charming.

No. 824 – PALM STUB – M. 41. Non-flint of the 80s; clear. Wine $25.00; goblet $35.00.

No. 827 – FLORIDA PALM, TIDAL – M. 95 – K. Bk. 3-110 and K. Bk. 8-148, 149, 150. Non-flint, clear, made by *Bryce Higbee, 1903.* Flat sauce $8.00; tumbler, pickle $17.00; 7", 8", 9" berry bowls $30.00; open sugar $20.00; spooner $30.00; celery $40.00; 9" cakestand $45.00; low covered jelly $35.00; covered butter $50.00; covered sugar $45.00; creamer $35.00; 12" cakestand $60.00. The four piece set has little feet.

No. 830 – BLOCK AND PALM – M. Bk. 2-136. Clear or milk glass made in 1890 in Beaver Falls, Pa.; non-flint. Flat sauce $8.00; celery $30.00; spooner $25.00; sugar shaker $45.00; goblet $30.00; pair salt and pepper shakers $40.00; water pitcher $50.00; covered butter $45.00; creamer $35.00; covered sugar $40.00; milk glass, 25% additional.

No. 833 – PALM LEAF FAN – K. Bk. 2-63. Non-flint of the early 90s. If one likes the sparkle of imitation cut, this pattern has more design merit than most. Comes in many pieces; flat sauces $8.00; bowls $20.00; spooner $30.00; open sugar $20.00; celery $40.00; wine $35.00; creamer $35.00; water pitcher $60.00; open compote $40.00; covered sugar $40.00; covered butter $50.00; large plate $35.00; large cakestand $75.00; covered compote $75.00.

No. 836 – PANELLED STIPPLED SCROLL – M. 173. This is really not an old goblet for it was made in the early 1920s. Comes in clear $8.00; amber $10.00; blue $12.00. *Look-alike version made 1920s and 1970s in clear, chartreuse green, amberina. Goblets, wines, footed sherberts, creamer and open sugar; called Old Sandwich by Duncan-Miller, 1924 – 1955.*

(Continued from Page 73)
No. 805 – OVAL MAPLE LEAF – L. 143. (Not pictured.) In this type the upright pieces are on stippled feet, are oval in shape and the finials are small grape bunch with leaves. Footed sauce, maple leaf $10.00; covered butter $80.00; creamer $55.00; covered sugar $70.00; covered compote $90.00; open vegetable dish $35.00; open sugar $30.00; covered vegetable $65.00; platter, diamond center, leaf edge $80.00; water pitcher $85.00; tumbler $40.00. Yellow 50% more; amber 25% more; blue 30% more; apple green 10% more; frosted 10% more. The Grant Peace plate with Grant's picture belongs here; it is better suited to decor than to table service; clear $65.00; yellow $90.00; *amber $85.00; apple green $185.00;* for service, there is:

No. 807 – ROUND MAPLE LEAF PLATE – L. 163. (Not pictured.) Plain round plate, with seven leaves in border and one in center, edges not serrated, or

No. 806 – SQUARE MAPLE LEAF – L. 158 calls it variant. This has the heavy serrated edge and combines beautifully. Plate $40.00.

No. 809 – LONG MAPLE LEAF – K. Bk. 4-144. Non-flint of the 80s. Creamer $45.00; open sugar $40.00; covered sugar $55.00.

839
Lotus and Serpent

842
Anthemion

845
Hops Band

846
Flower Spray with Scrolls

659
Leaf and Flower

849
Wild Bouquet

No. 839 – LOTUS WITH SERPENT – L.V. 73A – M. 14 – K. Bk. 3-58 calls it GARDEN OF EDEN *(most common)*. This and the one below are twin non-flint patterns of the 70s; in clear and textured surfaces. Flat sauce $15.00; spooner $30.00; pickle dish $15.00; open sugar $35.00; salt dish, ends are lily pads $35.00; covered butter $85.00; creamer $50.00; bread plate with "Give us this etc." $40.00; goblet $275.00; covered sugar $60.00; *pitcher $80.00; cakestand $65.00; covered compote $95.00; mug $55.00.*

No. 840 – LOTUS – M. 14. (Not pictured.) Exactly the same as above, only this has no serpent. Values 20% less.

No; 842 – ANTHEMION – L. 58 – K. Bk. 5-137. Non-flint, clear. Attractive with stippled background which gives it so lacy an appearance that it can be mistaken for Lacy Sandwich if one forgets that the latter is flint glass. In fact, I saw the large plate in one of our swanky shops, which wouldn't deal in Pattern Glass, "So late, you know," marked with a tag which read, "Lacy Sandwich – rare." Large, square flat sauce $12.00; berry bowl $25.00; tumbler $30.00; spooner $30.00; curled edge plate $25.00; 10" round plate $25.00; water pitcher $60.00; covered sugar $40.00; covered butter $70.00. *Albany Glass, 1890. Also in blue and amber, rare in emerald.*

No. 843 – PANELLED ANTHEMION – K. Bk. 4-59. (Not pictured.) Like its contemporary, Anthemion, only this has leaves separated by panel. Value 10% less than Anthemion.

No. 845 – HOPS BAND – M. 31 – K. Bk. 3-19. Non-flint of the 70s, made in clear. Flat sauce $8.00; oval relish, spooner $20.00; footed salt $25.00; egg cup $30.00; open sugar $20.00; open compote $40.00; covered butter $65.00; celery $45.00; sugar $40.00; water pitcher $65.00; large cakestand $50.00; covered compote $80.00. Pitchers have applied handles. *King & Son.*

No. 846 – FLOWER SPRAY WITH SCROLLS – K. Bk. 2-107 and Bk. 7-207 calls it INTAGLIO *(most common)*. Non-flint, made by Northwood in Indiana, Pennsylvania, in 1898. Belknap-310 calls it GOLDEN DAISY AND CUSTARD ROSE. (How flowery can one get?) Made in custard, white, canary, opalescent and blue opalescent; the latter being very popular now. *Removing gilt is not recommended as it lowers value presently.* Comes in collared sauces which are very large and practical for dessert dishes $40.00; large collared bowl $75.00; creamer $75.00; covered sugar $160.00; tumbler $70.00. These prices are for opalescent blue; clear with opalescent 30% of this. *Pitcher $225.00; covered butter $175.00; custard with good gold and green trim 100% higher; canary opal 30% higher.*

No. 659 – LEAF AND FLOWER – L.V. 50, 75. Medium heavy, non-flint, made in Wheeling, W. Va., in the 1890s. Comes in clear, clear and frosted with amber or green flowers (shown) and castor bottles have been reported in red. Sugar and creamer are squat and a pleasing shape. It is very popular now; it has many characteristics of much earlier glass. Clear: tumbler $30.00; flat sauce $20.00; long flat celery tray $40.00; waste or finger bowl $45.00; pair salt and pepper shakers $50.00; water pitcher $75.00; creamer $45.00; covered butter dish $70.00; covered sugar $45.00; castor set $140.00. In clear and frosted 25% more; with amber 90% more; with green 90% more; with red 100% more. *Hobbs, Brockunier & Co.*

No. 849 – WILD BOUQUET – Hitherto unlisted. Contemporary of Flower Scrolls with Spray. *Green 50% higher. Made in white, blue and opalescent. Rare in custard, 100% more. Northwood, 1902.*

No. 859 – STIPPLED CLOVER – L. 141. (Not pictured.) Clear, stippled, non-flint of the 80s. Not well known, seldom seen. Three leafed clovers scattered on a stippled background. Wine $60.00; goblet $75.00; creamer $60.00; covered butter $85.00; covered sugar $75.00; large cakestand $80.00.

No. 860 – STIPPLED WOODFLOWER – L. 136. (Not pictured.) Clear, with allover stippled background of the 80s. Not known. On this stippled background is a naturalistic pattern of leaves which resemble HOLLY LEAVES, only here there is a tiny blossom also. Finial is pretty upright leaf. Open sugar $20.00; covered sugar $45.00; creamer $35.00; covered butter $65.00.

861
Heavy Panelled
Grape

864
Late Panelled Grape

867
Early Magnet
and Grape Decanter

870
Magnet and Grape
with Frosted Leaf

873
Magnet and Grape
Stippled Leaf

876
Grape and Festoon
Stippled Leaf

879
Grape and Festoon
with Shield

882
Stippled
Grape and Festoon

No. 861 – PANELLED GRAPE – L. 64 – M. 95 – K. Bk. 3-61. Also known as HEAVY PANELLED GRAPE. Clear non-flint, made in Indiana as late as 1903; probably made first in the late 80s. The siren of Pattern Glass, pretty in too evident a way and so very, very false; probably the most frequently reproduced pattern. PRACTICALLY ALL ONE SEES IS REPRODUCTION. If you can't resist its lure, buy it at gift shops. Old suffers in value because of collectors' boycott. Oval sauces $8.00; bowls $20.00; spooner $30.00; open sugar $20.00; sherbet cup $8.00; low footed open compotes $20.00; toothpick $25.00; ale or parfait, 6" tall $35.00; cordial $25.00; tumbler $20.00; celery $35.00; lemonade, tall open compote $40.00; creamer $35.00; butter $45.00; goblet $35.00; covered sugar $40.00; syrup $60.00; water pitcher $60.00. *Reproduced in clear, milk glass, purple, canary opalescent. Kokomo Jenkins #507, 1901.*

No. 864 – LATE PANELLED GRAPE – L. 65 – M. 86. K. Bk. 1-94 calls another pattern, Darling Grape (listed on the next sheet), by this name. Clear, non-flint of the 1900s. The goblet in this or Darling Grape can be used with Heavy Panelled Grape if one is discouraged in trying to find them in the old. Sauce dish, deep and large $8.00; large open bowl $20.00; same bowl covered $35.00; goblets $30.00; creamer $25.00; butter, syrup $45.00; water pitcher, covered sugar $45.00; wine $35.00. *Kokomo Jenkins #807, 1910.*

No. 867 – EARLY MAGNET AND GRAPE CUT – The decanter is an interesting piece because it was trimmed with a cut magnet and panels and the grapes were engraved. It is probably a Pittsburgh piece and is the source of the design of the pressed pattern of the same name. It is most interesting to note how patterns were originated, copied and adapted by the same and competing firms. This decanter $500.00. *Other pieces are extremely rare: goblet $300.00; champagne $250.00; wine $200.00.*

No. 870 – MAGNET AND GRAPE, FROSTED LEAF – L. 63 – M. 147 and M. 13. There are three types of this fine flint of the 60s in the goblet. The earliest follows the line of most of the earliest goblets, bell tone and a short thick stem (M. 147); the second has a knob stem, is flint but the stem is not as thick and is longer, and while flint, not the ringing bell tone of the first or the very scarce famous one of the group, FROSTED MAGNET AND GRAPE WITH AMERICAN SHIELD. (See dedication page.) The difference is found only in the goblets; other pieces are in common for the Frosted Leaf variety. Flat sauce $20.00; spooner $100.00; frosted salt $60.00; egg cup $75.00; water tumbler $120.00; whiskey tumbler $160.00; goblet $100.00; goblet, low stem $90.00; covered butter $180.00; covered sugar $130.00; creamer $175.00; open compote $130.00; decanter, pint $170.00; with original stopper

$250.00; rare wine jug with spigot and inscription, "Try me $2,000.00. Finials are acorns, handles are applied. *Non-flint 60% less, covered bowl $175.00; celery $160.00; covered compote $160.00; champagne $185.00; wine $145.00. Goblet reproduced in flint, marked MMA.*

No. 873 – MAGNET AND GRAPE, STIPPLED LEAF – L. 62 – M. 98 also MAGNET AND GRAPE, CLEAR LEAF – M. 98. Clear, non-flint of the 70s. Only difference between the two is that in one the leaves are stippled, while in the other they are left clear. Finials acorns; applied handles. Not comparable in quality or demand with the frosted leaf variety. Flat 4" sauce $8.00; footed salt $25.00; goblet $40.00; egg cup $20.00; tumbler $30.00; wine $50.00; covered butter $65.00; covered sugar $80.00; covered compote $55.00; creamer $40.00.

No. 876 – GRAPE AND FESTOON, STIPPLED LEAF – L. 63 – M. Bk. 1-51 and in Bk. 2-61 shows the same goblet. Also comes with clear leaf. Non-flint of the 70s, made in Pittsburgh; applied handles, finials are acorns. Flat sauce $10.00; spooner $40.00; oval relish $15.00; footed salt, open sugar, mugs $30.00; egg cup $35.00; open compote $80.00; 6" plate $20.00; celery $45.00; wine $50.00; covered butter $60.00; covered sugar $55.00; covered compote $130.00; creamer $50.00; water pitcher $100.00; *goblet $42.00.*

No. 877 – GRAPE AND FESTOON, VEINED LEAF – M. 148. (Not pictured.) Another form of above pattern; same values.

No. 879 – GRAPE AND FESTOON WITH SHIELD – M. 28. Another form of the same family. Values 10% higher. *Mug found in amber and cobalt $45.00 – 65.00.*

No. 880 – GRAPE AND FESTOON, SMALL AMERICAN SHIELD – M. Bk. 2-56. (Not pictured.) In this, a small American shield is in center of panel formed by festoons. Of the same family as two above. Only goblet $40.00. These festoons have been used on odd pieces with no grapes; I've found miniature mug with only the festoons $35.00.

No. 882 – STIPPLED GRAPE AND FESTOON, CLEAR LEAF – L. 63 – M. 85 and STIPPLED GRAPE AND FESTOON, STIPPLED LEAF – M. 51. Clear and stippled, non-flint of the 70s. This form with the stippled background is the scarcest of the grape and festoon family. Applied handles, acorn finials. Flat sauce $10.00; spooner $40.00; oval relish $20.00; open sugar $25.00; egg cup $35.00; goblet $40.00; open compote, celery $45.00; covered butter $65.00; covered sugar, covered compote, creamer $65.00; water pitcher $95.00. *Doyle #28.*

885
Grape with Overlapping
Foliage

888
Arched Grape

891
Darling Grape

894
Grape with
Thumbprint Band

897
Ramsay **Grape**

900
Keystone Grape

903
Panelled
Grape **Band**

906
Early Panelled Grape Band

No. 885 – GRAPE WITH OVERLAPPING FOLIAGE – L. 164 No. 14 – K. Bk. 2-48. Milk white and clear, found with patent date of 1870. Spooner $40.00; open sugar $20.00; covered sugar $50.00; creamer $60.00; milk glass 50% more. *Hobbs Brockunier.*

No. 888 – ARCHED GRAPE – L. 64 – M. 51. Dainty, non-flint of the late 70s; clear only. Flat sauce $10.00; spooner $40.00; open sugar $20.00; covered butter $65.00; covered sugar; $55.00; water pitcher $85.00; celery $50.00; goblet $45.00; creamer $40.00. Most attractive on purple linen with gold band Haviland. *Boston & Sandwich, 1870s.*

No. 891 – DARLING GRAPE – M. 120. Clear, non-flint of the early 1900s frequently found with a gilt band. Spooner, open sugar $25.00; goblet $25.00; covered butter $45.00; covered sugar, creamer $25.00. *Indiana Glass (Dunkirk) #154.*

No. 894 – GRAPE WITH THUMBPRINT BAND – L. 164 No. 4 – M. 84. Clear, non-flint of the 90s. Flat sauce $3.00; goblet, fair impression as most often found $25.00; goblet with strong impression $30.00; spooner, open sugar $25.00;

tumbler $25.00; creamer $30.00; covered butter $40.00; covered sugar $35.00; syrup $45.00.

No. 897 – RAMSAY GRAPE – L. 154 No. 16 – M. 84. Clear, non-flint of the 90s. Goblet $35.00; flat sauce $8.00.

No. 900 – KEYSTONE GRAPE – L. 164 No. 13 – M. 84. Non-flint of the 80s. Clear only. Goblet $30.00. – *Scott Christmas 2001*

No. 903 – PANELLED GRAPE BAND – L.V. 32 – M. 28. Non-flint of the late 70s. Pitchers have applied handles. Flat sauce $10.00; footed sauce $12.00; oval relish $20.00; spooner $35.00; goblet $35.00; open sugar $25.00; egg cup $30.00; covered butter $65.00; covered sugar $40.00; creamer $35.00; covered compote $70.00; pitcher $80.00. *Richards & Hartley.*

No. 906 – EARLY PANELLED GRAPE BAND – L.V. 79 No. 7 and 8 – M. Bk. 2-21. Clear, non-flint of the early 70s. Pitchers have applied handles. Goblet $40.00; egg cup $35.00; covered butter $70.00; celery $50.00; creamer $45.00; covered sugar $50.00; water pitcher $85.00.

909
Grape Band

912
Grape with
Gothic Arches

915
Banded Beaded
Grape Medallion

918
Loganberry and Grape

921
Strawberry and Currant

924
Grape and Wheat Plate

927
Grape with Vine

No. 909 – GRAPE BAND – L. 64 – M. 51. Made in flint in the late 50s and in non-flint from the late 60s. The flint is bell toned and brilliant and has all the qualities of a very early pattern. Handles of both types are applied. Prices quoted are for non-flint which is type most commonly found. The non-flint comes in normal impression and in a very heavy one in which the grapes stand out a distance from the glass; in the flint the glass is heavy but there is only one type of impression. Flat sauce $6.00; footed salt $25.00; spooner $35.00; open sugar $20.00; goblet $45.00; egg cup $25.00; creamer $55.00; covered butter $65.00; wine $30.00; open compote $35.00; covered sugar $50.00; covered compote $65.00; water pitcher $95.00; Flint 80% more. *Bryce Walker & Co.*

No. 910 – BRADFORD GRAPE – (Not pictured.) K. Bk. 5-25 – L.V. 22 calls it BRADFORD BLACKBERRY . But Mrs. Kamm, who knew her botany, asserts it is grape and I believe she is right because there are tendrils shown and blackberries do not have tendrils. This is fine heavy flint, wide panels, scalloped at the top of each. A grapevine, not unlike that on Grape Band, runs around the pieces almost at the middle. Pitchers $150.00; have beautifully applied handles. Goblet $95.00; wine $85.00; creamer $80.00; covered sugar $85.00; champagne $110.00. *Boston & Sandwich, 1850s – 60s.*

No. 912 – GRAPE AND GOTHIC ARCHES – K. Bk. 1-99 – L. 177 shows it in OPAQUE CREAM COLOR – M. 65 shows the opaque and calls it CREAM GRAPE. It was also made in clear, non-flint in the 90s. Values for custard; goblet $140.00; covered sugar $180.00; water pitcher $450.00; creamer $165.00; clear 25% of this. *Master berry $180.00; sauce $80.00. Occasionally found in green, 40% more. Also found in custard with nutmeg, 10% more. Northwood, 1890s.*

No. 915 – BANDED BEADED GRAPE MEDALLION – M. 85 – L. 66 – K. Bk. 8-7. Non-flint, clear, no trouble to date for the pickle dish has "mould patented, May 11, 1869," printed on the bottom. Bases are stippled, with three medallions on each; in one type there is a bunch of grapes in the medallion and this one is said "to have design on foot" and is worth 10% more than those which do not have it. Handles are applied, finials are acorns. Flat sauce $8.00; spooner $38.00; footed salt $20.00; dated relish $20.00; goblet $40.00; small size lady's goblet $35.00; egg cup $35.00; champagne $90.00; covered butter $80.00; creamer, covered sugar $65.00; water pitcher $125.00; covered bowls $60.00; covered compote $125.00; castor set $140.00. *Occasionally found in flint, 60% more. Boston Silver Glass Co. Possibly Sandwich after.*

No. 916 – BEADED GRAPE MEDALLION – M. 85 – L. 66. (Not pictured.) Same as above only no band at top. Same values. *Boston Silver Glass Co.*

No. 918 – LOGANBERRY AND GRAPE – L. 151 – M. 114. On the opposite side is a bunch of grapes. Non-flint of the late 80s. Possibly used for commercial jelly container as quality is generally poor. Goblet $25.00; water pitcher $40.00.

No. 921 – STRAWBERRY AND CURRANT – L. 151 – M. 71 – K. Bk. 5-2. Clear, non-flint of the 90s. Footed sauce $10.00; tumbler, spooner $30.00; open compote $40.00; covered sugar, creamer $45.00; water pitcher $60.00; covered compote $75.00; open sugar $20.00; goblet $40.00; *rare syrup with applied handle $125.00.* Market flooded with reproduction goblets in clear, opalescent and colors in which they were never made. *Dalzell, Gilmore & Leighton, 1890s.*

No. 924 – GRAPE AND WHEAT PLATE – Hitherto unlisted. Non-flint 6" plate of the 70s; should be other pieces. On plate 113, Mrs. Lee shows a 6" grape plate which looks as if it might belong to Grapes With Overlapping Foilage, previously listed.

No. 927 – GRAPE WITH VINE – K. Bk. 2-60. Non-flint of the 90s. Originally came with red paint and gilt. Flat sauce $5.00; spooner $25.00; plate $15.00; bowls $15.00; creamer $30.00; covered butter $45.00; covered sugar $35.00; covered compote $45.00.

No. 928 – BEADED GRAPE *CALIFORNIA* – L. 63 – M. 79. (Not pictured). Non-flint of the 90s, made in clear and a most popular emerald green. Square in shape, erect pieces rather than squatty and easily distinguished by beading which divides into panels and lines tops of all but drinking vessels, in which case it is slightly below the top. Square, flat sauces $15.00; relish, handled olive dish $20.00; spooner $40.00; square toothpick holder $45.00; rectangular flat celery, square bowls, open sugar $30.00; tall celery $55.00; open compote $65.00; creamer $45.00; wine $55.00; tumbler $35.00; pair salt and pepper shakers $70.00; cruet $95.00; small cakestand $125.00; covered butter $85.00; square plate $40.00; covered sugar, flat $65.00; covered sugar on collared base $45.00; oblong bread tray $85.00; pitcher $85.00 – 110.00; goblet $35.00. Green 20% more. Reproduced. *U.S. Glass, 1899.*

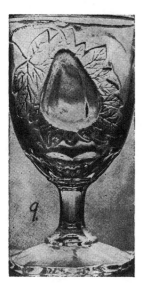

933
Baltimore Pear

936
Sugar Pear

942
Fruit Panels

945
Barley

948
Wheat and Barley

954
Panelled Wheat

951
Wheat Sheaf

No. 933 – BALTIMORE PEAR – L. 66, 154 No. 16 – M. 86 – K. Bk. 1-31. Clear, non-flint of the 80s. Has been known in some sections as TWIN PEAR, DOUBLE PEAR and FIG. Made by Adams of Pittsburgh. Sugar and spooner have at times, long individual bar handles. Flat sauce $8.00; with collared base or footed $15.00; pickle, open sugar, spooner $25.00; open compote, bowls $35.00; covered butter $80.00; celery $50.00; creamer $35.00; 10" plate $40.00; 9" cakestand $65.00; covered bowls $45.00; covered sugar $50.00; 10" cakestand $85.00; water pitcher $110.00; covered compote $50.00; goblet $40.00; high covered compote $95.00. *Reproduced goblet, cup & saucer, plate. Adams & Co., 1874, U.S. Glass, 1890s.*

No. 936 – SUGAR PEAR – M. 116. Clear, non-flint of the 90s. All I've seen were poor quality glass with the tell-tale lines of the commercial jelly container around the top. For this quality $25.00. *A clear one of good quality would be worth $35.00.*

No. 937 – PEAR, *BARTLETT PEAR* – L. 153, No. 4 – L.V. 72 – M. 59. (Not pictured.) This type has wide clear band over half width of goblet bowl; below this band is a group of two pears and three leaves, hanging at an angle from a curved stem. Non-flint, clear, of the 80s. Flat sauce $10.00; spooner $40.00; open sugar $25.00; creamer $45.00; covered sugar $50.00; goblet $45.00. *George Duncan & Sons, 1885.*

No. 942 – FRUIT PANELS – M. 60. Clear, non-flint of the 80s. Frequently found with weak impression, goblet $30.00 – 40.00; according to the strength of impression.

No. 945 – BARLEY – L. 113, 116 – M. 97 – K. Bk. 1-34. Non-flint of the late 80s; clear, any colored piece, rare, 100% more. Scalloped edges with beading add charm; plates are now hard to find so many use the platters as service plates. Honeys or flat sauces $8.00; 4", 5" footed sauces $10.00; open sugar $18.00; vegetable dish $15.00; open compote, goblet $35.00; celery $30.00; 6" plate $35.00; platter $35.00; cakestand $45.00; jam jar $70.00; covered sugar $40.00; covered butter $50.00; pitcher $60.00; covered compote $65.00; wheelbarrow relish $60.00. *Campbell Jones & Co.; wheelbarrow patented by Bryce Higbee is not part of pattern.*

No. 948 – WHEAT AND BARLEY – L. 50, 114 – M. 112 – K. Bk. 1-42. Non-flint, made by Bryce Bros. of Pittsburgh in the late 80s. Comes in clear, yellow, amber and blue. Has been known as OATS AND BARLEY and as HOPS AND BARLEY. Flat sauce $10.00; handled nappy $15.00; footed sauce $15.00; spooner $25.00; open sugar $20.00; relish $15.00;

bowls $25.00; tall jelly compote $35.00; tumbler $25.00; mug $25.00; goblets $35.00; open compote $35.00; 7" plate $20.00; salt and pepper shakers $45.00; small cakestand $35.00; large cakestand $50.00; covered sugar $35.00; water pitcher $50.00; covered butter $50.00; covered compote $50.00. Canary 75% more, blue 60% more. *Creamer & goblet reproduced. Amber 25% more.*

No. 952 – WHEAT AND MAPLE LEAF PLATTER – L. 188. (Not pictured.) Scalloped edge, clear, non-flint of the 70s. In the center of the platter is a wheat sheaf and at each side of handles is a maple leaf, around the edge, "Give us etc." Rather scarce, platter $45.00.

No. 953 – PLAIN SHEAF OF WHEAT PLATTER – (Not pictured.) This is the deep platter with folded rim which is seen frequently in non-flint, clear and in milk glass, has the lettering "Give us etc." Clear $45.00; milk glass $55.00. *Rarely found in blue $200.00.*

No. 954 – PANELLED WHEAT – L. 172, 173, 173A – K. Bk. 1-41. One of the choicest milk glass patterns but is also found in clear glass. Of the 70s, finials are wheat sheaves, handles are molded. In the milk glass the sugar comes in three types, one is rimless, one with wide rim, and one in which the wide rim is slotted for spoons; butter comes in both flat and with collared base. Milk glass: flat sauce $20.00; spooner $50.00; egg cup, tapered flat relish $45.00; flat covered butter $40.00; creamer $55.00; butter with collared base $90.00; sugar with slotted edge (covered) $80.00; covered sugar $70.00; goblet $50.00; water pitcher $100.00; covered compote $95.00; open compote $45.00; open sugar $30.00. Clear glass: flat sauce $15.00; spooner $35.00; relish, open sugar $20.00; covered butter $50.00; creamer $45.00; covered sugar $50.00; covered compote $75.00; goblet $45.00. *Hobbs Brockunier.*

No. 951 – WHEAT SHEAF – M. 69. Interesting, non-flint of the late 70s. Only goblet $35.00.

No. 955 – ROUND PANELLED WHEAT – M. Bk. 2-160 (not pictured) calls this PANELLED WHEAT but that pattern name is used for one above. In this, clear, non-flint of the late 80s, a sheaf of wheat hangs inverted from the opening of a circular panel formed by two rounded parallel lines which enclose wheat grains between them. Spooner $35.00; open sugar $20.00; goblet $40.00; covered butter $55.00; covered sugar $45.00; creamer $40.00; castor bottles each $30.00. *Central Glass #234.*

852
Branches

858
Apple Tree

674
Lacy Daisy

939
Bosc Pear

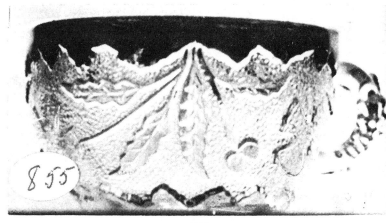

855
Four Petal Flower

No. 852 – BRANCHES – L. 190 No. 1. Non-flint of the late 80s. Creamer $50.00; open sugar $25.00; covered sugar $55.00; *spooner $45.00.*

No. 853 – BRANCHED TREE – K. Bk. 4-124. (Not pictured.) Non-flint of the 90s, probably made in Indiana. Entire water pitcher covered with branches, no leaves. Water pitcher $70.00.

No. 854 – TREE BARK – K. 1-49. (Not pictured.) Entire water pitcher textured like tree bark with exception of narrow band at top and wider band around collared base. These areas are covered with vertical prisms. There was a number of these novelty water pitchers in non-flint, made in Indiana, for premiums. Water pitcher $70.00.

No. 855 – FOUR PETAL FLOWER, *DELAWARE* – K. Bk. 1-101. Non-flint, of the late 90s. Entire body of pieces are textured; sugar and creamer are squat, very similar to this cup in shape. Comes in *rose flash*, green, and clear with wide gilt band. Very flashy, late, appeals to those who must have color, regardless of quality; therefore in demand. Prices quoted are for clear; oval or round large sauce $15.00; cup and saucer $25.00; pitcher $75.00; covered sugar $65.00; large bowl $45.00; pair salt and pepper shakers $300.00; green 80% more. *Rose flash 100% more. Butter $85.00; banana boat $55.00; tumbler $25.00; toothpick $45.00.*

No. 858 – ORANGE TREE – Hitherto unlisted. Just found a piece of lustered glass, carnival glass, I could endorse. Small goblet, 5¼" tall. Luster is golden, subtly applied and reaches only to the stem. When light plays through the piece it looks as if it were the fairies' orchard. Goblet $90.00; *mug $45.00; tumbler $50.00; hatpin holder $75.00. Fenton, 1911.*

No. 674 – LACY DAISY – K. Bk. 2-73 – L. 44 calls it DAISY. Rare in color. I've never heard of goblet nor tumbler but one could use Pittsburgh Daisy goblet listed below, it is of same weight and texture and embodies this motif along with a dozen superfluous ones. Flat sauce $8.00; individual salt dips $10.00; spooner $25.00; open sugar $20.00; several sizes of plates $15.00 – 20.00; sherbet cups $4.00; creamer $20.00; covered sugar $25.00; flat master salts $12.00; child's set $20.00. Although this is a late glass, its sparkle has won many friends and it is in heavy demand. Non-flint colored pieces rare, 100% more. *J.B. Higbee 1908, New Martinsville 1915.*

No. 675 – *FLORAL OVAL* – M. Bk. 2-69. (Not pictured.) Non-flint of the *1900s*. Has panel of daisy design as above and the remainder of the goblet is of the imitation cut glass variety. Made in full setting, but not worth listing; goblet combines well, however, with Lacy Daisy above. Goblet $25.00. *J.B. Higbee, 1910, New Martinsville, 1916.*

No. 939 – BOSC PEAR – K. Bk. 7-27. Very late, clear non-flint of the 1920s. Shown here for comparison with the other pear patterns. Creamer $15.00; *covered butter $45.00.*

No. 940 – SWEET PEAR, *AVOCADO* – K. Bk. 4-111. (Not pictured.) The writer states this is the one M. 116 calls Sugar Pear (above). This is an error for this is a much later pattern, contemporary of Bosc Pear, above. This is very similar in shape to Bosc Pear, but the entire body is covered with pear leaves, among which, on each side, hang two pears. Creamer $15.00. I realize that some writers state that these creamers are to be found in antique shops, today, and I'll agree that I've seen them in shops bearing a sign, ANTIQUES, and I've seen them in so-called ANTIQUE SHOWS, but. . . ? *Indiana Glass (Dunkirk), 1923.*

FRUIT PITCHERS – (Not pictured.) A group of interesting creamers, milk pitchers and water pitchers was produced in non-flint in the late 80s and 90s in Indiana and Ohio. The fruit differs on opposite sides. Like Strawberry and Currant, the body of each piece seems to fit into scalloped bottom and each has a tall stem; the handles are alike and interesting, just before they join the body of the piece, they burst into a group of elongated leaves, which meet the pitcher. *These are part of the Strawberry and Currant pattern.*

No. 930 – CHERRY AND FIG – K. Bk. 1-46. Cherries on one side, figs on reverse. $65.00.

No. 918 – LOGANBERRY AND GRAPE – See above. $65.00.

No. 931 – RASPBERRY AND GRAPE – K. Bk. 5-2. Berries on long stem cover one side, grapes on the other. $65.00.

No. 932 – FRUIT CORNUCOPIA – K. Bk. 2-124 calls this CORNUCOPIA but as that name has been used for a geometric the added word is necessary. On one side is a basket like cornucopia (I've hear it erroneously called Horn of Plenty) filled with fruits, on the reverse it is covered with long sprays of cherry branches with blossoms and fruits. Pitcher $70.00. *All by Dalzell Gilmore and Leighton, 1890s.*

957
Strawberry

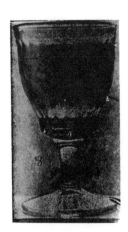

960
Falcon Strawberry

969
Currant

972
Way's Currant

975
Gooseberry

978
Blackberry

981
Early Harvest Blackberry

984
Naturalistic Blackberry

No. 957 – STRAWBERRY – L. 142, 151, 152 – M. 31 calls if FAIRFAX STRAWBERRY – K. Bk. 5-7. Clear and milk glass, of the late 60s, some of which was made at Sandwich. Applied handles, berry finials. Clear: flat sauce $15.00; oval relish $25.00; spooner $45.00; footed salt $35.00; open sugar $25.00; egg cup $40.00; open compote $45.00; creamer $75.00; covered butter $65.00; covered sugar $70.00; covered compote $80.00; celery $50.00. Milk glass: relish, footed salt $40.00; spooner $50.00; egg cup $45.00; open sugar $30.00; covered butter $70.00; creamer $85.00; covered sugar $75.00; low covered compote, tall covered compote $110.00; water pitcher $135.00. *Egg cup & goblet reproduced. Bryce Walker, 1870.*

No. 960 – FALCON STRAWBERRY – M. 52. Clear, non-flint, made in Indiana in the 90s. Goblet $35.00; sherbet cups $8.00.

No. 969 – CURRANT – L. 139 – M. Bk. 59 – K. Bk. 8-8. Lee 153 No. 20 lists a currant of poorer quality and Millard-60 lists A DOUBLE ROW CURRANT. Frequently in the fruits we find a poorer quality made later and sold for commercial jelly containers. The first Currant was fine, non-flint, made in the 70s, clear only. Pitchers have applied handles and finials are a tree branch. Goblet of poor quality $30.00. For fine quality: flat sauce $10.00; footed sauce $15.00; relish $20.00; spooner $35.00; footed salt $35.00; oval dish $20.00; open sugar $20.00; footed tumbler $35.00; wine $30.00; goblet $35.00; cordial $30.00; small cakestand $65.00; covered butter $80.00; creamer $45.00; large cakestand $90.00; covered sugar $65.00. *Campbell Jones & Co., 1870s. Pitchers $85.00.*

No. 972 – WAY'S CURRANT – M. 157. Later currant of the 80s. Clear, non-flint; only goblet $25.00.

No. 975 – GOOSEBERRY – L. 166 – M. 132 – K. Bk. 4-66. Clear, non-flint of the 80s. Clear and milk glass; while the other pitchers do not have an applied handle, I've had the syrup pitcher which did. Berry forms small handles at sides of spooner, sugar, etc. Some of this pattern was made at Sandwich. Flat sauce $10.00; spooner $35.00; open sugar $30.00; tumbler $40.00; mug $45.00; open compote $40.00; creamer $35.00; handled tumbler $55.00; covered butter $60.00; covered sugar $50.00; water pitcher $170.00; covered compote $85.00. Milk glass: sauce $15.00; goblet $45.00; covered butter $75.00; creamer $50.00; covered sugar $60.00. *Reproduced wines & goblets in clear & milk glass. Hobbs Brockunier, 1870s.*

No. 978 – BLACKBERRY – L. 142 – M. 132 calls it MESSEREAU BLACKBERRY. Contemporary of Gooseberry above. *10% more than Gooseberry. Reproduced. Hobbs Brockunier, 1870s.*

No. 981 – EARLY HARVEST BLACKBERRY – M. Bk. 2-46. Non-flint of the 70s. Clear and I've seen one lovely deep blue, almost cobalt, but without the red overtones of the latter color. Clear $40.00; cobalt blue $200.00.

No. 984 – NATURALISTIC BLACKBERRY – L. 153 No. 6 calls this BLACKBERRY VARIANT. Clear non-flint of the late 70s. Only goblet $40.00.

No. 964 – STRAWBERRY WITH ROMAN KEY BAND – M. Bk. 2-19 – Kamm Bk. 4-89 calls it PANELLED STRAWBERRY. Late, non-flint (not pictured). Flared, tall bowled goblet with band of Roman key running horizontally around, panels, and naturalistic strawberries and leaves hang, hiding part of the Roman Key band. Goblet, creamer $35.00; covered butter $50.00; covered sugar $40.00. *Indiana Glass (Dunkirk), 1911.*

No. 965 – FALMOUTH STRAWBERRY – M. Bk. 2-39. (Not pictured.) Clear, non-flint of the 1900s. Only goblet which has a very short, wide panelled body, ribbed at the bottom and a tall stem with trimmed knob near top. Berries hang from 1/8" wide band which circles the goblet just beneath the scallops at the top of the panels. Goblet $30.00. This pattern and the one above show the transition to the poorly designed goblets of the late 90s and the 1900s. Note the number of meaningless decorative elements, unusual shapes with harsh lines, panelled, trim at base of bowl, lines around the top, scallops, etc., and on this, God's lovely berries in this maze of man-made decor. They not only gild the lily, but trim the berry.

No. 966 – INVERTED STRAWBERRY – M. Bk. 2-38. (Not pictured.) Short, flared, rounded bowl on long stem; berries impressed toward inside of goblet in intaglio fashion. Companion to Late Thistle, L. 187. Non-flint. Goblet, large plate $45.00; punch cups $15.00; *pitcher $65.00; 2-pc. punch bowl $110.00. Also found in emerald with gold, 40% more. Cambridge Glass, 1915, #2870. Reproduced table set in cobalt, pink, clear.*

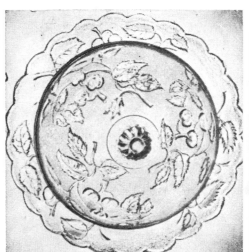

987
Cherry

990
Panelled Cherry

993
Stippled Cherry

996
Berry Cluster

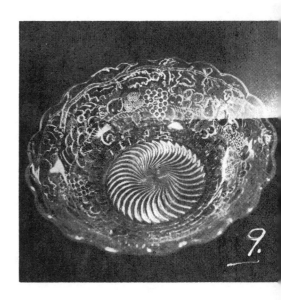

999
Barberry

1002
Fruit in Oval Panels

1005
Diamond Panelled
Fruits

1008
Frosted Fruits

No. 987 – CHERRY – L. 19, 66, 155 – M. 114. Clear and a scarce milk white, made by Bakewell, Pears of Pittsburgh, in the 70s. Pitchers have applied handles and the lovely fruit finial is on covered pieces. Flat sauce $20.00; spooner $45.00; open sugar $25.00; goblet $45.00; butter $75.00; open compote $45.00; covered sugar $60.00; covered compote $85.00; creamer $50.00. Milk glass 50% more. Goblet now reproduced in clear and milk glass.

No. 990 – PANELLED CHERRY – L. 79 – M. 132 – K. Bk. 5-63. Clear, non-flint of the 1900s. Flat sauce $8.00; toothpick $20.00; tumbler, open sugar, square mug, marked "Sweetheart" on the bottom, goblet $25.00 – 30.00; creamer $30.00; covered butter $50.00; water pitcher $65.00; syrup $70.00; covered sugar $35.00; spooner, open sugar $25.00. *Kokomo/Jenkins #475, 1904.*

No. 993 – STIPPLED CHERRY – L. 124, 145, 146 – K. Bk. 4-132. Clear stippled, non-flint of the late 80s. Erect pieces are separated into panels by upright sprays of conventionalized leaves. No goblets which limits the number of collectors. Value greatly reduced if soap residue in the stippling dulls it. Flat sauce $8.00; berry bowls $20.00; spooner, open sugar $30.00; tumbler $25.00; 6" plate $20.00; celery $35.00; mug $25.00; bread plate with "Give us, etc.," $40.00; covered sugar $35.00; covered butter $45.00; water pitcher $50.00. *Lancaster Glass Co., 1880s.*

No. 996 – BERRY CLUSTER – K. Bk. 3-33. Attractive, non-flint, berry pattern of the 80s. Spooner $35.00; open sugar $20.00; creamer $40.00; covered sugar $45.00.

No. 999 – BARBERRY – L. 135, 139, 142 – M. 59 – K. Bk. 1-12. Made in Ohio in the late 70s or early 80s. Non-flint, comes with round or oval berries; handles are applied, finials are interesting conch shells. Had been known as PEPPER BERRY by some. Another pattern in which a thinner, poorer quality is found at times and which was another commercial jelly container. This quality goblet $25.00; flat sauce $10.00; footed sauce $15.00; oval dishes, spooner $35.00; relish $15.00; cup plate $30.00; open sugar $25.00; footed salts $25.00; goblets, wines, 6" plate, open compotes $35.00; celery $45.00; butter $55.00; with wide rim and design on edge $85.00; water pitcher $110.00; sugar $50.00; low covered compote $80.00; tall covered compote $95.00; *syrup $150.00.* Scarce pieces in color; amber, blue 100% more. *Occasionally found in flint, 80% more. McKee Bros.*

No. 1002 – FRUIT IN OVAL PANELS – M. 66 shows this in milk glass and calls it FRUIT PANELS, a name too similar to one already used. Non-flint clear and milk glass of the 80s. Goblet, clear $40.00; milk glass $55.00.

No. 1005 – DIAMOND PANEL FRUITS – M. Bk. 2-3 – K. Bk. 5-129 calls it WILD FRUITS. Clear, non-flint of the late 90s. Goblet $35.00. The mold may have been found for now this is reproduced in clear and colors.

No. 1008 – FROSTED FRUITS – L.V. 34. Non-flint of the late 80s. Clear sauce dish $30.00; tumbler $90.00; water pitcher $210.00; berry bowl, makes attractive center piece $85.00. *Editor's note: The stippled background is so fine that it appears frosted. Actual frosting has not been reported.*

No. 929 – GRAPE WITH HOLLY BAND – K. Bk. 4-33. (Not pictured.) Non-flint of the late 90s. Band of prisms at top and bottom, space between filled with grapes and leaves and for good measure, a band of conventionalized holly trims the base. When I speak of poor design in some of this late ware, I mean lack of design; some factories had stocks of different patterns and these were put together by workmen, sans rhyme, reason or suitability. When one sees a preponderance of this type of glass in a shop it generally means the dealer is more interested in stock which can be obtained with little outlay of time or capital. Of little value as old glass.

No. 930 – PALM BEACH – L.V. 58. (Not pictured.) Another late grape similar in shape to Grape with Vine; this has large woody vines, forming irregular triangular panels in which hang the clusters and small leaves, a large leaf is between each grouping. Handles are the woody vine and finials a conventionalized bunch of grapes. Made in Pittsburgh in the 1900s in clear and opalescent. Fingerbowl creamer, tumbler $50.00; sauce $25.00; water pitcher $220.00; covered sugar $90.00; butter $150.00. Prices are for yellow, blue, 10% less, *clear 30% less. U.S. Glass #15119, circa 1909.*

1011
Cardinal

1014
Parrot

1017
Owl and Possum

1020
Owl in Horseshoe

1023
Flying Birds

1026
Birds in Swamp

1029
Birds at Fountain

1032
Humming Bird

No. 1011 – CARDINAL BIRD OR CARDINAL – L. 98, 100 – M. 158 – K. Bk. 1-33. Clear, non-flint of the 70s. Has been called BLUE JAY. One type of covered butter dish has three birds, labeled "Redbird-Pewitt-Titmouse," and this one is worth $150.00; other covered butter $100.00; flat sauce $10.00; footed sauce $15.00; spooner $40.00; open sugar $25.00; creamer $50.00; covered sugar $70.00; water pitcher $180.00; goblet $45.00; very collectible. Cakestand $110.00. *Goblet reproduced.*

No. 1012 – PANELLED CARDINAL – M. Bk. 2-111. (Not pictured.) In a large oval panel on each side of the goblet is a branch on which rests the bird. Stem enlarges to bulbous knob at the bottom. Clear, non-flint of the 70s. Scarce. $95.00.

No. 1014 – PARROT – L. 100 – M. 95 – K. Bk. 8-67. Has also been known as OWL IN FAN. Clear, non-flint of the late 80s. Goblet $50.00; rather plentiful; wine, scarce $120.00.

No. 1017 – OWL AND POSSUM – L. 100 – M. 36. Opposite side shows possum in the tree. Clear, non-flint of the 80s. Goblet $150.00; water pitcher $220.00; sauce $30.00. Goblet now reproduced.

No. 1020 – OWL IN HORSESHOE – M. 62. Scarce, non-flint of the 80s. Only goblet $150.00.

No. 1023 – FLYING BIRDS – M. 111 – L. 164 No. 6. Clear, non-flint of the 70s. Only goblet $130.00.

No. 1026 – BIRDS IN SWAMP – M. 158. Non-flint of the 80s. Clear $85.00; amber $110.00; blue $150.00.

No. 1029 – BIRDS AT FOUNTAIN – M. 167. Clear, non-flint of the early 80s. Flat sauce $15.00; small flat bowl $17.00; goblet $50.00; miniature mug $85.00. Should be other pieces. *Cakestand $85.00.*

No. 1032 – HUMMING BIRD – L.V. 35 – K. Bk. 4-25 – M. 101 calls it FLYING ROBIN. It has been known as BIRD AND FERN and in Texas as THUNDER BIRD. Attractive, non-flint of the late 80s; comes in clear, canary, amber, and blue. Flat sauce $15.00; spooner $40.00; footed sauce $20.00; finger bowl $25.00; goblet, celery $65.00; water pitcher $110.00; creamer $50.00; covered butter $75.00; tray for water set $80.00; covered sugar $65.00; *wine $75.00.* Canary 80% more, blue 75% more, *amber 50% more.*

MOLD MARKS

Often I hear people speak proudly of their pattern in two or three molds. The number of molds in pressed glass has absolutely NO meaning as to value, age, or anything else pertinent to it. It may be because there is an entirely different type of glass, sometimes called Three Mold Blown that this error has become so common and so difficult to correct. DISREGARD ENTIRELY THE NUMBER OF MOLD MARKS. When you hear one discuss them as of having importance you can be assured that the person in question is not a profound student of the glass.

TRADE MARKS — THE BEE

At times we find different markings on the bottom of pieces, very much like the trademarks used by the present day glass factories, the "H" design of Heisey; the "I" of the Illinois Glass Co., etc. On some of our old patterns, I've found it frequently in Panelled Thistle, there is a small bee in the bottom of the pieces. I believe the winged insect to be the trademark of Bryce Higbee and Co., a factory which operated in the Pittsbrugh district from 1879 till the early 1900s. *Actually J.B. Higbee, 1907–1919.*

1059
Frosted Eagle

1062
Jumbo

1068
Horse, Cat and Rabbit

1071
Squirrel

1077
Grasshopper

1080
Frog and Spider

1083
Spider Web

No. 1059 – FROSTED EAGLE, *OLD ABE* – K. Bk. 6-62. Bk. 5-22. Clear and frosted, non-flint, made in Ohio in the 70s. The finials of the covered pieces are a frosted eagle. Spooner $55.00; open sugar $45.00; celery $65.00; covered butter $185.00; covered sugar $110.00; covered compote $220.00; *water pitcher (illus.) $125.00. Old Abe was a military mascot of the Civil War.*

No. 1060 – JUMBO AND BARNUM – (Not pictured). L. 94 shows one type of the big elephant patterns; note on the covered compote that the design of the base is the same as that of Eagle, above, while the spoon rack has a differing base. I've found the compote with the same base as the spoon rack also. I believe most of these were products in the novelty line and were not necessarily a complete pattern. In Jumbo and Barnum, however, there is a four piece set, the finials being elephants, and Barnum's head is at the base of where the handles are applied. The spooner, the celery and the covered sugar are handled and the elephant is the finial on covered pieces. About 10 years ago I showed a piece of this with Barnum's head to a Chicago lawyer, then 88 years old, who as a young man had worked in the offices of Armour and Co. P.T. Barnum visited the city as a guest of Armour and it was this young man's assignment to show him the city and the "yards" in particular. He identified the head as a good likeness of Barnum. The spoon rack was considered very rare, but as frequently happens when a piece is so listed, many have appeared. Spoon rack, covered compote pieces with Barnum's head: spooner $150.00; creamer $125.00; covered sugar $550.00; covered butter $475.00; celery $135.00. There are numerous unrelated elephant pieces such as *JUMBO AND BARNUM, Canton Glass 1884, elephant with short tail and long tusks and spoon rack. Aetna Glass, 1884, elephant with long tail with tuffed end and short tusks.*

No. 1062 – JUMBO GOBLET – M. 36. Non-flint of the 80s. Evidently made by same firm as made Horse, Cat, and Rabbit as the border is the same. Very rare and in demand. Goblet $1,000.00+. *Iowa City, 1881.*

No. 1063 – ELEPHANT MATCHHOLDER – L.V. 103. (Not pictured.) Elephant head with trappings made to hang on to wall. Clear $85.00; amber, blue $100.00. Reproduced.

No. 1064 – ELEPHANT CASTOR SET – (Not pictured.) Three elephants' heads form container for castor bottles, which are squat with rounded bottoms to fit into heads. A metal handle comes up through the center. With bottles $650.00; without bottles $400.00. *Blue 200% more.*

No. 1065 – ELEPHANT TOOTHPICK – L. 127. Fancy little elephant in all of his circus trappings carries a box on his back for matches or toothpicks. Scarce $90.00.

No. 1067 – PLAIN JUMBO – K. Bk. 5-14. (Not pictured.) Mrs. Kamm shows a pattern in which the squat elongated creamer has no sign of the elephant, but the butter dish and sugar cover carry and elephant finial. Spooner, open sugar $110.00; creamer $170.00; covered butter $300.00; covered sugar $200.00.

No. 1068 – HORSE, CAT AND RABBIT – M. 15. Another non-flint of the animal era of the 80s. One side has the horse, one the cat, and the other the rabbit, all the same size. Scarce and in demand, goblet $750.00.

No. 1071 – SQUIRREL – L. 100 – M. 103 – K. Bk. 5-128. Another of the very desirable animal patterns of the 80s. Finials are squirrels. Flat sauce $30.00; footed sauce $35.00; open sugar $125.00; covered butter $300.00; covered sugar $220.00; water pitcher $300.00; goblet extremely rare and in demand $600.00. *Lamp $300.00. Bakewell & Pears, lamp with hand $600.00.*

No. 1075 – SQUIRREL IN BOWER – K. Bk. 4-60. (Not pictured.) Later, possibly made in Indiana in the 90s as a group of naturalistic water pitchers were. In this the squirrel is in natural setting; twig handle. Clear $225.00; *chocolate $650.00. Indiana tumbler & goblet, 1900.*

No. 1076 – SQUIRREL WITH NUT – K. Bk. 5-128. Contemporary of above, title describes it; clear handle; same value. *1075 & 1076 are two styles of same pattern.*

No. 1077 – GRASSHOPPER WITH INSECT – GRASSHOPPER WITHOUT INSECT – L.V. 38 – K. Bk. 1-88. Shown is creamer without insect, when grasshopper is present, he is climbing up the side directly above the floral motif. Many pieces including large deep plate have the three short, rounded feet. Flat sauce $15.00; footed sauce $20.00; open sugar $30.00; spooner $45.00; celery $50.00; creamer $45.00; covered butter $75.00; low coverd bowl $45.00; large plate $30.00; covered sugar $85.00; tall covered compote $80.00. Without insect 30% less. I've never seen an old goblet but one has been listed; it would be a rarity. But now I'm wondering if listed one is reproduction goblet now on the market. In the reproduction goblet, the insect is wretchedly crude and never made by the maker who put out the finely molded one on the other pieces. *Grasshopper also found in amber, 40% more, creamer, sugar, footed sauce & covered compote known in canary, 100% more. Goblet is not original to set, Metz was right!*

No. 1080 – FROG AND SPIDER – M. 165. Non-flint, rare goblet of the 80s. $300.00.

No. 1083 – SPIDER WEB – Hitherto unlisted. This is a little glass, 2" high, about which I'd like to know more. I've been told it was Russian and contained caviar. On the base is a crown and below this is a shield trademark but this has the word "trade mark" in English, so I doubt its foreign origin. Nicely finished around the top and bears no sign of having a cover. Help wanted.

1086
Monkey

1092
Pigs in Corn

1095
Lion

1098
Square Lion Heads

1101
Polar Bear

1104
Deer and Pine Tree

1107
Deer and Doe
with Lily-of-the-Valley

1110
Elk and Doe

No. 1086 – MONKEY – L. 94A – K. Bk. 4-81. Clear and fiery opalescent non-flint of the 80s. As it becomes better known, prices and demand are soaring, and rightly so. Finials are monkeys. Open sugar $110.00; mug $95.00; pickle jar $150.00; tumbler $110.00; waste bowl $90.00; celery $100.00; covered butter $210.00; creamer $150.00; covered sugar $190.00; water pitcher $350.00. In opalescent 100% more. *Valley Glass Co., Beaver Falls, PA, 1890s. Amber stain 400% more.*

No. 1087 – LION AND BABOON – K. Bk. 3-57. (Not pictured.) Another clear, non-flint humorous design of the 80s. Pieces panelled, under spout is a small baboon, and a lion's head is at top of textured handle. Four animals' legs merge with narrowed lower part of the dish as if helping to support it. Spooner $45.00; tumbler $90.00; creamer $125.00; covered butter $180.00; covered sugar $140.00.

No. 1088 – GOAT'S HEAD – K. Bk. 3-108. (Not pictured.) Another of the animals family. The base, triangular, has three supporting wide legs, each of which is covered with long whiskers and horns which extend from the goat's head to meet the adjoining one. Finials are goats' heads. I remember this was one pattern I passed up in my first days of collecting because my favorite author did not list it and I concluded it was a fake. Now 30 years later, I know the opposite is true; the ones we see too often may be the fakes and these seldom-seen pieces can be the collector's joy. Spooner $150.00; open sugar $90.00; celery $170.00; covered butter $250.00; covered sugar $275.00; creamer $150.00. *Hobbs, Brockunier, 1877.*

No. 1089 – DANCING GOAT – K. Bk. 7-73. (Not pictured.) Tall ale glass; dart similar to that used in pattern. Dart separates glass into two panels, in each of which a full length goat stands and dances. Non-flint of the late 80s. Think what fun for a recreation room, worth $175.00 even if they were used in advertising beer.

No. 1090 – DRAGON – L.V. 36 – M. Bk. 2-130. (Not pictured.) Another little known member of the animal group. The dragon hisses his way around the bottom of the body of the pieces. Flat sauce $40.00; open sugar $120.00; creamer $250.00; goblet $1,000.00. *McKee Bros. 1870.*

No. 1091 – GARGOYLE – M. Bk. 2-130. (Not pictured.) Tall, formal appearing goblet with gargoyles covering most of the bowl. Fancy ring knob at top of stem. Only goblet $200.00. *BellAire Goblet, 1880s.*

No. 1092 – PIGS IN CORN – M. 36 – K. Bk. 8-67. For an all American goblet this is it! Only goblet, much wanted and scarce $700.00.

No. 1095 – LION – L. 90, 91, 92, 93 – L.V. 2 – M. 149 – K. Bk. 8-67. McKerin, plate 211, shows a goblet made for "Tillie – 1879" and so engraved; this dates it. Clear and frosted. Rampant lion sits on haunches with paws on log; crouching lions, sometimes called "praying lion," is slightly smaller; these are the finials. Two sizes footed sauces $25.00 – 30.00; spooner $80.00; oval relish $45.00; covered sugar $110.00; open compote $85.00; goblet $80.00; celery $90.00; bread plate $100.00; wine $250.00; butter $150.00; covered jam jar $100.00; covered round compote $200.00; covered oval compote $180.00; water pitcher $350.00; syrup pitcher $1,000.00; champagne $225.00; footed master salt $300.00. A listed lamp is swirled with a lion's head protruding from each side and is a rarity as are the milk pitcher $400.00; cheese dish $550.00; cologne bottles $375.00; and any colored piece. These bring from $800.00+. Reproduced. *Gillinder & Sons, 1877.*

No. 1096 – LION'S HEAD – L. 93 – K. Bk. 5-4. (Not pictured.) Belonging to family above but finials are only lion's heads. The stems are plain; these are worth 20% less than pieces with stem of lion's heads. There is no goblet in this type. *The value of this is 20% less than Lion. Reproduced. Gillinder & Sons, 1877.*

No. 1098 – SQUARE LION'S HEADS – M. 168 calls it CLEAR LION'S HEADS, K. Bk. 5-83 calls it ATLANTA (preferred name). This is later than the other Lion, being made in the 90s. Pieces are all square. Flat sauce $30.00; berry bowls, open sugar, spooner $65.00; covered butter $95.00; goblet, creamer $65.00; covered sugar $95.00; covered compote, large cakestand $130.00. *Frosted 20% more, stain 100% more. Goblet reproduced.*

No. 1101 – POLAR BEAR – L. 91, 94 – M. 72, 73. Clear, or clear and frosted, non-flint of the 70s, made in Ohio. Goblet shows bear in one panel and seals on ice on the other. Has been known as ARCTIC, ICEBERG, and NORTH POLE. All clear 40% less. Ice or waste bowl $120.00; goblet $150.00; oval or round water tray $225.00; water pitcher $300.00. *Crystal Glass Co., 1883.*

(Continued on Page 99)

1113
Lion in Jungle

1116
Three Presidents

1119
Boat Scene

1122
Buck and Doe

1125
Butterflies and Flowers

1128
Dog with Rabbit
in Mouth

1131
Dog, Rabbit at Foot

1134
Conventional Band

No. 1113 – LION IN THE JUNGLE – Hitherto unlisted. This is one of the goblets which went through the Chicago fire. Its surface is pitted and darkened. Goblet $130.00.

No. 1114 – IBEX – Hitherto unlisted. (Not pictured.) Companion to one above; this came out so dark it could not be photographed. Shows the ibex in natural habitat. Goblet $115.00.

No. 1116 – THREE PRESIDENTS – Hitherto unlisted. Note the perfection of the etching. Rare. Goblet $100.00. *Washington, Lincoln, Garfield.*

No. 1119 – BOAT SCENE – Hitherto unlisted. Look carefully and you will see the boat in the scenic band. Only goblet $65.00.

No. 1122 – BUCK AND DOE – Hitherto unlisted. Another of the family. Only goblet $85.00.

No. 1125 – BUTTERFLIES AND FLOWERS – Not hitherto listed. Clear, non-flint of the early 70s. Compote $80.00.

No. 1128 – DOG, RABBIT IN MOUTH – Hitherto unlisted. Contemporary of the other early etched. Goblet $115.00.

No. 1131 – DOG, RABBIT AT FOOT – Hitherto unlisted. Another of the same family. This is the story of a hunt. Goblet $115.00.

No. 1134 – CONVENTIONAL BAND – K. Bk. 1-19. The geometric is designed as well as the naturalistic in this period. Creamer $30.00; goblet $35.00; covered sugar $40.00; spooner $30.00.

No. 1135 – DEER AND DOG – L. 101 – M. Bk. 2-38. (Not pictured.) Clear and etched of early 70s. Scene shows hunter with gun and his dog out among the trees. Finials are a lovely dog. Here is one of the vagaries of values in pattern glass; in the goblet in this pattern, there are two shapes, one has angular bowl, like the covered sugar, etc., and is worth $60.00. The other, which is "U" shaped and does not match shape of other pieces of the set, is the scarce one for which goblet collectors hanker and is worth $75.00. Footed sauce $25.00; spooner, open sugar $70.00; open compote $95.00; creamer $85.00; covered sugar, covered compote $150.00; celery $95.00; water pitcher $190.00; covered butter $140.00.

No. 1136 – CAMEL CARAVAN – M. Bk. 2-75. (Not pictured.) Shows camels among the palm trees, and caravan resting. Contemporary of Deer and Dog.

No. 1136 – OASIS – K. Bk. 1-1. Contemporary of Deer and Dog. (Not pictured.) Shows man leading horse which has its load on back, one on side, and woman at crude water hole, dipping water on the other. There are differing scenes on differing pieces. Compote has Arabs among palms, scenes along Nile, pyramids, palms, and everything one could imagine. Prices same as for Deer and Dog. This etched glass has been neglected and I feel it is partly because it is so difficult to draw or photograph. It is comparatively early; I have two goblets which went through the Chicago fire of 1871. I have seen blown sauces so decorated. Shapes are graceful and etching superior. There were later etched goblets in which there was nothing but simple fern or berry etched decor, not comparable to the earlier work.

No. 1078 – BORDERED GRASSHOPPER – (Not pictured.) Hitherto unlisted. Years ago I saw the grasshopper with insect which had a border of diamonds around the top; in amber and in clear. Open sugar $50.00; in amber $85.00.

No. 1079 – LONG SPEAR – K. Bk. 8-57. (Not pictured.) Same as grasshopper without insect, only this has a dart and leaves added to the floral unit; no insect. Values same as for Grasshopper without the insect, its contemporary.

(Continued from Page 97)
No. 1104 – DEER AND PINE TREE – L. 119 – M. 119 – K. Bk. 4-31. Non-flint of the 80s; comes in clear, yellow, apple green and amber, the latter being the scarcest. No round plates so rectangulr platter are used for service. Pieces are rectangular. Flat sauce $20.00; footed sauce $25.00; spooner $75.00; open sugar, oblong pickle $35.00; bowls $55.00; mugs $65.00; open compote $65.00; goblet $65.00; creamer $70.00; covered butter $110.00; water pitcher $130.00; platter $70.00; very large water tray $70.00; covered jam jar $110.00; covered sugar $95.00; cakestand $125.00. There is a small mug which has the deer and pine tree but not the geometric border, which combines beautifully, mug $30.00. Yellow 100% more, apple green 80% more, blue 80% more, or amber 40% more. Goblet now reproduced. *Belmont & McKee, 1886.*

No. 1107 – DEER AND DOE WITH LILY-OF-THE-VALLEY – M. 36 – L. 164 No. 17. Non-flint, clear, of the 80s. Only goblet $150.00.

No. 1110 – ELK AND DOE – M. 11 – K. Bk. 8-69 calls it THREE DEER. Contemporary of above. Only goblet $185.00.

1162
Drum

1165
Preparedness

1168
Ribbed Opal

1172
Swirled Opal

1175
Crossbar Opal

1178
Arched Leaf

No. 1162 – DRUM – K. Bk. 7-47. Clear, non-flint diminutive set, made by Bryce Higbee, in Pennsylvania, in the 80s. Finials are tiny cannon. Spooner $60.00; creamer $70.00; covered sugar $80.00; covered mustard $70.00; covered butter $85.00. How happy a child, sick in bed would be to find these on his tray.

No. 1165 – PREPAREDNESS TOOTHPICK – Not all late glass is without merit. Made in 1917, the detail is so carefully worked out that the tiny stars on the sailor's middy are plainly visible. If one has a tiny budget, buys like this at $65.00 are worthwhile. Of course, they are not antique; they are just nice old things with a future. *Editor's note: After 40 years, this item is quite valuable.*

No. 1168 – RIBBED OPAL – L. 147 and in L.V. – 69 calls it BEATTY RIB. Made by A.J. Beatty Co., in Tiffin, Ohio, in the late 80s. Beautiful opalescent, blue opalescent and a few pieces of a very rare yellow opalescent. Always sought after by collectors. Sauce dish $20.00; salt shaker $60.00; finger bowl $35.00; other bowls $60.00; individual creamer, small mug $35.00; large creamer $40.00; large handled mug $60.00; toothpick $45.00; sugar shaker $120.00; tumbler $40.00; covered sugar $50.00; rectangular deep relishes $25.00; covered butter $85.00; water pitcher $185.00; cracker jar $170.00. In blue opalescent 30% more; yellow opalescent 150% more.

No. 1172 – SWIRLED OPAL – Contemporary of above. *Prices 30% higher than above Beatty Swirled.*

No. 1175 – CROSSBAR OPAL – Contemporary of Ribbed *Opal. Same values as Beatty Swirled & Betty Honeycomb.*

No. 1178 – ARCHED LEAF – L. 28, 73 – M. 94. Clear, which comes in a non-flint and a fine sparkling flint. Of the early 70s. Large plate, goblet, non-flint $50.00. In flint: footed salt $45.00; large plate $80.00; goblet $85.00. This belonged on an earlier page but the number of patterns and the pages in classifications do not always correspond. At times, I've put a non-flint later pattern near an earlier one with which it has been confused, but here this one just did not fit, before this.

1181
Actress

1184
Classic Medallion

1187
Girl with Fan

1190
Valentine

1193
Three Face

1196
Three Face Medallion

1199
Portrait

1202
Baby Face

No. 1181 – ACTRESS – L. 164 No. 11 – M. 80 – K. Bk. 4-5. Also has been known as THEATRICAL. Clear and clear and frosted, made by La Belle Glass Co. at Bridgeport, Ohio, about 1875. Identified by stippled, elongated shell-like ornament which is on every piece, on the opposite sides of upright pieces and at the corners of the others. The name Theatrical has been preferred by some because some pieces have scenes, notably Robinson and Crane as the Two Drominos (so marked) on the base of the cheese dish and the Lone Fisherman (not marked) on the cover of the same. One type of bread tray and the celery has scenes from Pinafore. There are all clear pieces, pieces with frosting on lower part of body of the piece and around the top and rare pieces where only the stem and base are frosted. It is wise to combine all types. Kate Claxton, Lotta Crabtree, Annie Pilxey, Adelaide Neilson, Maggie Mitchell, Mary Anderson, Fanny Davenport, Stuart Robson (Father of May Robson of Hollywood fame), Sanderson Moffat and William H. Crane are the actors and actresses shown. Prices quoted are for clear, combined with frosted, all clear 20% less. Flat sauce $20.00; footed sauces 4", 4½", 5" $25.00; spooner $75.00; relishes, 3 sizes $40.00; open compote $140.00; flat pickle dish with "Love's request is pickles," $50.00; covered butter, bread tray, scene from Pinafore, creamer $110.00; bread tray, Miss Neilson $85.00; 6" – 10" covered compotes $320.00; milk pitcher, 6½" tall $310.00; celery $150.00; cakestand $180.00; cheese dish $300.00; covered sugar $120.00; goblet $100.00; water pitcher $300.00. *Pickle dish reproduced; champagne $150.00.*

No. 1184 – CLASSIC MEDALLION – K. Bk. 1-24 – L.V. 36 calls it CAMEO, but I prefer the name which is not one used to describe a kind of glass. Clear, non-flint of the 80s, frequently found with a poor impression. Remember, however, poor impressions are not a sign of a reproduction but of using a worn mold which old companies used to do. Footed sauce $15.00; several sizes of footed bowls $40.00; open sugar, spooner $30.00; celery, open compote $35.00; water pitcher $90.00; covered sugar $45.00; covered compote $60.00; creamer $40.00; covered butter $50.00.

No. 1187 – GIRL WITH FAN – L. 153 No. 12 – M. 121. Clear, non-flint, made by Bellaire Glass Co. in Ohio in the mid 80s. Only goblet $85.00. Goblet now reproduced.

No. 1190 – VALENTINE – M. 78 – L. 164 No. 12 – L.V. 54 calls it TRILBY. Clear, non-flint, made by U.S. Glass Co. in Pittsburgh in the late 90s. Match holder $80.00; cologne bottle (does not have head in the medallion) with original heart shaped stopper $185.00; goblet $110.00; heart shaped butter dish $95.00; water pitcher $250.00; sugar $100.00; and creamer $85.00.

No. 1193 – THREE FACE – L. 89. 91 – L.V. 7 – M. 149 – K. Bk. 3-11. Clear and frosted non-flint of the 70s *made by Geo Duncan & Sons, 1878,* Pittsburgh. Mrs. Miller was the model for the three faces; her granddaughter, a Chicago resident, told me this. Duncan & Miller wasn't formed until 1900, so could not have made three faces. Mrs. Lee reports one of the lamps as having been found in amethyst and values it at $200.00*. It is most certainly unique and worth it; when one considers the value of a rare stamp or coin, he realizes that glass has not reached its peak. It's an exception to the clear, and it's the exceptional that brings money. Footed sauces, 2 sizes $30.00; spooner $95.00; salt dips $40.00; salt shakers, each $45.00; goblet $100.00; celery with scallop top $175.00; covered compotes, several sizes $200.00 – 3050.00; open compote $85.00 – 150.00; creamer $150.00; covered butter $150.00; creamer with face under spout $170.00; cakestands, 4 sizes $200.00 – 500.00; wines $160.00; claret $110.00; hollow stemmed champagnes $800.00; covered sugar $150.00; lamp $200.00 – 500.00; water pitcher $850.00; milk pitcher $850.00; cracker jar $850.00; *compote covered $300.00 – 500.00; compote scallop top large $400.00; celery with scallop top $250.00.* Covered cracker jar is flat, has wide ribs and a geometric scroll around the bottom and top; finial is the three faces. At times this pattern, like all others, is found etched or initialed; initialing detracts 10%, but they are fine to have as a basis of comparison with the reproductions. Reproduced. *No record of colored ware, lamp was probably sun-turned.*

No. 1196 – THREE FACED MEDALLION – L. 154 No. 2 – M. Bk. 2-8 – K. Bk. 7-68 calls is CAMEO. Clear, non-flint of the 80s. Goblet $70.00. There is a platter with this medallion in the center and much decoration extending to the edges; platter $75.00.

No. 1199 – PORTRAIT – M. 70. Clear, non-flint of the early 80s. Goblet has three differing medallions; in one a man; in the second, a woman; in the third a boy. This is the same goblet used by Millard for the picture in his book. I've never heard of another. I'd value it at $250.00; unless many more are reported. I'd appreciate reports.

No. 1200 – GRANT and WILSON – M. 150. (Not pictured.) In the oval panel is Grant's picture on one side and on the other is his popular vice-president, Wilson, who went into office with Grant, but who died in 1875 before fulfilling his term. Evidently this is a goblet of the early 70s. Scare $250.00. Goblet is exactly same shape as Pan. Cardinal. *Goblet is Greeley & Brown, Presidential campaign of 1872.*

(Continued on page 105)

**1035
Ostrich Looking
at the Moon**

**1038
Bird and Strawberry**

**1041
Dolphin**

**1044
Heron**

**1047
Swan**

**1050
Swimming Swan**

**1053
Frosted Stork**

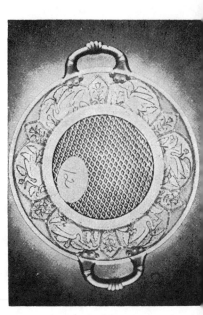

**1056
Swan and Flower**

No. 1035 – OSTRICH LOOKING AT THE MOON – M. 157 – K. Bk. 8-67 calls it MOON AND STORK. Clear, non-flint of the late 70s and a beauty. The man in the moon is only a rim but he has a smiling face and the ostrich, or stork, if you must, stands among the dainty flowers looking at the moon through a lorgnette which is hung about his neck by a ribbon. This WAS mold making. Only goblet $100.00 and I predict it will go much higher.

No. 1038 – BIRD AND STRAWBERRY – M. Bk. 2 – 75-K. Bk. 2-85 calls it BLUEBIRD. Non-flint of the 1900s. As manufactured, berries and leaves were found crudely colored, leaves in green, berries in red and birds in blue. Bowls and some sauces are on three little feet. Flat sauce $20.00; footed sauce $40.00; spooner $60.00; heart shaped relish $45.00; wines $80.00; tumbler $50.00; covered butter $120.00; goblet $210.00; large cakestand, covered sugar $75.00. *Color 90% more, Indiana Glass (Dunkirk) 1914.*

No. 1041 – DOLPHIN – L.V. 68 – M. Bk. 2-110 – K. Bk. 3-7. Clear or clear with dolphin and lower parts of bowls frosted. Scarce, non-flint of the 80s. Finials are tiny dolphins. Much in demand. Spooner $80.00; butter $155.00; open compote $55.00; creamer $65.00; covered sugar $10.00; goblet $250.00. *Hobbs Brockunier 1880s.*

No. 1044 – HERON – K. Bk. 4-24 call this BLUE HERON but that is apt to confuse title with glass color so I'm shortening it. The glass is decorated in the same manner as Cupid & Psyche, low fine stippling and fine lines, very difficult to photograph. *Values similiar to Clear Stork.*

No. 1047 – SWAN – L. 77 – M. 17 – K. Bk. 1-63. Rare, non-flint of the 80s. Clear and very rare in yellow, amber, dark blue. Flat sauce $20.00; footed sauces $30.00; spooner $100.00; open oval bowl $80.00; open sugar $50.00; creamer $85.00; covered pickle or jam jar $150.00; butter $150.00; water pitcher $400.00; oval covered dish, covered sugar $150.00; goblet $95.00. The oval covered dish and covered sugar have a clear lid with swan finial but I've had a covered butter in which the cover had the same meshed background with clear panel containing swan. I believe they were made both ways; we should not become panicky when we see these differences in handling the same pattern and conclude they are fakes; the fakers don't make this type of mistake. Amber 140% more, blue and canary 200% more. *Canton Glass, 1882.*

No. 1050 – SWIMMING SWAN – M. Bk. 2-160 and in 161 is SITTING SWAN so very like that it is difficult to find the point of variance. K. Bk. 5-127 calls it SWAN WITH TREE. Clear, non-flint of the 80s. Goblet $125.00; water pitcher $180.00.

No. 1056 – SWAN AND FLOWER – Hitherto unlisted. The handles are similar to those used by the Iowa Glass Co. and this may be one of the novelty plates produced there in the 80s. Non-flint, clear plate $65.00; I've just seen it in a fine clear medium blue, plate $120.00.

No. 1053 – FROSTED STORK – L. 68, 99, 100 – M. 61 – Bk. 3-65. Clear or clear and frosted, non-flint of the early 80s. The details of the stork's activities differ from scene to scene on the same piece; and another piece may show other activities; spooner will all be the same, but will differ from the goblets which will all be the same. Spooner $55.00; deep oval dish, waste bowl $65.00; water pitcher $230.00; pickle or jam jar $150.00; covered butter $100.00; goblet $85.00; round handled plate $85.00; large tray for water set $125.00; covered sugar $110.00; flat sauce $25.00; platters $85.00. Now reproduced: *oval bread plate and goblet.*

No. 1057 – CLEAR STORK – M. 61. (Not pictured.) The basic scenes are the same as above, but there are differences in two items in the pattern; I've had a covered sugar in this with a geometric finial and one with a stork finial. The goblets in this which I've seen had a ringed stem, but they may have been made with a plain stem. Covered sugar with geometric finial $80.00; with stork finial $95.00. Other clear 35% less than frosted. Now reproduced.

No. 1058 – FLAMINGO – M. 61. (Not pictured.) In this, the bird is not in a panel but reaches from the top band to the bottom of the goblet body. Many ringed stem. Clear, scarce, non-flint of the 80s. Only goblet $90.00.

(Continued from Page 103)
No. 1202 – BABY FACE – L. 89 – M. 149. Clear and frosted, non-flint, made in the 70s. Salt dip $60.00; goblet $225.00; covered butter $450.00; covered sugar $450.00; covered compote $450.00; water pitcher $500.00. *Goblet and wine reproduced. McKee & Bros. Glass Co. 1875.*

1140
Stippled Peppers

1143
Pineapple

1144
Butterfly and Fan

Late Butterfly
1147

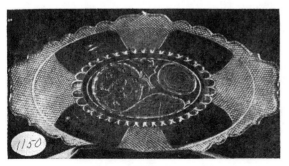

1150
Vegetables

1153
Lord's Supper Tray

No. 1140 – STIPPLED PEPPERS – M. 139. Interesting, clear, non-flint made at the Sandwich factory in the 70s. Pitchers have applied handles. Sauce $8.00; footed salt $15.00; footed tumbler $25.00; goblet $30.00; egg cup $25.00; spooner $30.00; creamer, covered sugar $40.00. Deserves to be better known.

No. 1143 – PINEAPPLE – L.V. 38. Clear, non-flint of the 70s. Spooner, open sugar $35.00; tumbler $35.00; covered butter $65.00; covered sugar $45.00; celery $45.00; *cakestand $50.00. No goblet.*

No. 1144 – BUTTERFLY AND FAN – M. 140 – L.V. 32 calls it FAN and K. Bk. 2-16 calls it JAPANESE and Bk. 7-76 calls it BIRD IN RING. Differing names due to fact that it is another of those patterns in which the scenes differ in the differing pieces. Made by Richars & Hartley Glass Co. in Tarentum, Pa., in 1881. Non-flint, clear only. Creamer footed, as is sugar, etc. Footed sauce $150.00; open sugar, spooner $35.00; open compote $35.00; goblet $50.00; covered butter $100.00; creamer $35.00; covered sugar, covered compote $100.00; celery $80.00. *Aka Parrot and Fan. Card tray, Book II, found in blue, amber, canary 100% more.*

No. 1145 – BUTTERFLY HANDLES – (Not pictured.) L.V. calls this BUTTERFLY. Non-flint, clear or clear with frosted handles, made in mid 80s. Pieces are plain, with handles in form of a butterfly. Pieces are plain, with handles if form of a butterfly. Pickle dish $20.00; spooner $45.00; oval relish $20.00; handled, covered mustard $45.00; creamer, pair salt and pepper shakers $55.00; celery $65.00; covered sugar $85.00; covered butter $90.00.

No. 1147 – LATE BUTTERFLY – L.V. 28 – M. Bk. 2-31. Late 90s, made to look like cut glass. Comes with butterflies in red or amber and this type is worth 50% more. Flat sauce $5.00; bowl $15.00; tumbler $25.00; spooner $30.00; wine $25.00; celery $40.00; goblet $30.00; covered butter $45.00; covered sugar $40.00; creamer $30.00; water pitcher $50.00; are prices for clear.

No. 1150 – VEGETABLES – Hitherto unlisted. Evidently, a relish dish with its tomato, onion and squash. There is a tall celery which has a stalk of celery on each side but it is not stippled as this is. I believe they are odd novelties. Clear, non-flint of the 80s. Relish $25.00; celery $40.00.

No. 1153 – LORD'S SUPPER BREAD TRAY – L. 133. Clear, non-flint of the 90s. Popular because of its subject. Plate $75.00. Orginally was painted on back with red and gold; easily removed with varnish remover. *Reproduced several times. Model Flint Glass Co., rarely found with open edges $90.00.*

No. 1154 – CUCUMBER – K. Bk. 8 Pl. 34. (Not pictured.) Novelty dish for pickles in form of cucumber; the cover has a small cucumber finial. Clear $45.00; green $65.00.

No. 1155 – FROSTED ARTICHOKE – L.V. 24. (Not pictured.) K. Bk. 7-78. Comes in all clear, clear with all petals frosted, clear with alternating petals frosted. In this the leaves or petals come up from base to top row where there is a single leaf. Non-flint made in the 90s in many forms but no old goblets have been found. Spooner $60.00; bowls $45.00; tumblers $60.00; bowl, vase, footed sauce $25.00; flat sauce $20.00; finger bowl and plate $20.00; cruet $130.00; original stopper, celery $85.00; night lamp without shade $350.00; covered butter $130.00; covered sugar $110.00; creamer $70.00; bulbous water pitcher $180.00; cakestand $140.00; scalloped edge compote $95.00; covered compote $140.00; large glass lamp $250.00; tankard water pitcher $225.00. I've found a bobeche and I wonder if they were candlesticks; bobeche $50.00. Prices given are for any combination of clear and frosted. All clear 40% less. A reproduction goblet in the clear and frosted is out. *Fostoria Glass.*

No. 1156 – CABBAGE LEAF – L. 65. (Not pictured.) Non-flint of the 80s, comes stippled or frosted and clear. Surface practically all covered with cabbage leaves; in upright pieces a clear liner goes part way down to set in the leaves. In the covered pieces, the leaves come together at the top and bunnies peek out from the leaves. Years ago, I found the remains of a set in a family and there were plates, covered with the leaves and with the rabbits' head peeping out. There was no goblet and no tumbler has been reported but I suspect there was one because from this family I learned the date was the late 80s and I've found many patterns of that era with tumblers only. Sauce dish $30.00; spooner $55.00; covered sugar $75.00; covered butter $110.00; water pitcher $165.00; celery $90.00; leaf pickle $45.00; plates, creamer $65.00. Prices given are for frosted, stippled 20% less. A few pieces in old amber have been found. 50% more. Reproduced in most forms, particularly in color.

1229
Classic

1232
Cupid and Venus

1235
Psyche and Cupid

1238
Minerva

1241
Bearded Man

1247
Cupid's Hunt

1250
Ceres

No. 1229 – CLASSIC – L. 97, 98 – M. 74 – K. Bk. 4-108. Clear and frosted, non-flint of the late 70s. Made in Pittsburgh. Much difficulty was encountered in removing pieces with little feet from mold, so collared base was adopted; this brings about 80% of the footed type. Large plates come with warrior center or with pictures of Cleveland, Hendrichs, Blaine or Logan. On the shoulder of Blaine or Logan can be found "Jacobus, Scul." Jacobus was the unexcelled mold maker, who made the Westward Ho molds, also. The mold making on the Logan plate is considered about the finest example of the mold maker's art; while artistically the design might leave something to be desired the workmanship is so careful that one can almost feel the whipcord of the coat. Finials are acorns and twigs. Prices quoted are for footed specimens. Sauce dish $35.00; spooner $130.00; covered butter $200.00; warrior plate $180.00; celery $140.00; covered compotes, various sizes $250.00 – 300.00; covered sugar (very large) $225.00; water pitcher $325.00; portrait plate $230.00; goblet $300.00. *Gillinder & Sons, 1875.*

No. 1232 – CUPID AND VENUS – L. 70, 92, 111 – M. 121 – K. Bk. 1-29. Clear, non-flint, made in Pennsylvania in the late 70s; was known as GUARDIAN ANGEL. Large plates have been found in amber & canary and are worth 50% more. Flat sauce $10.00; footed sauces, 3 sizes $10.00 – 15.00; spooner $40.00; open sugar $45.00; open compote $45.00; 10" plate $45.00; jam jar $95.00; wine $95.00; goblet $80.00; champagne $100.00; covered butter $95.00; covered sugar $75.00; covered compote $125.00. *Richards & Hartley.*

No. 1235 – PSYCHE AND CUPID – L. 75 – M. 121 – K. Bk. 4-3. Clear, non-flint of the 70s. This is another pattern in which the design is put on in extremely fine texture, resembling stippling. It must have been extremely difficult for the mold maker, but it does give a lovely silvery appearance, though difficult to photograph. three sizes of footed sauces $15.00 – 20.00; spooner $50.00; open sugar $40.00; celery $45.00; goblet $45.00; water pitcher $90.00; creamer $60.00; wine $50.00; covered butter $75.00; covered sugar $65.00; covered compote $100.00.

No. 1238 – MINERVA – L. 121, 115 – M. 54 – K. Bk. 1-42. Clear, non-flint, made at the Sandwich factory in the 70s. Rows of tiny dewdrops add sparkle to this now scarce pattern. Flat sauce $8.00; footed sauce $20.00; oval pickle with "Love's request is pickles," deep rectangular relish dishes $30.00 – 50.00; oval platter $75.00; large or small plate $70.00; water pitcher $200.00; covered compotes $100.00 – 180.00; covered sugar $75.00; covered butter $85.00; rare goblets $110.00; covered jam jar $180.00; open sugar $45.00; open compotes $100.00. *Adams & Co.*

No. 1241 – BEARDED MAN – L.V. 33 – K. Bk. 1-89 calls it OLD MAN OF THE WOODS. Has been called NEPTUNE, SANTA CLAUS, OLD MAN. Clear, non-flint of the early 80s; finials are Maltese crosses. Spooner $50.00; open sugar $40.00; celery $45.00; many sizes open compotes $60.00 – 80.00; covered butter $85.00; creamer $50.00; covered sugar $75.00; covered compotes $90.00. *Aka Queen Anne, LaBelle Glassworks.*

Nos. 1244 – 1247 – CUPIDS' HUNT – Hitherto unlisted. Clear, non-flint of the 70s, décor same type as Cupid and Psyche. Several sizes footed sauces $30.00; footed bowls, relish dish, has lion in scene in bottom $50.00. Two views of sauce shown as story continues around the bowl; there are two horseshoes, one on either side of the bowl, containing a Cupid; the scene is on the shore of a lake and there are Cupids in a canoe, one with a fishnet, one with a horn; there are Cupids with a bow and arrow, Cupids with a spear and wild game, including a deer along the shore who has just been hit. They must be hunting. Wish I knew the myth or story.

No. 1250 – CERES – K. Bk. 2-51. Clear and milk glass of the 70s. Open sugar $30.00; creamer $45.00; covered sugar $50.00; tumbler $35.00. Milk glass 50% more; purple marble glass 200% more. *Profile, Atterbury Glass Co., 1870s.*

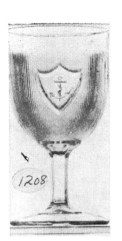

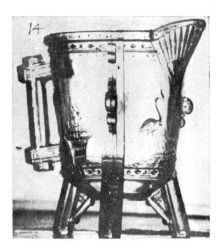

1205
Westward Ho

1208
Rhode Island

1211
Capitol Building

1214
Oriental

1217
Egyptian

1220
Canadian

1223
Cape Cod

1226
New England

No. 1205 – WESTWARD HO – L. 89, 91, 92 – M. 79 – K. Bk. 1-18. Clear and frosted non-flint, made by Gillinder and Co., in the 70s. Mold was made by Jacobus, an artisan of such great skill that it has not been possible to reproduce it so that it can fool a real glass student. The goblet has been reproduced at least four different times and scattered back in the hinterlands, even as far as Canada. Butter dish $250.00; celery $150.00; jam jar, covered $250.00; covered sugar $250.00; wine $300.00; footed sauces, 3½", 4", 4½" $40.00 – 45.00; oval pickle $50.00; spooner $100.00; goblet $150.00; covered compotes $250.00 – 350.00; small covered compote $180.00; water pitcher $450.00; *creamer $150.00; milk pitcher $850.00.* An extremely heavy impression of this pattern with squarer bowl was made in the four-piece set and the goblet, M. Bk. 2-40, has never been reproduced and is worth 10% more. A platter has been reported with log cabin handles and I wonder if this is the one which belonged to the heavy. I've never seen a reproduction in that form. I believe the mug and the goblet left clear were made later, but I have no proof yet. Reproduced in most forms. *No tumbler in original. Gillinder & Sons, 1879.*

No. 1208 – RHODE ISLAND – M. Bk. 2-7. Clear, non-flint of the late 70s; extremely rare goblet $500.00.

No. 1209 – SHIELD AND ANCHOR – M. 143. (Not pictured.) Contemporary of above and just the same only background is clear and not ribbed. Only goblet $65.00.

No. 1211 – CAPITOL BUILDING – Heretofore unlisted and here only as basis of comparison. Souvenir glass, about 50 years old but being misrepresented every day. Even the picture shows the difference in workmanship between it and Rhode Island. Sauces $15.00; goblet $60.00. Different pieces have different buildings; this is its sole interest. *Fenton.*

No. 1214 – ORIENTAL – L.V. 72 – K. Bk. 7-77. Clear, non-flint of the late 80s. Different scenes, motif on different pieces, scrolls, circles, triangles, bars, flowers, fish, fans, flower pots, etc. These things are not designed; they are like Topsy, they just grew. Spooner, open sugar $40.00; creamer, covered sugar $50.00. *Geo Duncan & Sons, 1880. Also Grace Richards & Hartley.*

No. 1217 – EGYPTIAN – L. 11, 18 – M. 82 – K. Bk. 1-32 calls it PARTHENON. Clear, non-flint of the 70s; some goblets have "Ruins of the Parthenon" under the building picture, others do not; both are old. One should realize the fakers would not make such obvious mistakes; different molds were used as some wore out; some factories copied the work of competitors and changed them slightly. Flat sauce $15.00; oblong pickle, footed sauce $20.00; spooner, open sugar $45.00; 6", 8", 10" plates $35.00 – 50.00; goblets $50.00; covered butter $90.00; creamer $60.00; celery $80.00; platter with Cleopatra center $80.00; platter with Mormon tabernacle, rare $350.00; covered sugar $95.00; compotes, sphinx on base $270.00 – 350.00. *Adams & Co. Mormon platter reproduced.*

No. 1220 – CANADIAN – L. 111, 112, 113 – M. 35 – K. Bk. 1-40. Clear, scenic, non-flint of the 70s. Flat sauce $15.00; wine $50.00; spooner $60.00; handled bowl $65.00; open sugar $35.00; celery $75.00; goblet $50.00; covered butter $100.00; water pitcher $150.00; covered sugar $90.00; covered compote $90.00 – 130.00.

No. 1223 – CAPE COD – L. 114, 115 – M. 176 – K. Bk. 8-68. Clear and stippled, non-flint of the 70s. Sauce $15.00; spooner $40.00; open sugar $35.00; handled bowl $45.00; open compote $60.00; wine $60.00; celery $75.00; goblet $50.00; 10" handled plate $55.00; covered butter $65.00; milk pitcher $75.00; water pitcher $95.00; covered jam jar $100.00; covered sugar $55.00; covered compotes $100.00 – 200.00; large, handled plate $60.00.

No. 1226 – NEW ENGLAND – M. 70. Clear and stippled, non-flint of the late 70s. Only goblet $50.00; covered pickle jar $110.00. Should be other pieces.

No. 1224 – HUNDRED LEAVED IVY – L. 115. (Not pictured). First sauce in row. This is not part of Cape Cod but I've found enough pieces to see another distinct pattern; this has the stippled background with the ivy leaves and the panels are separated by the same prisms of conventionalized leaves as are used in Cape Cod, and in Hundred Leaved Rose. Large, footed plate $65.00; flat sauce $8.00; spooner $45.00.

1277
U. S. Coin—Dime

1280
U. S. Coin
Half Dollar

1283
Columbian Coin

1286
Liberty Bell

1289
Pittsburgh Centennial

1292
Philadelphia Centennial

1295
Washington Centennial

1298
New England Centennial

No. 1277 – UNITED STATES COIN, DIME – M. Bk. 2-12. – L.V. 16, 17, 18, 19 – K. Bk. 3-80 – K. Bk. 8-156, 157.

No. 1280 – UNITED STATES COIN, HALF DOLLAR – M. Bk. 2-19. Also called FROSTED COIN. Great difference in value between United States Coin and Columbian Coin, below. The coin pattern is the outstanding example that it is scarcity and not age, that is the determining factor when it comes to value. This is non-flint, made only for a few months in 1892, at Wheeling, W. Va., when the Treasury Department stopped its manufacture because real coins were used in the molds. In some cases, the coins were left clear, in some, frosted, and in some, gilded. An attempted reproduction was stopped by the government in Indiana a few years ago; a few toothpick holders reached the market. Prices have skyrocketed and are still on the way upward. Flat sauces $120.00; footed sauce $200.00; bowl, scalloped top, from 6" – 9" $280.00 – 350.00; finger or waste bowl $300.00; open sugar $200.00; covered sugar $450.00; creamer $650.00; syrup $800.00; spooner $375.00; celery $400.00; handled mug, beer mug $425.00; pickle dish, narrow, slanting edge $325.00; bread tray $350.00; rectangular 8" dish, straight sides $350.00; tumbler $250.00; wine $400.00; claret, champagne $600.00; goblets $750.00; large goblet, flared top, originally catalogued as large ale $600.00; epergne $1,200.00; cakestand $500.00; tray for water set $380.00; pair salt and pepper shakers $300.00; toothpick $300.00; water pitchers $1,200.00; covered compotes $550.00 – 700.00; many types lamps with square fonts $600.00; many types of lamps with round fonts $500.00; lamps with coins on stems, only $400.00. A few pieces, notably lamps, have a 20-cent piece also. I checked with the Treasury Department and found that a twenty-cent coin was minted here in 4 years, 1875, 1876, 1877, 1878. I was surprised to find we ever had such a coin. Clear, not frosted, 40% of this; same for gilded as for clear. *Central Glass.*

No. 1283 – COLUMBIAN COIN – M. 106. When manufacture of the coin pattern was stopped with U.S. coins, the manufacturers turned to using South American or Columbian coins. Open sugar, spooner $50.00; creamer $80.00; syrup pitcher $300.00; goblet $75.00; covered butter $225.00; lamp $150.00; water pitcher $175.00; covered sugar $95.00; cruet $150.00 (there is a demand created by many cruet collectors); covered butter $110.00; toothpick holder $450.00; tumbler $50.00. Reproduced in tumblers, toothpicks, and goblets.

No. 1286 – LIBERTY BELL – L. 58, 113 – M. 29 – K. Bk. 1-27 calls it by name of another pattern, Centennial. Clear, few pieces in milk glass, made by Gillinder and Co., in 1876. The story is told that this pattern was designed by the grandson of Deming Jarves, who was commissioned to do so by the officials of the Philadelphia Centennial Exposition. They made the mug with the snake handle there for it is so inscribed. A glass replica of the liberty bell was made by Libby Glass Co. for the Chicago World's fair in 1893; this too, is so inscribed. Pitchers have lovely reeded applied handles. Flat sauce $25.00; flat handled nappies $50.00; footed sauces $35.00; oval, relish $75.00; small open salts $40.00; salt shakers $100.00; form of bell, bells with covers for candy or ornament, bell made by Libby $95.00; open sugar $35.00; open compote $50.00; platters with signers $75.00; larger platter, no signers $95.00; covered butter dish $150.00; creamer $115.00; covered sugar $110.00; water pitcher $900.00; miniature set $550.00; goblet $70.00; milk white platters with signer $350.00; milk white platter with John Hancock's name $350.00. *Adams & Co., 1875.*

No. 1289 – PITTSBURGH CENTENNIAL – M. 83. Another non-flint of this time. Only goblet, clear $160.00. Some have the word, "Centennial," on the foot. *Thomas Cook & Co., 1875.*

No. 1292 – PHILADELPHIA CENTENNIAL – M. 29 – L. 164 No. 5. Another goblet produced in quantities at this time. Only goblet $95.00.

No. 1295 – WASHINGTON CENTENNIAL – L. 117 – L.V. 51 – M. Bk. 2-20 – K. Bk. 2-124 calls it CHAIN WITH DIAMONDS. Another of the exposition patterns, this one made by Gillinder & Co. Handles are applied, platter has Washington's head, flat oval relish has claw handles and is marked, "Centennial 1776 – 1876." Other platters are marked "The Nation's birthplace, Independence Hall," and another shows Carpenter's Hall. Platters $130.00; flat sauces $15.00; open salt $35.00; oval relish $60.00; open sugar $35.00; oval bowls $30.00; open compotes $50.00; egg cups $12.00; wine $65.00; celery $50.00; goblet $55.00; champagne $75.00; covered butter $95.00; water pitcher $150.00; creamer $95.00; covered compotes, covered sugar $90.00; cakestand $70.00 – 130.00; *rare syrup pitcher $195.00.*

No. 1298 – NEW ENGLAND CENTENNIAL – M. 117. This is probably the least known of the goblets of the centennial and it is the most unusual. On the opposite side, instead of the eagle are the figures "1776" and a cannon, outlined by the stars. Scarce $180.00. Only goblet.

1253
Powder and Shot

1256
Garfield Drape

1259
G. A. R.

1262
Scottish Rite

1265
Odd Fellow

1268
Knob Stem Horseshoe

1271
Horseshoe

1274
Horseshoe Stem

N. 1253 – POWDER AND SHOT – L. 79 – M. 98 – K. Bk. 4-23. Stippled and clear, non-flint, made in the early 70s; fragments found tell us that this was made at the Sandwich factory; may have been made elsewhere, too. I've listed this as non-flint and it generally is but I've seen a flint goblet* in it; this happens at times, possibly the ingredients were at hand and used. As American as the Fourth of July; lovely applied handles on pitchers. Spooner $40.00; egg cups $50.00; salts $20.00; open sugar $25.00; goblet $65.00; covered butter $100.00; celery $65.00; covered sugar $75.00; creamer $65.00; open compotes $60.00; covered compotes $100.00; rare castor set $250.00. *Boston & Sandwich, 1870. *Flint actually found often.*

No. 1256 – GARFIELD DRAPE – L. 98, 104, 165 – M. 133 – K. Bk. 1-26. Clear, non-flint of the 80s. Flat sauce $12.00; footed sauce $15.00; oval relish $25.00; open sugar $30.00; open compote $50.00; memorial plate with Garfield and "We mourn our loss," $85.00; same large plate with star center $65.00; cakestand $110.00; creamer $60.00; covered sugar $75.00; spooner $90.00; water pitcher $100.00; goblet $50.00. *Adams & Co., 1881. Aka Canadian Drape.*

No. 259 – G.A.R. – M. 80. Non-flint and this one for the Milwaukee encampment is dated 1889; were put out for Minneapolis meeting, also. Non-flint, clear, goblet $150.00; platter $180.00. *Other dates as well.*

No. 1262 – SCOTTISH RITE – M. 69. Rather thin, non-flint of the 80s; clear, only goblet $45.00.

No. 1265 – ODD FELLOW – M. 54. Non-flint of the late 80s; clear only. Practically the same as knob stem Horseshoe only the prayer rug space is taken over by the lodge emblem. Goblet $55.00.

No. 1268 – KNOB STEM HORSESHOE – M. 54. See Horseshoe below.

No. 1271 – HORESHOE OR GOOD LUCK – L. 112, 131, 133 – M. 54 – K. Bk. 1-66. Has also been called PRAYER RUG. Clear, non-flint of the 80s. In goblet and celery there are two forms, plain stem and knob stem; finials are small horseshoes. Evidently made by several factories as we find slight variations in the design; some have two rugs some have three; slight variations in size of creamers, etc. This does not mean reproduction, as well informed dealers and collectors know from handling great quantities of glass. Flat sauce $10.00; footed sauces, 3" and 4" $15.00; deep oval bowls, finger bowls $85.00; covered oval bowls $200.00; goblet, plain stem $45.00; knob stem $50.00; tiny salt dip, shaped like horseshoe $30.00; large horseshoe master salts $100.00; spooner, open sugar $40.00; oval relish $25.00; platter $60.00; with double horseshoe handles $75.00; celery $50.00; pitcher, covered jam jar $125.00; 7", 8", 10" plates $65.00; wine $300.00; creamer $65.00; covered butter $110.00; scarce cheese dish, bottom has scene with woman churning $300.00; small cakestand $80.00; large cakestand $100.00; wine is extremely rare. *Adams & Co., 1881.*

No. 1274 – HORSESHOE STEM – M. Bk. 2 – 16. Clear, non-flint of the mid 80s. Footed sauce $15.00; spooner, open sugar $35.00; cakestand $85.00; goblet $90.00; creamer $65.00; covered sugar $75.00; open compote $55.00; covered compote $110.00. *O'Hara Glass, 1880.*

NOTE: The Wheelbarrow salt with pewter wheel mistakenly identified as "Barley," has foliage identical to "Good Luck," not "Barley."

1301
Stippled Star

1304
Stippled Sandbur

1307
Lined Stars

1310
Inverted Thumbprint
with Star

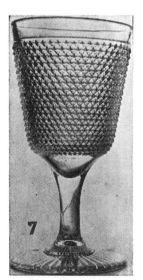

1313
Star Rosetted

1317
Chain with Star

1319
Shrine

1322
Eastern Star

No. 1301 – STIPPLED STAR – L. 147 – M. 38. Unusually interesting, non-flint pattern, made by Gillinder in Pittsburgh in the 70s. Clear only. Flat sauce $15.00; spooner $30.00; open sugar, footed sauce $20.00; egg cup $35.00; open compote $40.00 – 45.00; creamer $55.00; covered sugar $55.00; covered compote $75.00; celery $40.00; goblet $25.00. *Gillinder, 1870. Goblet reproduced in colors.*

No. 1302 – EFFULGENT STAR – M. Bk. 2-122 (Not pictured.) Clear, non-flint of the 80s. Below a wide plain band extending almost halfway down the body of the goblet are rows of stars which protrude out sharply from the piece. They are smaller than stars in above and larger than those in Stippled Star, bulb stem. Goblet $45.00. Mug $35.00. See below.

No. 1302 – STAR GALAXY – K. Bk. 8-78. (Not pictured.) The cake plate is shown here under this name by Kamm but it is the cake plate of Effulgent Star above, so there is probably a set. Cake plate $65.00.

No. 1304 – STIPPLED SANDBUR – M. Bk. 2-41 – K. Bk. 1-101 calls it STIPPLED STAR VARIANT. Clear, non-flint of the early 90s. Though late, the goblet has characteristics of earlier design. Large, flat sauce $7.00; spooner, wine, open sugar $20.00; bowls, celery $25.00; creamer $25.00; covered butter $45.00; covered sugar $40.00; covered compote $55.00; goblet $25.00. *Beatty-Brady, 1902.*

No. 1307 – LINED STARS – M. 107. Contemporary of above. Only goblet $25.00.

No. 1310 – INVERTED THUMBPRINT AND STAR – M. 170. Clear, non-flint of the late 70s. Goblet only; clear $18.00; canary $40.00; amber $20.00; blue or green $35.00. *Bellaire Goblet, 1880; U.S. Glass, 1891.*

No. 1313 – STAR ROSETTED – L. 98, 131 – M. 38. Very attractive, non-flint of the 80s. A large plate in the pattern, with inscription on the border, "A good mother makes a happy home," is much in demand, $30.00; flat sauce $6.00; footed sauce $10.00; oval pickle $15.00; spooner $22.00; open sugar $20.00; open compote $15.00 – 20.00; covered butter $45.00; creamer, covered sugar $50.00; covered compote $50.00 – 65.00.

No. 1314 – STAR AND FEATHER PLATE – L. 135. These 7" plates have a border of the same star design and a center of stars surrounded by feathers; they are used with the above. They come in clear $18.00; canary $45.00; amber $25.00; blue or green $30.00. Plates of this type widely reproduced.

No. 1317 – CHAIN WITH STAR – L. 132 – M. 175 – K. Bk. 8-12. Quaint, non-flint, clear pattern of the 80s. Flat sauce $10.00; footed sauce $15.00; spooner $25.00; open sugar $20.00; oval pickle $20.00; open compote $30.00; large, handled bread plate $40.00; 7" plate, water pitcher $55.00; covered butter $45.00; creamer $30.00; covered sugar $35.00; covered compote $35.00. *Bryce, U.S. Glass. Also Burlington Glassworks, Canada.*

No. 1316 – CHAIN AND STAR BAND – M. 23. (Not pictured.) Clear, non-flint of the 90s and very different from the older one above. Around the top of the goblet are two rows of chain links and between them is a row of stars. Around the lower part of the goblet bowl is a row of diamonds containing tiny stars. Only goblet $30.00.

No. 1319 – SHRINE – L.V. 35 – M 111. Clear, non-flint of the 80s. Sauces $20.00; spooner $35.00; open sugar bowls $25.00; tumbler, jelly compote $30.00; creamer $40.00; covered butter $50.00; covered sugar $55.00; goblet $65.00; platter $45.00. In demand, becoming hard to find. *Beatty-Brady, 1904.*

No. 1322 – EASTERN STAR – M. 70. Clear, non-flint of the 80s. I can't agree with Dr. Millard when he compares this to the early flint, Sandwich Star. This goblet is light and really a member of the honeycomb family. Only goblet $25.00. *King & Son, 1875, U.S. Glass, 1891.*

1325
Dewdrop with
Small Star

1328
Star and Palm

1331
Drapery Band
with Stars

1334
Leverne

1337
Block and Star
Spear Point

1340
Sawtooth and Star

1343
Star and Oval

1347
Honeycomb with Star

No. 1325 – DEWDROP WITH SMALL STAR – L. 154 No. 4 – M. 15 – K. Bk. 7-71 calls it Dewdrop with Star but there is an important pattern known by that name for years. Clear, non-flint of the late 80s; only goblet $35.00.

No. 1326 – DEWDROP WITH STAR – L. 73 – K. Bk. 3-67. (Not pictured.) Beautiful, non-flint of the 80s; pattern has no matching goblet but Dewdrop combines about the best. Creamer has applied handle; design consists of full length prisms and band of dewdrops with large stars of dewdrops in the center of the bottoms. These large stars are of dewdrops. The pieces are large, the handles are applied. Very large domed lids on butter and cheese dish. Many sizes of flat sauces and bowls $10.00 – 15.00; footed salt $20.00; large spooner $25.00; oval pickle $12.00; many sizes of plates from 4½" to large 11", one with sheaf of wheat in center $15.00 – 35.00; lamp, tall glass with patent mark 1876 in base $95.00; covered sugar $45.00; creamer $35.00; celery $40.00; large cakestand $85.00; water pitcher $125.00; cheese dish is large plate with huge domed cover $125.00; covered butter $50.00. Very few try to collect a setting in this, but the indidivual pieces are striking for decor. Colored & clear footed salts and sauces, 7", 11" plate now copiously reproduced. *Campbell, Jones & Co. 1877.*

No. 1328 – STAR AND PALM – M. Bk. 2-26. Clear, non-flint of the late 80s. Only goblet $15.00.

No. 1331 – DRAPERY BAND WITH STARS – M. 168. Comtemporary of above. Only goblet $25.00. *Doyle & Co., 1885.*

No. 1334 – LEVERNE – M. 168 – K. Bk. 2-122 calls it STAR IN HONEYCOMB. Non-flint of the early 70s. Pitchers have applied handles. Flat sauce $10.00; footed sauce $12.00; spooner $45.00; oval relish $12.00; celery $40.00; open sugar $30.00; open compote $45.00; covered butter $75.00; creamer $40.00; covered sugar $55.00; covered compote, water pitcher $120.00; large cakestand $85.00. *Wine occasionally blue or amber 30% more. Bryce Bros., 1880; U.S. Glass 1891.*

No. 1337 – BLOCK AND STAR SPEAR POINT – M. Bk. 2-110 and M. Bk. 2-18 shows it in red top and calls it BLOCK AND STAR. K. Bk. 1-113 calls it WAFFLE AND STAR BAND. Goblet $25.00 with red $240.00. Other pieces are so awkward they have little value as this is a late pattern of the early 1900s. *OMN Tarentum's Verono.*

No. 1340 – SAWTOOTH AND STAR – L.V. 47 – K. Bk. 2-52 and Bk. 5-46. Made first in 1892 and reissued in 1898. Came flased with red, also, so Kamm calls it RUBY STAR. Flat sauce $7.50; small bowls $10.00; spooner $30.00; sugar shaker $35.00; pickle dish $25.00; curet $45.00; goblet $35.00; syrup $55.00; compote $40.00; creamer $30.00; covered butter $45.00; cup and saucer $30.00; covered sugar $40.00; with red flashing 100% more. *OMN O'Hara's Diamond, 1890.*

No. 1343 – STAR AND OVAL – L.V. 68 – K. Bk. 2-36 calls it LENS AND STAR. Non-flint, made in Pittsburgh in the late 80s. Sauce $10.00; spooner $25.00; waste bowl $12.00; tumbler $20.00; creamer $35.00; celery $40.00; water pitcher $90.00; handled tray $35.00. When name is etched on any piece value is reduced about 40% as it limits sale.

No. 1347 – HONEYCOMB WITH STAR – L. 102 – K. Bk. 5-62 calls is STARRED HONEYCOMB. Non-flint, made by Fostoria Glass Co. in 1905. Poor design in flat creamer and sugar, no goblet seen. Flat sauce $8.00; spooner, open sugar, tumbler $20.00; cruet $25.00; creamer $20.00; covered sugar $25.00.

1352
Legged Banded Star

1367
Pert

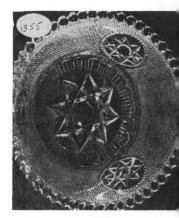

1355
Shimmering Star

1358
American Shield

1361
Roman Cross

1364
Barred Star

1349
Banded Prism Bar

No. 1349 – BANDED PRISM BAR – M. Bk. 2-53 – K. Bk. 7-73 calls it DOYLE'S 40, its trade name. Clear, non-flint made in 1891 but well designed for so late. Flat sauce $7.00; footed sauce $12.00; spooner $30.00; open sugar $20.00; open compote $35.00; covered butter $50.00; creamer $40.00; cakestand $75.00; covered sugar $45.00; covered compote $50.00.

No. 1352 – LEGGED BANDED STAR – L.V. 67 – K. Bk. 4-110. Called Banded Star by them but another pattern has that name. Clear, non-flint of mid-80s. All pieces on feet. Salt $15.00; sauce $20.00; open sugar $25.00; spooner $35.00; bowls $25.00; celery $40.00; open compote $30.00; water pitcher $45.00; interesting shapes in covered bowls $55.00; covered butter $70.00; creamer $45.00; covered sugar $60.00.

No. 1355 – SHIMMERING STAR – L.V. 79 No. 16, 17 – K. Bk. 2-55. Sparkling, non-flint, clear, of the 80s. As in many of the later patterns, the creamers and sugars are smaller than in the early ones but the sauce dishes are large enough to be practical. Flat sauce $5.00; spooner $20.00; open sugar $15.00; tumbler $15.00; creamer $30.00; covered butter $45.00; covered sugar $35.00; cakestand $55.00.

No. 1358 – AMERICAN SHIELD – K. Bk. 3-58 calls this CENTENNIAL SHIELD, which is too near to the name of another pattern. This is known in a heavy four-piece set, clear, brilliant, non-flint, probably made for the centennial in 1876. The butter lies horizontally but should not be confused with the later Banner Butter (L.V. 76) which is lighter in weight and which has a small shield finial, value $130.00. This butter has no finial and the top is rounded. Spooner shown $150.00; creamer $110.00; covered butter $250.00; covered sugar $190.00; rare and in demand.

No. 1361 – ROMAN CROSS – M. Bk. 2-31. Slight variation of the block theme but same general family. Same values.

No. 1362 – GREEK CROSS BAND – M. Bk. 2-53. (Not pictured.) Just one band of cross practically the same as Roman Cross above, slightly above center of goblet body. Stem larger at top, narrows toward bottom. Same values.

No. 1364 – BARRED STAR – L.V. 49 – M. 99 calls it SPARTAN. Clear, non-flint, made by Gillinder & Co. of Pittsburgh in the early 80s. Flat sauce $7.00; spooner $15.00; bowls $10.00; open sugar $12.00; tumbler $15.00; goblet $15.00; lamp $85.00; creamer $15.00; covered butter $35.00; covered sugar $25.00.

No. 1367 – PERT – L.V. 35. Clear, non-flint, small four-piece table set of the 80s. Creamer, 3½" tall, about the size of Ribbed Forget-Me-Not. Spooner $20.00; covered sugar $25.00; covered butter $45.00; creamer $20.00. The small sets are fine for a family of two or for bridge tables.

1370
Buckle

1373
Banded Buckle

1376
Diamond Rosettes

1379
Buckle with Star

1382
Late Buckle

1385
My Lady's Workbox

1388
Aegis

1391
Oval Panels

No. 1370 – BUCKLE – L. 62, 102 – M. 110 – K. Bk. 5-8. Clear, flint and non-flint, of the 70s, made in Pittsburgh by several factories, over a long period of years, which accounts for it in flint and non-flint. Flint worth 50% more; occasional colored piece worth 300% more. Handles are applied; finials are conventionalized acorn with diamonds at base. Prices quoted are for non-flint. Flat sauce $8.00; spooner $35.00; oval relish $18.00; tumbler $40.00; footed salt $20.00; open bowls $30.00; egg cup $35.00; open sugar $25.00; wine $45.00; covered butter $50.00; covered sugar $65.00; creamer $110.00; covered compote $65.00; champagne $95.00; water pitcher possibly unique $650.00+.

No. 1373 – BANDED BUCKLE – L. 102 – M. 110 – K. Bk. 4-9. Contemporary of Buckle above. Value 20% less, except water pitcher $250.00. *King & Son, 1875, OMN Union.*

No. 1376 – DIAMOND ROSETTE – M. Bk. 2-165. Contemporary of above. Value 20% less.

No. 1379 – BUCKLE WITH STAR – L. 166 – M. 110 – K. Bk. 1-22 calls it LATE BUCKLE. Non-flint of mid 80s. Clear, molded handles. Finials are Maltese crosses. Flat sauce $9.00; oval relish $15.00; spooner $35.00; oval or round bowls $25.00; footed salt $20.00; open sugar $25.00; open compote $30.00; wine $35.00; tumbler $45.00; goblet $40.00; handled tumbler $50.00; covered mustard $65.00; syrup $95.00; covered butter $50.00; covered sugar $45.00; covered bowl, covered compote $65.00; cakestand $45.00. *Bryce Bros. OMN Orient, 1880; U.S. Glass, 1891.*

No. 1382 – LATE BUCKLE – L. 72 – M. 109 calls it BELT BUCKLE – K. Bk. 2-13 calls it JASPER. Contemporary of Buckle with Star. Same values. *Bryce Bros.; 1880, U.S. Glass, 1891.*

No. 1385 – MY LADY'S WORKBOX – M. 69. Contemporary of Buckle with Star, above. *Goblet $25.00. 20% less.*

No. 1388 – AEGIS – M. Bk. 2-82 – L.V. 79 No. 5, 6 – K. Bk. 1-60 calls it BEAD AND BAR MEDALLION. Another contemporary of Buckle and Star, above 10% less. *McKee Bros., 1880s.*

No. 1391 – OVAL PANELS – L. 62 – M. 26. Non-flint made in Pennsylvania in the late 80s. Only goblets. Clear $20.00; yellow $45.00; amber $25.00; blue $40.00.

VALUATIONS — NOT THE LAST WORD

Valuations are a guide — not a dogmatic rule; allow variations either way. At times when a piece is given a high valuation, scouts hunt them and we find many more than we knew existed. Then we have to revise valuation downward. Values must be higher in the extreme west to cover buying trips and shipping.

At times, a dealer who loves old glass, can't resist a piece and pays too much for it. Pieces ripen and the values will get there eventually.

Condition is important. Very fine specimens have higher values.

HOW TALES GET STARTED

Recently as I entered a shop, the dealer said, "I want you to see this rare piece of Spanish Glass." Out came a piece of very late, ordinary Pattern Glass, which has been listed under the title of Cordova. It sounded Spanish, didn't it? You are entitled to ask a dealer to show you the pattern in a standard text.

1394
Roman Rosette

1397
Rosette

1400
Rosette Band

1403
Beaded Rosette

1406
Cord Rosette

1409
Frosted Medallion

1412
Diagonal Rosettes

1415
Pendleton

No. 1394 – ROMAN ROSETTE – L. 109, 135, 157 – L.V. 84 – M. 93 – K. Bk. 1-35. Non-flint of the 80s, comes in clear and clear flashed in red in different ways. At times, rosettes are red, again band and dot in center of rosette is red, etc. Clear, flat sauce $15.00; footed sauces $20.00; small bowls $12.00; spooner $25.00; open sugar $25.00; 8" bowls $20.00; creamer $30.00; mugs $20.00 – 35.00; oval relish, open jelly compote $20.00; 9" relish $20.00; pair salt and pepper shakers $45.00; oval platter $35.00; covered butter $55.00; celery $35.00; covered sugar $45.00; water pitcher $65.00; covered jelly compote $50.00; wine $45.00; covered honey dish $45.00; syrup pitcher $65.00; cordial $85.00 (rare); covered compote $75.00; castor set, 3 bottles in glass stand $75.00; with red or amber color in good condition, 50% more. Round plates, scarce, creamers, etc., plentiful. Goblet now reproduced. *Bryce Bros., 1875 – 85, U.S. Glass, 1894 – 98.*

No. 1397 – ROSETTE – L. 106 – M. 77 – K. Bk. 4-46. Made in Pittsburgh in the late 70s and again in Ohio in 1898. Clear, non-flint. Flat sauce $9.00; mug $25.00; spooner $20.00; relish $15.00; open sugar $25.00; goblet $35.00; wine $30.00; celery $35.00; 7" plate $12.00; large handled plate $25.00; creamer $25.00; covered butter $45.00; covered sugar $40.00; covered compote $50.00; cakestand $65.00; water pitcher $60.00. *Bryce Bros., 1889. OMN Magic, U.S. Glass, 1891.*

No. 1400 – ROSETTE BAND – M. Bk. 2-24 – K. Bk. 7-23 calls it DOUBLE DAISY. Contemporary of Roman Rosette. Sauce $15.00; wine $30.00; goblet, scarce $35.00; pair salt and pepper shakers $55.00; spooner $25.00; bowl $20.00; open sugar $25.00; creamer $30.00; covered butter $45.00; covered sugar $40.00; covered compote $65.00; cakestand $60.00.

No. 1401 – ROSETTE AND PALMS – M. 167 – L.V. 21. (Not pictured.) Contemporary of Roman Rosette; like Rosette Band only branches of palms grow up from between rosettes and stem has one small ring at center. Sauce $7.00; spooner $18.00; open sugar $20.00; wine $25.00; celery $25.00; open compote $20.00; 8" plate $15.00; goblet $25.00; water pitcher $45.00; covered butter $40.00; creamer $20.00; covered sugar $40.00; 10" plate $15.00.

No. 1403 – BEADED ROSETTE – M. 14. Clear, non-flint of the early 80s. Only goblet $25.00.

No. 1406 – CORD ROSETTE – M. 111. Clear, non-flint of the early 80s. Scarce goblet $65.00.

No. 1409 – FROSTED MEDALLION – M. Bk. 2-163 – K. Bk. 4-120 calls it SUNBURST ROSETTE. Clear, non-flint of the late 80s, stippled so finely that it gives the effect of a very white frosting. Body of pieces are entirely covered with the frosting only where the medallion is. Goblet has frosted knob with the medallion in the center of the stem. Oval bowl shown. Flat sauce $8.00; spooner $18.00; relish $10.00; oval bowls $12.00; open sugar $20.00; creamer $25.00; covered butter $45.00; goblet $30.00; water pitcher $45.00; covered sugar $40.00; covered compote $50.00.

No. 1412 – DIAGONAL ROSETTES – Hitherto unlisted. Non-flint of the late 80s. Creamer $25.00; open sugar $20.00; covered sugar $35.00. Should be other pieces. *Water pitcher $45.00. Known in amber, 15% more.*

No. 1415 – PENDLETON – M. 161. Clear of the late 60s and possibly early 70s. This goblet looks like an early flint one and was reported to me as such but when I checked it I found it was non-flint. It may exist in flint, however, as in some of this era we find early ones in flint and those of a few years later, in the lime glass. Non-flint goblet $20.00; flint $55.00.

1418
Stippled Medallion

1421
Buckle with
Diamond Band

1424
Stippled Scroll

1427
Heart

1430
Princess Feather

1433
Palmette

1436
Medallion

1439
Columbian Exposition

No. 1418 – STIPPLED MEDALLION – L. 28 – L.V. 29 – M. 71 – K. Bk. 8-13. Clear, non-flint of the late 60s; an occasional piece has been found in flint. Pitcher handles are applied. Spooner, open sugar, $30.00; goblet $40.00; covered butter $80.00; covered sugar $65.00; creamer $50.00. *Union Glass, 1880. Flint 50% more.*

No. 1421 – BUCKLE WITH DIAMOND BAND – L. 154 No. 18 – M. Bk. 2-133 – K. Bk. 1-51. Clear, non-flint of the early 70s. Goblet $40.00; spooner $35.00; creamer $45.00; butter $60.00; water pitcher $95.00; covered sugar $65.00.

No. 1424 – STIPPLED SCROLL – M. Bk. 2-101. Goblet, non-flint $35.00. *Geo. Duncan & Son, 1870s.*

No. 1427 – HEART – L. 24 – M. 94. Clear and stippled, non-flint made by Bakewell. Pears of Pittsburgh in the 70s. Only goblet $65.00.

No. 1430 – PRINCESS FEATHER – L. 19, 23, 109, 112, 135, 155 – M. 25. Non-flint, of the late 70s made by Bakewll, Pears & Co. of Pittsburgh and at Sandwich, in clear and milk glass. Again as in patterns of this time, pieces are sometimes found in flint; the milk glass pieces I've seen were flint. Also known as Rochelle and Lacy Medallion but it should not be confused with the Lacy Sandwich of the name. Pitchers have applied handles and finials are plumes. Honey dish, flat sauce $10.00; spooner $35.00; goblet $45.00; open sugar $30.00; open compote $45.00; plates 6", 7", 8", 9" $35.00 – 40.00; creamer $65.00; covered butter dish $40.00; handled cake plate $35.00; oval dishes $25.00 – 35.00; egg cup $40.00; water pitcher $95.00; covered compotes and covered bowls $65.00; covered sugar $65.00. In milk glass 100% more. *Occasionally found in flint, 50% more.*

No. 1433 – PALMETTE – L. 95, 112, 120, 129 – M. 25 – K. Bk. 4-20. The plate shown on p. 29 of Mrs. Lee is termed a Variant but seems to be the only plate made to go with it and it matches no other pattern. This plate comes in clear $30.00; amber $65.00; blue $85.00; otherwise the pattern is clear, non-flint of the 70s. Pitchers have applied handles and are scarce. Flat sauce $10.00; spooner $35.00; oval relish $20.00; footed salt $40.00; goblet $45.00; egg cup $40.00; celery $30.00; open sugar $25.00; castor bottles $20.00; tumbler $35.00; wine $65.00; covered butter $75.00; creamer, covered sugar $65.00; covered compote $85.00; cakestand $125.00; waste pitcher $135.00; milk pitcher $135.00. *Burlington Glass, 1880s. Aka Hearts & Spades.*

No. 1436 – MEDALLION – L. 102 – M. 35 – K. Bk. 5-19. Non-flint of the late 80s. Comes in clear, canary, amber, blue and green. Also known as SPADES. Flat sauce $6.00; spooner $30.00; open sugar $20.00; relish $15.00; goblet $35.00; castor bottle $35.00; tumbler $20.00; wine $20.00; egg cup $20.00; celery $40.00; covered butter $35.00; covered sugar $40.00; covered compote $45.00; water pitcher $55.00. Canary 100% more, amber 30% more, blue or green 80% more.

No. 1439 – COLUMBIAN EXPOSITION – M. 137. Clear and dark green, non-flint, made in the early 90s. Only goblet; clear $25.00; dark green $250.00+.

No. 1440 – COLUMBIAN EXPOSITION – RING STEM – M. Bk. 2-10. (Not pictured.) Same as its contemporary above but there is a very minor difference in the medallion, which is stippled and has several fleur-de-lis like motifs on the stippling. The stem has small ring. Only goblet $35.00.

1419
Selby

1420
Hour Glass

1425
Threaded

1428
Scalloped Diamond Point

1429
Sunburst Medallion

1431
Aberdeen

1438
Oaken Bucket

No. 1419 – SELBY – M. 67. Clear, non-flint of the 70s. Goblet $12.00; egg cup $15.00.

No. 1420 – HOUR GLASS – L.V. 56 – M. 58. Non-flint of the 80s in an interesting shape. Comes in clear, yellow, amber, and blue. Large sauce dish $12.00; wine $40.00; bowl $25.00; goblet $30.00; water pitcher $60.00; creamer $35.00; covered butter $55.00; covered sugar $40.00. Yellow, 100% more; amber 30% more; blue 60% more.

No. 1425 – THREADED – M. 72 – K. Bk. 3-15 calls it THREADING. Clear, non-flint of the late 80s; most pleasing in line. Not to be confused with the old blown Sandwich threaded glass. Footed sauce $10.00; open sugar $20.00; creamer $35.00; covered butter $45.00; covered sugar $40.00; covered compote $50.00; open compote $30.00. *Geo Duncan & Sons, 1880s.*

No. 1428 – SCALLOPED DIAMOND POINT – L.V. 50. Clear, non-flint of the 80s. No relation to the old flint Diamond point. Flat sauce $6.00; footed sauce $10.00; many sizes, round and oval bowls $10.00 – 25.00; small cakestands $35.00; large cakestands, 10", 11", 12" $45.00 – 75.00; covered sugar $40.00; covered cheese dish $65.00; covered butter $50.00; creamer $35.00; wine $25.00. *Central Glass, found in cobalt & cobalt with clear.*

No. 1429 – SUNBURST MEDALLION – M. Bk. 2-52 – K. Bk. 5-35 calls it DAISY MEDALLION. Clear, non-flint of the 80s. Goblet $35.00; open sugar $20.00; covered butter $60.00; creamer $40.00; covered sugar $50.00.

No. 1431 – ABERDEEN – M. 174. Clear, non-flint of the early 70s. Pitchers are graceful, bulbous and have applied handles. Flat sauce $10.00; open sugar $25.00; open compote $40.00; covered butter $65.00; covered sugar $55.00; water pitcher $100.00; creamer $45.00; covered compote $75.00. *Aka Interlocking Bands, Keyhole Band.*

No. 1438 – OAKEN BUCKET – L.V. 67 – K. Bk. 1-55. Non-flint, novelty set made in miniature and full size in clear, yellow, amber, blue, and a scarce amethyst. There are small toothpick or match holders in the form of a pail with wire handles. Toothpick holder $25.00; spooner $35.00; open sugar $20.00; covered sugar $45.00; covered butter $75.00; creamer $40.00. The small is as of much value as the large. Yellow 100% more, amber 65% more, blue 80% more, amethyst 125% of clear. *Aka Wooden Pail, Bryce, Higbee & Co., 1880s.*

COLLECTING VERSUS ACCUMULATING

Frequently, I hear of someone who has 600 pairs of salt shakers or 400 slippers or 500 butter pats. When questioned, I find the owner knows nothing of the quality or workmanship or history of his possessions; it is simply the glory of number. I think of a talk by Sinclair Lewis when he was trying to get his audience to see that number alone does not constitute worth. "Is a seventeen story building which is ugly any better than a two story hideous structure or is it more pleasant to spend an evening with twelve stupid people than with three bores?" he queried. To collect profitably, taste and information must grow with the collection.

1442
Cable

1445
Reticulated Cord

1448
Clear Panels with
Cord Band

1451
Curtain Tie Back

1454
Cord Drapery

1457
Curtain

1460
Cord and Tassel

1460
Cord and Tassel

No. 1442 – CABLE – L. 32, 36 – M. 37. Heavy, brilliant flint pattern of the 50s, shown here because it has been confused by novices with some of these later non-flint patterns. Comes in clear mostly but a few rarities have been found in opaque, blue opaque, and green opaque, and with an amber (silver stain) panel. These colored pieces would be very rare, 250% of clear. Flat sauce $20.00; goblets $110.00; wines $250.00; tumblers $175.00; lamps $135.00; decanters with stopper $350.00; lamps with marble bases $100.00; spooner $65.00; open compote, 10" $200.00; egg cup $75.00; footed salts $45.00; covered egg cup $600.00; 6" plate $75.00; celery $150.00; covered butter $165.00; footed tumbler $175.00 ex. rare; creamer rare $180.00; water pitcher, rare $600.00. *Boston & Sandwich, 1859. Aka Atlantic Cable, Cable Cord.*

No. 1443 – CABLE WITH RING – L. 58. (Not pictured.) Contemporary of above but few pieces have appeared. In this, the design unit consists of a ring through which pass short pieces of cable, there is a row of the cable around the top and bottom of the piece. No goblet nor tumbler has been reported. Flat sauce, honey dish $20.00; lamp $135.00; covered sugar $150.00; creamer $200.00.

No. 1445 – RETICULATED CORD – M. Bk. 2-139 – L. 154 No. 5. Non-flint of the 80s; color scarce. Covered pieces have interesting finials of horizontal bar, supported by uprights; molded handles. Flat sauce $6.00; spooner $25.00; relish $12.00; tumbler $20.00; open sugar $20.00; celery $35.00; 11" round plate $20.00; goblet $25.00; wine $20.00; covered butter $50.00; creamer $25.00; covered sugar $35.00; water pitcher $80.00; large cakestand $75.00. *Amber 25% more, canary 100% more, blue 50% more, O'Hara, 1891.*

No. 1448 – CLEAR PANELS WITH CORD BAND – M. 154 – K. Bk. 5-14 calls it ROPE BANDS. Well designed, clear, non-flint of the late 70s, which deserves to be better known. Flat sauce $6.00; footed sauce $10.00; spooner $30.00; relish $15.00; open sugar $20.00; goblet $25.00; most interesting platter $30.00; open compote $30.00; celery $25.00; creamer $25.00; small cakestand $35.00; covered sugar, large cakestand, covered compote $40.00. *OMN Argent, Bryce Bros., 1891.*

No. 1451 – CURTAIN TIE BACK – M. 35 – K. Bk. 3-118. Clear, non-flint of the mid 80s, made in many forms including two types of feet. Flat sauce $10.00; footed sauce $12.00; spooner $30.00; pickle $15.00; open sugar $20.00; goblet, either type of foot $30.00; celery $35.00; creamer $25.00; covered butter $40.00; bread tray $20.00; pair salt and pepper shakers $20.00; water pitcher $50.00; covered sugar $30.00; covered compotes $40.00. *Adams, 1880s. "President Taylor" platter, $450.00. He was Mormon leader after Brigham Young after 1887.*

No. 1454 – CORD DRAPERY – M. 58 – K. Bk. 1-78. Non-flint of the 1900s, comes in clear, amber, blue, and emerald green. Flat sauce $10.00; footed sauce $25.00; spooner $65.00; open sugar $40.00; relish $45.00; goblet $135.00; covered butter $90.00 – 140.00; water pitcher $90.00; pair salt and pepper shakers $150.00; covered sugar $40.00; wines $100.00. Colors scarce, 200% more. *Indiana Tumbler & Goblet. Two sizes of butters.*

No. 1457 – CURTAIN – L. 85 – M. 173 – K. Bk. 3-60. Clear, non-flint of the late 70s, made by Bryce Bros. of Pittsburgh. Flat sauce $10.00; collared sauce $12.00; spooner $30.00; pickle dish $20.00; open sugar $20.00; bowls 5" – 8", collared bases $20.00 – 30.00; open compote $40.00; finger bowl $30.00; long celery boat $25.00; plain top, tall celery $30.00; large mug $35.00; tumbler $40.00; scalloped top tall celery $35.00; 7" square plate $20.00; 8" cakestand $45.00; pair salt and pepper shakers $30.00; creamer $25.00; 9" cakestand $45.00; goblet $30.00; large square plate, tray for water set $35.00; covered butter dish $55.00; covered sugar $35.00; covered compote $55.00; water pitcher $45.00. *Bryce Bros., 1888. OMN Sultan. Milk pitcher $45.00.*

No. 1458 – DRAPED WINDOW – M. Bk. 2 – 152. (Not pictured.) Odd, clear non-flint goblet of the 80s, showing curtains draped over window. Scarce, just a novelty for goblet collectors. Goblet $1,200.00+. *Very rare.*

No. 1460 – CORD AND TASSEL – L. 116 – M. 127. Clear, non-flint of the early 70s, probably made in Ohio. Made by more than one factory for I've found lamp and syrup with applied handle and creamer with molded handle. Flat sauce $10.00; spooner $35.00; open sugar $20.00; wine $35.00; egg cup $30.00; compote $40.00; goblet $45.00; syrup, large cakestand $125.00. *LaBelle Glass, Central Glass, 1879. Bridge Port, Ontario, 1872.*

1463
Chain

1466
Chain and Shield

1469
Picket

1472
Rail Fence Band

1475
Ripple

1478
Herringbone Band

1481
Picket Band

1484
Scalloped Lines

No. 1463 – CHAIN – L. 132 – K. Bk. 1-26. In M. 175 that which is labeled Chain is Chain and Star of which he shows two slightly differing types. (Possibly corrected in later editions.) Well known, good simple conventional, non-flint of the early 80s. Clear only. Goblets vary slightly in size and shape but this is not noticeable at distance they are on the table. Flat sauce $8.00; footed sauce $10.00; spooner $25.00; oval relish $20.00; open sugar $20.00; 7" plates $30.00; goblet $30.00; wine $25.00; creamer $25.00; butter $40.00; 11" plate $30.00; cordial $25.00; water pitcher $85.00; covered sugar $40.00; covered compote $50.00. *Goblet has two known shapes, rounded bowls (shown) and tapered with flatter bottom.*

No. 1466 – CHAIN AND SHIELD – L. 105, 106 – M. 168. Clear, non-flint of the late 70s. Flat sauce $10.00; spooner $40.00; open sugar $40.00; wine $50.00; goblet $45.00; creamer $40.00; covered butter $60.00; oval platter $35.00; covered sugar $45.00. *Portland Glass.*

No. 1469 – PICKET – L. 107 – M. 175. Non-flint, made in Pittsburgh, in the late 80s. This pattern listed a few years ago as plentiful and not much in demand, is becoming hard to find. The serrated edges are usually a little rough and this may be a result of removing from mold; it's really not a defect; should be noted, however. Sauce dish flat $15.00; footed sauce $20.00; spooner $35.00; toothpick $35.00; handled square sauce, nappie $20.00; open compote $35.00; flat rectangular salt $35.00; open sugar $30.00; waste bowl $40.00; celery $45.00; small platter $20.00; creamer $45.00; covered butter $50.00; cakestand $90.00; covered jam jar $55.00; goblet $45.00; covered sugar $55.00; covered compote $85.00; tray for water set $65.00; water pitcher $75.00. *King & Sons, 1880s. Aka Picket Fence.*

No. 1472 – RAIL FENCE BAND – M. 155. Another, clear, non-flint of the 80s, would be interesting for ranch home. Only goblet $18.00.

No. 1475 – RIPPLE – L.V. 22 – Lee Sandwich 202 – M. 155 calls it RIPPLE BAND. Clear, non-flint, made in the later days of the Sandwich factory in the 70s. Pitchers have applied handles. Flat oval salt, flat sauce $10.00; oval bowls $20.00; spooner $25.00; goblet $35.00; 6" plate $15.00; open sugar $20.00; footed salt $20.00; egg cup $35.00; wine $30.00; champagne $40.00; lamp $75.00; open compote $35.00; covered butter $65.00; covered sugar $45.00; covered compote $60.00; creamer $40.00.

No. 1478 – HERRINGBONE BAND – K. Bk. 3-20. Contemporary of Ripple, possible made by another factory. Same values.

No. 1481 – PICKET BAND – K. Bk. 3-33 – M. 155 and M. Bk. 2-48 calls the same pattern STAVES WITH SCALLOPED BAND. Another of the Ripple family. Values the same.

NO. 1482 – TILE BAND – M. 155. (Not pictured.) In this the band is made up of three rows of brick-like tiles. Only goblet $35.00.

No. 1484 – SCALLOPED LINES – L.V. 21 – M. Bk. 2-14 calls it SCALLOPED BAND. Another of the same family as Ripple and it, too, was made at Sandwich in the later days of the factory. Values the same as for Ripple. *Sweeney, McCluney & Co., 1871.*

1487
Festoon

1490
Teardrop and Tassel

1493
Tidy

1496
Draped Top

1499
Stippled Swag

1502
Beaded Chain

1505
Dainty

1508
Garter Band

No. 1487 – FESTOON – L. 145, 166 – K. Bk. 1-93. Clear, non-flint of the late 90s. Flat sauce $8.00; bowls, including finger bowls $25.00; spooner $35.00; open sugar $25.00; oblong dishes $25.00; tumbler $35.00; covered butter $55.00; compote $40.00; creamer $35.00; cakestand $75.00; covered sugar $45.00; water pitcher $75.00; pickle jar $45.00; tray for water $30.00; 8", 9" plate $30.00; covered compotes $80.00.

No. 1490 – TEARDROP AND TASSEL – L. 78 – M. 93. Non-flint of the 1899 which comes in clear and colors peculiar to it, notably, green tint, bright grass green, medium blue with red overtones, scarce green, chartreuse milk glass, *Nile green, also rarely found in chocolate, amber & cobalt.* Goblet and wine are exceedingly scarce even in clear. Clear: wine $225.00; goblet $200.00; flat sauce $15.00; spooner $50.00; open sugar $45.00; oval bowls $65.00; round bowls $55.00; tumbler $50.00; open compote $45.00; pair salt and pepper shakers $300.00; creamer $45.00; covered butter $75.00; covered sugar $75.00; compote $80.00 – 125.00. Light green 60% more; blue 120% more; chartreuse milk glass 300% more. *Indiana tumbler & goblet (Greentown).*

No. 1493 – TIDY – K. Bk.-22 – L.V. 22 calls it DRAPERY VARIANT – M. 62 calls it STAYMAN. In a list of reproductions currently published, one method of detecting fakes stated is difference in measurements; this is dangerous, for in many patterns such as this one the width of the clear band varies greatly in the old ones. Molds became worn and new ones had to be made; different factories copied and changed ever-so-little. This is too important and too different a pattern to be listed as a variant; note most interesting finial of the sugar. Clear, non-flint of the 70s. Flat sauce $10.00; spooner $25.00; relish $15.00; oval vegetable dishes $20.00; egg cup $25.00; goblet $30.00; wine $20.00; celery $35.00; covered butter $65.00; covered sugar $45.00; covered compote $75.00; open sugar $20.00; open compote $40.00. *McKee Bros., 1880, Log finials.*

No. 1496 – DRAPED TOP – K. 6-34 and plate 63, 64 calls it RIVERSIDE VICTORIA – M. Bk. 2-92 calls it DRAPED RED TOP as he shows it with the red. Non-flint, made by Riverside Glass Co., Wellsburg, W. Va., in 1894. Most popular in red. Prices quoted for clear, with red 150% more in demand, toothpick $55.00; tumbler $30.00; each piece of small individual four-piece set $35.00; creamer $45.00; covered butter $85.00; pair of salt and pepper shakers $100.00; covered sugar $60.00; cakestand $75.00; covered compote $125.00; water pitcher $185.00; *syrup with pewter top (shown) $195.00. Also found with amber stain, 150% more.*

No. 1499 – STIPPLED SWAG – Hitherto unlisted. Non-flint of the 70s. Footed salt $20.00; spooner $25.00. Must be other pieces.

No. 1502 – BEADED CHAIN – L. V. 55 – M. Bk. 2-134 – plate 102, he calls the same pattern LOOPED CORD. Clear, non-flint of the 70s. Pitchers have applied handles. Flat sauce $10.00; spooner $20.00; goblet $20.00; relish $10.00; 6" plate $10.00; celery $25.00; covered butter $35.00; creamer $30.00; covered sugar $35.00.

No. 1505 – DAINTY – Hitherto unlisted. Light weight, non-flint of the late 80s. Only goblet $12.00.

No. 1508 – GARTER BAND – M. Bk. 2-95. Clear, non-flint of the late 80s. Goblet, wine, celery are pleasing but other pieces mediocre in line. Goblet $12.00; wine $10.00; celery $20.00; covered butter $25.00; covered sugar $25.00.

1511
Beaded Band

1514
Sheraton

1517
Fan Band

1520
Tailored Band

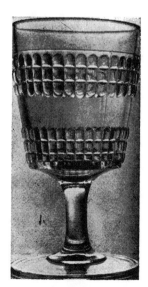

1523
Double Beaded Band

1526
Spirea Band

1529
Double Beetle Band

1532
Pleated Bands

No. 1511 – BEADED BAND – L. 61 – M. 97. Pleasing, simple, geometric, made in 1884, patent mark on syrup gives date. Flat sauce $10.00; footed sauce $10.00; relish $15.00; double relish $30.00; spooner $25.00; goblet $35.00; wine $35.00; open compote $25.00; open sugar $20.00; covered butter $45.00; water pitcher $90.00; covered pickle $65.00; syrup jug $90.00; creamer $30.00; covered sugar $45.00; covered compote $60.00. Colored rare, 100% more. *Burlington Glass. Aka Thousand Eye Band.*

No. 1512 – BOSWORTH – M. Bk. 2-19. (Not pictured.) Non-flint of the 1900s which has been confused by dealers who do not look up patterns with Beaded Band. In Bosworth, the shape is that of D. & B. with Narcissus, the stem and bowl are panelled, and the base is scalloped and ribbed. The goblet is flared, the trimming band of diamonds. Goblet $20.00; wine $20.00; other pieces awkward and of little value. *Indiana (Dunkirk) Glass, 1915.*

No. 1514 – SHERATON – L.V. 55 – M. 127 – K. Bk. 3-38. Non-flint of the early 80s comes in clear, amber and blue; colors found readily in Illinois, Indiana region which makes me think it was probably an Ohio pattern. Flat sauce $10.00; footed sauce $12.00; bowls $20.00; open sugar $20.00; open compote $30.00; creamer $30.00; water pitcher $75.00; small platter $35.00; covered butter $35.00; covered sugar $40.00; covered compote $75.00. Amber 30% more, blue 50% more. *Bryce, Higbee, 1885. OMN: Ida.*

No. 1517 – FAN BAND – K. Bk. 4-14 and Bk. 8-p. 16, 17. SCALLOPED FLOWER BAND – M. Bk. 2-25. Made by Bryce, Higbee, called YALE by them; McKee Glass Co. called Crowfoot, "Yale," two different companies, calling an entirely different pattern by the same name; this is the reason why it is not wise to try to continue using original trade names; it results in endless confusion. In the goblet, the band is around the lower part of the body. Footed sauce $10.00; waste bowl $20.00; spooner $20.00; open sugar $15.00; open compotes, celery $25.00; creamer $25.00; bread tray $20.00; tray for water set $30.00; covered butter $30.00; water pitcher $40.00; covered sugar $35.00; covered compotes $40.00.

No. 1520 – TAILORED BAND – Hitherto unlisted. We are not apt to think of these simple geometrics as being made in the late 70s or early 80s, however, I just found one marked "Sophie — 1880." These are an excellent choice to use with flowered Haviland. Only goblet $10.00.

No. 1523 – DOUBLE BEADED BAND – M. Bk. 2-138. Another of the early 80s family. Wine $12.00; goblet $15.00; should be other pieces.

No. 1526 – SPIREA BAND – L.V. 29 – M. 177 – K. Bk. 4-34. Non-flint of the mid 80s, comes in clear, 2 shades of amber, blue, apple green and canary. Flat sauce $8.00; footed sauce $10.00; spooner $25.00; wine $20.00; open sugar $20.00; goblet $25.00; cordial $25.00; covered butter $30.00; compote $25.00; creamer $25.00; celery $30.00; platter $15.00; water pitcher $65.00; covered sugar $35.00; covered compote $40.00. Yellow, green, 50% more; amber 20% more, blue 40% more. *(Green doubtful.) Bryce, Higbee, 1880s. OMN: Earl*

No. 1529 – DOUBLE BEETLE BAND – M. 102 – K. Bk. 3-47 calls it SMOCKING BANDS. Non-flint of the mid 80s, made in clear, yellow, amber and blue. Flat sauce $10.00; footed sauce $15.00; wine $25.00; spooner $25.00; goblet $30.00; covered butter $45.00; creamer $30.00; covered sugar $40.00. Yellow 100% more, amber 25% more, blue 40% more. *Yellow rare.*

No. 1532 – PLEATED BANDS – M. Bk. 2-66 – K. Bk. 8-77 calls it PETTICOAT FLUTING. Canadian, see Book #2 page 198.

1535
Portland Tree of Life

1538
Pittsburgh Tree of Life

1541
Snowdrop

1544
Shell and Tassel

1547
Frosted Circle

1550
Fleur-de-Lys

1553
Stippled Fleur-de-Lys

1556
Fleur-de-Lys and Drape

No. 1535 – PORTLAND TREE OF LIFE – L.V. 1 – M. 80 – K. Bk. 3-120. Non-flint, clear and textured, made by the Portland Glass Co. of Portland, Maine, in the late 60s or early 70s. Under the foot of this goblet is "P.G. Co." In some pieces, one can find the name "Davis" woven among the all-over pattern. Davis was a designer of the firm; pieces so marked are worth almost 50% more. Rare pieces have been found in color. Sauce dish $12.00; plate $25.00; footed tumbler $40.00; relish dish, bowls $20.00; wine $55.00; celery $80.00; champagne $75.00; water pitcher $135.00; open compote $100.00; goblet $65.00; creamer $55.00; cakestand $100.00; large rectangular ice cream tray $60.00; covered sugar $70.00; wine with applied handle $200.00; epergne, child's figure form stem $250.00. Any color 100% more. One should not confuse this with Sandwich Overshot which it resembles; Overshot is blown and so sharp it almost cuts the hand as it passes over the surface. *Pitcher on stand with mug on hook $900.00.*

Portland version: smooth rim, conical stems, main design separated from rim by clear marginal band with design covering bases & stems of some items. Only version found in color.

Duncan version: design covers entire piece, no marginal band bases. Stems not patterned. Items are melon-ribbed with hand stems and ribbed bases.

Sandwich version: design strongly defined with well-formed branches/stems/bases. Stems not patterned. Clear marginal rim as on Portland versions.

No. 1538 – PITTSBURGH TREE OF LIFE – L.V. 11 – K. Bk. 3-7 calls it TREE OF LIFE WITH HAND. Non-flint, clear, textured and frosted, made by Duncan's Sons of Pittsburgh in 1884. Because of charm of the stems and finials which are hands holding balls, and the recent publicity given to the glass of the Pittsburgh area, the demand and price of this pattern is soaring. Sauces $15.00; 6" plates $35.00; berry dishes in shape of a leaf, finger bowls $45.00; ice cream tray $75.00; pieces with hand and ball stem: sauce $15.00; open sugar bowl $40.00; covered butter $85.00; covered sugar $75.00; celery $65.00. There seems to be no goblet with hand stem. *Spooner $40.00; pitcher $175.00.*

No. 1541 – SNOWDROP – Millard Bk. 2-31 calls this ASHLAND, but I've heard from a well informed glass dealer that she saw a page of an old catalog of the Portland Glass Co. and Snowdrop was its trade name. It described it well, it is altogether lovely. Non-flint, clear and textured. I've just seen a pretty tray for ice cream and leaf shaped ice cream dishes. The tray had large scalloped inverted shell on each end. Goblet $40.00; ice cream tray $75.00; leaf dishes $20.00 each.

No. 1544 – SHELL AND TASSEL – L. 97, 105, 157 – K. 3-59 – M. 143. On p. 134, Bk. 2 – Millard lists the same pattern as SHELL AND SPIKE. Clear (a few rare, colored pieces), non-flint of the early 80s made by Duncan & Co. of Pittsburgh. Comes in two forms; square which has shell-like finial and round in which the finial is a dog. There is only one type of goblet $85.00. For square: footed sauce $20.00; handled nappie $20.00; shell salt $25.00; spooner $45.00; covered sugar $85.00; *oyster plate $225.00;* celery $65.00; covered butter $125.00; large square platter $60.00; water pitcher $85.00; flat sauces shaped like shell $20.00. Round form: spooner $45.00; covered sugar $100.00; celery $55.00; small, deep oval bowl $20.00; large deep oval bowl $30.00; handled footed sauce $10.00; large oval tray $75.00; pair salt and pepper shakers $225.00; pair vases $125.00; covered jam jar $65.00. Goblet now copiously reproduced. Colored 100% more. *Butter $65.00; pitcher $95.00.*

No. 1547 – FROSTED CIRCLE – L. 76, 96, 131 – L.V. 83 – M. 94 – K. Bk. 4-19, Bk. 6-85. Clear, or clear and frosted, made by Bryce Bros. of Pittsburgh and reissued by the U.S. Glass Co. in 1892. Flat sauce $8.00; footed sauce $20.00; spooner $30.00; 4 sizes of bowls $20.00 – 30.00; oval relish $25.00; open sugar $25.00; tumbler $35.00; open compote $30.00; salt shaker $25.00; pair $65.00; covered sugar $45.00; wine $30.00; goblet $40.00; large plate $30.00; cakestand $45.00; covered compote $85.00; covered butter $65.00; vinegar cruet with same stopper $65.00; without stopper $35.00. Goblet now reproduced.

No. 1548 – CLEAR CIRCLE – M. 109. Same as frosted above only circles are not frosted; value 20% less than the frosted.

No. 1550 – FLEUR-DE-LIS – M. 97. Clear, non-flint of the early 80s. Only goblet $35.00.

No. 1553 – STIPPLED FLEUR-DE-LIS – M. 173 – K. Bk. 1-84 calls it FROSTED FLEUR-DE-LIS. Pleasing stippled, non-flint of the late 80s. Comes in clear, amber and blue. Wine $24.00; goblet $35.00; covered butter $55.00; creamer $40.00; covered sugar $45.00; cakestand, small $35.00; large $55.00.

No. 1556 – FLEUR-DE-LIS AND DRAPE – L.V. 59 – M. Bk. 2-14 and K. Bk. 3-50 call it FLEUR-DE-LIS AND TASSEL. Made by Adams and Co. in Pittsburgh in the late 80s and reissued by the U.S. Glass Co. in the early 1900s. Non-flint, clear and green. Saucer, sauce dish $10.00; spooner $20.00; oval relish, long oval celery tray $10.00; salt shaker $20.00; cup $10.00; bowls, open sugar $15.00; tall celery $25.00; goblet $20.00; compote $30.00; covered mustard cup and saucer $45.00; flat covered butter $35.00; 7", 8" plates $20.00; footed covered butter $45.00; water pitcher $65.00; creamer $25.00; covered sugar $40.00. Emerald green 60% more.

1559
Diamond Quilted

1562
Fishscale

1565
Fishbone

1577
Broken Column

1580
Cut Log

1571
Jacob's Ladder

1574
Late Jacob's Ladder

1568
Feather

No. 1559 – DIAMOND QUILTED – L. 104 – M. 151. One of the finest of the non-flint patterns of the 80s. Non-flint, comes in lovely colors clear, canary, 2 shades of amber, light blue, periwinkle blue, light and a very dark amethyst. As modern as tomorrow, with a classic simplicity that blends with traditional or primitive. Flat sauce $8.00; individual or master salt $10.00; wine $15.00; footed sauce, 2 sizes $10.00 – 12.00; spooner $30.00; goblet $25.00; tumbler $25.00; celery $35.00; creamer $25.00; open compote $20.00; covered butter $40.00; round water tray $40.00; water pitcher $50.00; covered sugar $40.00; small covered compote $15.00; round or oval bowls $15.00; large covered compote $55.00. Canary 100% of this, amber 50% of this, light blue 75% of this; dark amethyst 200% of this with exception of the goblet which is worth $75.00; light amethyst 150% of this. Goblet now clumsily reproduced in color as are master salts. *Aka Quilted Diamond.*

No. 1562 – FISHSCALE – L. 120, 156 – M. 87 – K. Bk. 1-58. Clear, non-flint of the 80s, made in Pittsburgh. Round and square plates are becoming scarce. Flat sauce $7.00; footed sauce $10.00; spooner $30.00; large mug $35.00; footed jelly $20.00; syrup $100.00; celery $30.00; creamer $25.00; small cakestand $45.00; butter $40.00; plates $25.00; large cakestand $70.00; water pitcher $55.00; covered sugar $40.00; covered compote $55.00; pair salt and pepper shakers $85.00. *Bryce Bros.*

No. 1565 – FISHBONE – M. Bk. 2-93. Clear, non-flint of the 70s. At times, one might wonder what value there is in some of these patterns which seem to have so little design interest. They serve a definite purpose; if one's decor is getting "too busy," too much pattern in evidence a grouping of goblets of this type will be a fine, muted accompaniment. Scenic or highly decorated china can use these. Only goblet $15.00. *Glass poor quality, gray.*

No. 1568 – FEATHER – L.V. 57 – M. 30 – K. Bk .1-73 calls it FINECUT AND FEATHER. Has also been known as INDIANA SWIRL. Clear and green, non-flint, made in Indiana in the 90s. Comes in many different qualities of glass, prices quoted are for fine, clear quality. Flat sauce $12.00; footed sauce $15.00; bowls $20.00; relish $18.00; spooner $30.00; small cakestand $65.00; creamer $35.00; wine $50.00; goblet $60.00; cordial, tiny, rare $95.00; syrup $175.00; banana dish $10.00; large cakestand $110.00; pair salt and pepper shakers $125.00; covered compote $125.00; toothpick $90.00; water pitcher $75.00; celery, flat $35.00; footed jelly $20.00. In one type of the pattern the quill runs to top of piece and ends in a scallop, in the other there is a narrow geometric border around the top; in wines, I've quoted price for those which have rounded quill at the top; the type that ends with a straight line across the top is worth 20% less. Emerald green 200% more. A rare type has band of amber or red around the edge; this type is worth 300% more, also. *Aka Doric, Prince's Feather.*

No. 1571 – JACOB'S LADDER – L. 50, 57 – M. 74 – K. Bk. 1-22. Clear, non-flint made by Bryce Bros. of Pittsburgh in the late 70s. Few pieces in amber, yellow and blue have been found. Finial is Maltese cross; syrup comes with metal top, one type of which has a knight's head in metal $125.00. Flat sauces 3½", 4", 5" $8.00 – 12.00; footed sauces $15.00; oval relish $20.00; spooner $35.00; open sugar $30.00; mug $100.00; wine $35.00; round bowls $25.00; castor bottle $30.00; footed salt $35.00; tumbler $35.00; celery $45.00; cakestand $55.00; jam jar $75.00; syrup, plain top $40.00; handled tumbler $55.00; covered butter $65.00; water pitcher $150.00; 11", 12" cakestand $95.00; covered sugar $55.00; covered compote $80.00 – 125.00; goblet $60.00; complete 5 bottle castor set $350.00; rare compote with dolphin stem $400.00.

No. 1574 – LATE JACOB'S LADDER – K. Bk. 1-96. Clear, non-flint of the late 90s. Lacks charm of line of earlier pattern shown above. Is put here as an example of a bargain piece sold by uniformed dealer as Jacob's Ladder.

No. 1577 – BROKEN COLUMN – L.V. 71 – M. 139 – K. Bk. 4-116. Clear and clear with red notches, made by Columbia Glass Co. in Findlay, Ohio, and carried on by U.S. Glass Co. after the merger. Has been called IRISH COLUMN, NOTCHED RIB, and BAMBOO, but the latter is a different pattern. Flat sauce $10.00; open bowls $40.00; pickle dish $25.00; salt shaker $45.00; goblet $85.00; wine $80.00; water pitcher $90.00; covered butter $85.00; creamer $45.00; water bottle $75.00; cracker jar $85.00; sugar shaker $45.00; plates $25.00 – 40.00; cup and saucer $50.00; covered compote $100.00; covered sugar $70.00; banana dish $150.00; large cakestand $95.00. With red dots 100% more. Reproduced cobalt cup $80.00.

No. 1578 – BAMBOO – K. Bk. 8, plate 79. (Not pictured.) Contemporary of Broken Column; made by *LaBelle Glass.* In Bamboo, the rows end with a scallop, while in Broken Column, the lines end on one of the notches, forming a decided indentation. In Broken Column, in the four piece set, the design goes to the top of the piece, while in Bamboo, there is a wide marginal plain band. I've never seen a goblet in Bamboo, but there is a tumbler; it, too, comes with red notches, value 100% more than listing for all clear which is given. Flat sauce $8.00; spooner $35.00; open sugar $30.00; bowls $20.00; celery $35.00; covered butter $45.00; water pitcher $65.00; covered sugar $50.00; creamer $45.00; tumbler $30.00.

(Continued on page 143)

1583
Double Spear

1586
Job's Tears

1589
Panelled Beads

1592
Ribbed Sawtooth

1595
Washboard

1598
Prism Arc

1601
Seashell

1604
Frosted Foot

No. 1583 – DOUBLE SPEAR – L. 132 – M. 173 – K. Bk. 1-23. Clear, non-flint of the early 80s. Design is simple and lines of covered pieces are chaste and interesting; finials are quaint, petalled flower. Simple, flat butter makes pleasing candy dish. Flat sauce $7.00; footed sauce $10.00; spooner $20.00; egg cup $15.00; open sugar $15.00; goblet $20.00; open compote $25.00; celery $30.00; creamer $20.00; butter $45.00; water pitcher $50.00; covered sugar $40.00; covered compote $55.00.

No. 1586 – JOB'S TEARS – M. 101. Clear, non-flint of the mid 80s. Wine $20.00; goblet $25.00; creamer $40.00; celery $45.00; covered butter $55.00; covered sugar $50.00. *Adams & Co., 1875 – 1889.*

No. 1589 – PANELLED BEADS – M. Bk. 2-99. Clear, non-flint of the late 80s. Only goblet $25.00.

No. 1592 – RIBBED SAWTOOTH – K. Bk. 2-30. Clear, non-flint. Here is a very late pattern with some design interest. I'm showing it here as I've seen it sold as much earlier glass. Mrs. Kamm speaks of it as having a fair resonance; I have this before me and if one thinks of resonance in terms of the tone one gets from flint glass, this has none. At times in patterns of the 70s or 80s we find a non-flint pattern in which an occasional piece will contain some lead and have some tone, possibly because the ingredient was left and was handy but we do not find this in the glass of the nineties. I'm always amused when I see collectors tapping patterns we know to be non-flint, because it tells absolutely nothing. Covered butter, covered sugar $45.00; creamer $30.00; pair salt and pepper shakers $36.00. I've seen neither goblet nor tumbler. *Columbia Glass, 1891, Adonis (preferred).*

No. 1595 – WASHBOARD – K. Bk. 2-127 and Bk. 6-Plate 13. Non-flint, made by McKee & Bros. of Pittsburgh, in 1897, in clear, canary, deep blue. Flat sauce $7.00; round and oval bowls $20.00; spooner $25.00; relish $15.00; tumbler $20.00; salt shaker $25.00; celery $30.00; open compote $20.00; water pitcher $50.00; 11" plate $45.00; syrup $55.00; covered butter $45.00; covered sugar $40.00; large cakestand $50.00; creamer $30.00. Yellow 100% more, deep blue 75% more. Known for years as PLEAT AND TUCK. *OMN: Adonis.*

No. 1598 – PRISM ARC – M. Bk. 2-47 – K. Bk. 5-134 calls it X-LOGS. Clear, non-flint of the mid 80s with most interesting stem. Wine $20.00; goblet $25.00; creamer $20.00; cakestand $40.00; covered sugar $35.00. Should be other pieces. *Milk pitcher $35.00.*

No. 1601 – SEASHELL – L.V. 20 – K. Bk. 4-1 – M. Bk. 2-66 calls it BOSWELL. Finials are pretty shells. Non-flint of the late 70s, very different in line, with pretty scrolled design on the stem; deserves to be much better known. Open sugar $20.00; spooner $25.00; footed sauce $12.00; covered butter $35.00; creamer $25.00; goblet $35.00; covered sugar $30.00; covered compote $30.00.

No. 1604 – FROSTED FOOT – M. Bk. 2-117. Clear and frosted, non-flint of the late 70s. Only goblet $25.00. Would combine nicely with the four piece set of Three Face.

(Continued from page 141)
No. 1580 – CUT LOG – L.V. 53 – M. 30 – K. Bk. 1-115 calls it CAT'S EYE AND BLOCK. Clear, non-flint of the 80s. Flat sauce $15.00; footed sauce $20.00; mug $20.00; tumbler $45.00; celery $30.00; small creamer $20.00; mustard $35.00; round handled olive dish $25.00; rectangular pickle $40.00; wine $25.00; open compote $35.00; small cakestand $65.00; covered butter $75.00; cruet with patterned stopper $70.00; water pitcher $95.00; goblet $60.00; creamer $50.00; covered sugar $65.00; square honey dish $90.00; large cakestand $130.00; large water pitcher with applied handle $85.00. Large cakestand is stunning. *OMN Ethol Bryce, Higbee. Two styles of pitchers: one is tall & thin lemonade pitcher, other squat like large creamer.*

1607
Dakota

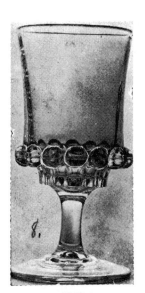

1610
Atlas

1613
Cannon Ball

1616
Ball and Swirl

1619
Crystal Wedding

1622
Teardrop

1625
King's Crown

1628
Fancy King's Crown

No. 1607 – DAKOTA – L.V. 67 – K. Bk. 4-8 – M. Bk. 2-151 shows the spooner of this pattern and lists it as THUMBPRINT BAND. Known for years as BABY THUMBPRINT. *Originally produced in 2 distinct forms: 1. A "hotel" set characterized by ruffled edges & flat bases. 2. "Household" set characterized by plain edges & pedestaled, circular bases. Both in complete table sets & either plain or copper wheel in panel.*

Clear, non-flint made in the late 80s by Doyle & Co. of Pittsburgh and reissued by the U.S. Glass Co. in 1891 after they had absorbed the former firm. Pattern has such simple lines that it is as modern as tomorrow, yet combines beautifully with traditional. The etched is much more in demand and commands about 40% more than the plain variety. In the attic of an old relative, I found, just lately, a huge cover, with deep sides, such as are used in bakeries and restaurants to cover the pile of doughnuts or rolls, in this pattern. It was at least 15" in diameter and 5" deep. It had bird and berry etching; I should have not believed it if anyone else had told me she had seen this piece. Value of cover $300.00 – 375.00; flat sauce $20.00; footed sauce $25.00; mug $20.00; spooner $30.00; tumbler $45.00; berry bowls $45.00; pepper sauce bottle $75.00; open sugar $20.00; wine $40.00; open compote $30.00 – 50.00; salt and pepper shakers $130.00; goblet $35.00; covered butter $50.00; waste pitcher $125.00; cruet $125.00; covered sugar $65.00; large cakestand $85.00; covered compote $60.00 – 135.00. A customer reports a plate, I've never seen one but this may be like the cake cover. Non-etched 20% more; ruby 50% more. *Cobalt sauce $80.00; dome for cakestand $800.00.*

No. 1610 – ATLAS – L.V. 26 – K. Bk. 2-15 – M. Bk. 2-9 calls it CRYSTAL BALL. Good, non-flint geometric, made by Bryce Bros., Mt. Pleasant, Pa., in 1889. Fairly heavy, it combines well with Ironstone china. Many forms but goblets and wines are hard to find in this as well as in the similar patterns, Ball and Swirl and Cannonball, so it is wise to combine them; it's much more interesting, too. At times, with flashed with red, which adds to value because there are so many more collectors for the ruby. Footed sauce $15.00; spooner $30.00; bowls $20.00; goblet $60.00; wine $35.00; creamer $30.00; butter $45.00; water pitchers, two types $55.00; covered sugar $40.00; cakestand $60.00.

No. 1611 – THOUSAND EYE BAND – M. Bk. 2-151. (Not pictured.) Another contemporary of this family, ornamented with balls. Shaped like Dakota, this has a row of balls around the bottom edge of the goblet bowl. There is a row of balls, midway of the stem, forming a knob. Clear, non-flint of the early 90s. Goblet $25.00; wine $15.00.

No. 1613 – CANNON BALL – L.V. 72 – M. 88. L.V. 72 shows Cannon Ball goblet and a creamer and celery called Atlas, however they are an entirely different pattern from what is shown as Atlas on p. 26. I believe this form of the family should be termed BULLET. Cannon Ball is contemporary of Atlas. Same values.

No. 1616 – BALL AND SWIRL – L.V. 27 – M. Bk. 2-32 shows a similar one with the top frosted; comes with red flashed top, also. Note that in the true pattern the stems are swirled. Made in Ohio in the early 90s. Mug, footed sauce $15.00; spooner $20.00; open sugar $20.00; tumbler $15.00; wine $25.00; open compote $30.00; goblet $25.00; butter $45.00; creamer $20.00; syrup $45.00; water pitcher $40.00. Frosted or color flashed 25% more. *McKee Bros., 1894, Aka Ray.*

No. 1617 – TALL BALL AND SWIRL – K. Bk. 2-106 calls this BALL AND SWIRL, VARIANT. (Not pictured.) Flat, tankard type creamers in which the swirls extend halfway up the piece in one shown here and in others they do not extend so far. Handles are swirled. These creamers are to be found in abundance in the resale shops all through Illinois and Indiana; they are not more than 25 years old; may have been mustard container $20.00.

No. 1618 – BALL AND SWIRL BAND – M. Bk. 2-32. (Not pictured.) Mentioned above, under Ball and Swirl which it resembles but this does not have swirled stem. Instead, this has a stem knob made up of band of rounded prisms. Frosted $15.00; clear $12.00.

No. 1619 – CRYSTAL WEDDING – L.V. 48 – K. Bk. 3-74 – B. Bk. 2-43 calls it COLLINS. Made by Adams and Co. in Pittsburgh in the late 80s. Non-flint comes in clear, in frosted and with red flashing. The original name being thus some of our clever manufacturers of gift store items made up stories about this being a bowl used on anniversaries and REPRODUCED IT IN CLEAR, MILK GLASS, and ENAMELED TRIM and dubbed it "The Old Wedding Bowl." Many pieces even goblets REPRODUCED. Flat sauce $15.00; footed sauces $20.00; spooner $35.00; open sugar $20.00; bowls $65.00 – 85.00; tumblers $35.00; open compotes $40.00 – 50.00; celery $35.00; salt and pepper shakers $65.00; goblet $55.00; wine $50.00; water pitcher $75.00; creamer $65.00; covered butter $50.00; covered sugar $60.00; covered compote $75.00; banana dish $125.00; amber or ruby stained 100% more. *Some reproduced colors are painted over clear glass.*

(Continued on page 147)

1631
Pineapple Stem

1634
Prism and **Flute**

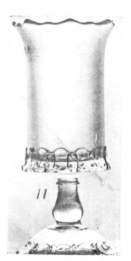

1637
Apollo

1640
Shield and Band

1643
Quatrefoil

1647
Lakewood

1650
Droplet Band

1653
Sawtooth Bottom

No. 1631 – PINEAPPLE STEM – M. Bk. 2-73 – L.V. 54 calls it PAVONIA. Non-flint, clear, made in Pittsburgh in the late 80s. Because of its simplicity, this pattern is enhanced by etching, which is more in demand and which is worth 40% more than the plain. Prices quoted are for etched. Pineapple knob at base of stem come sin two sizes. 3 sizes of footed sauces $15.00; tumbler $35.00; spooner $45.00; open sugar $35.00; open compotes $40.00; covered butter $75.00; tankard lemonade pitcher $95.00; small cakestand $55.00; goblets $35.00; wine $35.00; salt and pepper shaker $15.00; pair $60.00; large cakestand $85.00; covered sugar $45.00; covered compote $65.00. *Ripley 1885, U.S. Glass, 1891.*

No. 1634 – PRISM AND FLUTE – L. 15, 16 – M. 126. Has also been known as PRISM but there is an old flint pattern by that name, the added word works for clarity. Non-flint, clear, made by Bakewell, Pears in Pittsburgh in the late 70s. Goblet $20.00. *Mostly found in flint. Goblet $45.00; egg cup $20.00.*

No. 1635 – LOOP WITH PRISM BAND – K. Bk. 2-121. (Not pictured.) Contemporary of Prism and Flute above. Same values. Has same type of band of prisms, but below them the space is occupied by long loops instead of being left plain. Applied handles, also.

No. 1637 – APOLLO – L.V. 62 – K. Bk. 3-6. Clear, non-flint of the late 70s, made by Adams & Co., of Pittsburgh. Note the difference between this and Shield Band which is similar. In Apollo the border consists of ovals and oval prisms which are indented. In Shield Band the border is of more angular units and they seem to be added to the body of the piece. In Shield Band the border is repeated around the outer edge of the bases. Flat sauce $10.00; footed sauce $15.00; pickle dish $18.00; spooner $30.00; open compotes, innumerable bowls $10.00 – 25.00; goblet $25.00; open sugar $25.00; wine $35.00; celery $35.00; tray for water set $30.00; covered butter $55.00; cakestand $65.00; creamer $35.00; covered sugar $45.00; covered compotes $65.00. *Found all clear, frosted borders, frosted bowls. Frosting 25% more.*

No. 1640 – SHIELD BAND – M. Bk. 2-70 and in Bk. 1-149 calls the same pattern with frosted top (shown) FROSTED FESTAL BALL. I suggest the same name for both as we are apt to find any pattern frosted. Contemporary of Apollo; same values.

No. 1643 – QUATREFOIL – Hitherto unlisted. This pattern, in such pieces as bowls and compotes, is plentiful in Illinois, but I've never seen a goblet, nor a tumbler. Clear, non-flint, which looks as if it belonged to the 80s. Decor consists of a band of quatrefoil which is stippled in the same man-

ner as Psyche and Cupid; finial is stipple quatrefoil. Bowls $10.00; open compote $20.00; covered compote $35.00.

No. 1647 – LAKEWOOD – M. Bk. 2-75. Pleasing, non-flint of the 80s. Only goblet $12.00.

No. 1650 – DROPLET BAND – M. Bk. 2-57 shows this with frosted goblet bowl, decorated with grapes and leaves in yellow and calls it YELLOW VINTAGE – FROSTED. In this type I've seen bowls $10.00; tankard waste pitcher $45.00; tumbler $15.00. In clear goblet $18.00. Undoubtedly there are other pieces in both.

No. 1653 – SAWTOOTH BOTTOM – M. Bk. 2-33. Clear, non-flint of the 80s. Etching adds greatly to these goblets with plain bowls. Only goblet $20.00. Each time I see such an interesting stem, I can't help but think how interesting it would be to collect goblets or wines with stem interest as connecting factor. *Aka Noonday Sun, King Glass Co., 1888.*

(Continued from page 145)
No. 1622 – TEARDROP – L.V. 69 – K. Bk. 3-23 calls it TEARDROP AND THUMBPRINT – M. 154 erroneously calls this Crystal Wedding. Non-flint, made by Ripley & Co., Pittsburgh, in 1890. Non-flint, clear and pretty cobalt blue. Flat sauce $7.00; footed sauce $10.00; spooner $15.00; tumbler $15.00; relish $10.00; bowls $12.00; open sugar $15.00; wine $15.00; goblet $20.00; celery $25.00; open compote $20.00; syrup $40.00; water pitcher $45.00; creamer $25.00; covered butter $30.00; covered sugar $30.00. Cobalt blue 100% more.

No. 1623 – MARTHA'S TEARS – M. 103. (Not pictured.) K. Bk. 4-117 calls it TEARDROP BANDS and in Bk. 8-plates 68, 69. Made by Greensburg Glass Co. in 1889. Excellent, simple, non-flint which has a future. Around base of some pieces is a double band of small teardrops, one pointing up and meeting the point of the opposite one which points down. Flat sauce $6.00; footed sauce $10.00; tumbler $20.00; waste bowl $15.00; rectangular deep relish $12.00; goblet $20.00; wine $20.00; salt shaker $15.00; large plate $10.00; celery $20.00; creamer $20.00; covered butter $40.00; covered sugar $25.00; cakestand $30.00; tray for water set $25.00; 6", 7", 8" bowls $10.00 – 20.00.

(Continued on page 149)

1656
Scroll

1659
Seeley

1662
Flat Panel

1665
St. Bernard

1668
Eight-O-Eight

1671
Fan and Star

1674
Fancy Foot

1677
Pillow Encircled

No. 1656 – SCROLL – L. 140 – M. 86 – K. Bk. 7-70 calls it STIPPLED SCROLL. Clear, non-flint of the 70s; finials are acorns. Flat sauce $10.00; spooner $25.00; footed salt $15.00; goblet $35.00; footed tumbler $25.00; open sugar $20.00; open compote $20.00; covered butter $50.00; creamer $25.00; covered sugar $35.00; covered compote $45.00. *Geo. Duncan, 1870s. Not same as Metz's Stippled Scroll.*

No. 1659 – SEELEY – M. Bk. 2-27 – K. Bk. 8-35. Clear, non-flint of the late 80s or early 90s. Goblet $15.00; creamer $20.00; covered butter $25.00; covered sugar $25.00.

No. 1662 – FLAT PANEL – L.V. 51 – K. Bk. 8-60 calls it PLEATING. First issued in the 80s by Bryce Bros. and Gillinder in Pittsburgh. Reissued by U.S. Glass Co. in 1891 and made in Indiana as late as 1903. Non-flint in clear and flashed with red. Sauces $7.00; bowls $10.00; spooner $15.00; open sugar $12.00; creamer $20.00; water pitcher $40.00; cakestand $40.00; covered butter $40.00; covered sugar $35.00; with red flashings 50% additional.

No. 1665 – ST. BERNARD – K. Bk. 5-61 and plate 13. Made by Fostoria Glass Co. in Moundsville, W. Va., in 1894. Covered pieces have dog finial and dog is in bottom of sauces, bowls, etc. Not the fine modeling found in some of the earlier dog patterns. Flat sauce $10.00; open sugar $20.00; berry bowl $35.00; covered sugar $75.00; covered compote $65.00; covered jam jar $55.00; creamer $35.00; goblet $35.00. *Aka Czar.*

No. 1668 – EIGHT-O-EIGHT – K. Bk. 4-78. Contemporary of King's Crown. Clear, non-flint of the early 90s. Spooner $65.00; open sugar $30.00; tumbler $35.00; 9" plate $60.00; waste pitcher $70.00; covered butter $110.00; creamer $45.00; covered sugar $65.00; covered compote $110.00. *OMN Indiana. Rare in cobalt blue, +200%; green, +50%. Tankard $115.00.*

No. 1671 – FAN AND STAR – L.V. 66 – K. Bk. 4-28 calls it CHALLINOR – No. 304 this firm having made it in the 80s. Non-flint, though a milk white rimmed with color has been listed. Spooner $25.00; bowls $18.00; sauces $10.00; celery $30.00; open compote $35.00; water pitcher $60.00; goblet $20.00; covered butter $45.00; creamer $30.00; covered compote $50.00. *Opaque white +50%, Challinor & Taylor, 1885.*

No. 1674 – FANCY FOOT – Hitherto unlisted. Non-flint of the 80s. Decor consists of raised leaf-like unit, stippled, about ⅛" thick on foot. Creamer $35.00. Covered sugar has been reported so there should be more. Most attractive.

No. 1677 – PILLOW ENCIRCLED – K. Bk. 2-129 – L.V. 53 shows the form with red flashing and calls it RUBY ROSETTE. Clear, and ruby flashed of the early 90s. Prices for clear: Sauce dish $15.00; toothpick $75.00; individual creamer, spooner $40.00; bowls $35.00; open compote $35.00 – 55.00; open sugar $20.00; creamer $55.00; covered butter $75.00; covered sugar $50.00; covered compote $70.00 – 90.00; with red flashing (Ruby Rosette) 75% more. *Etched +50%.*

(Continued from page 147)
NO. 1625 – KING'S CROWN – L. 162 – M. 46 – K. Bk. 1-102 call this RUBY THUMBPRINT CLEAR. Most collectors, however, call the clear version KING'S CROWN and save the other title for the ruby which would seem more logical. Late 1890s, but deservedly popular, made in all clear, clear with gilt top and gilt, green or amethyst thumbprints and an all-over olive green and cobalt blue, the latter two being exceedingly scarce. Clear and red reproduced copiously in most forms. The gilt may be completely or partially removed which is what most decorators do, leaving just a little to brighten it; so if the gilt is worn, it does not detract from the value. But the ruby top must not be worn or scratched or discolored if piece is to command full price. This ruby flashed glass discolors if exposed to strong sunlight for long period of time, so it does not make desirable window pieces. Prices are ruby stained, vintage etched tumbler $25.00; oval relish $35.00; spooner $40.00; toothpick $35.00; individual creamer $35.00; handled round olive dish $25.00; tumbler $25.00; various sized bowls $15.00 – 45.00; square plate $35.00; creamer $50.00; open compote $55.00; scalloped edge (never had a lid) covered butter $65.00; tankard type water pitcher $125.00; cup and saucer $50.00; pair salt and pepper shakers $95.00; covered sugar $65.00; banana dish $350.00; covered honey dish $110.00; bulbous water pitcher $150.00; goblet $35.00; castor set glass, complete with 4 bottles $185.00, punch bowl, very large $175.00; wine $35.00; champagne $40.00; covered cheese dish $180.00. I've seen a huge community punch bowl with plate almost 36" in diameter in the Ruby which was never made in this size in the old. Cobalt blue or green (all I've seen had souvenir markings) same as ruby. In the ruby, souvenir marked pieces 50% of vintage etched, ruby not etched 75% of vintage etched, clear 33% of ruby.

No. 1626 – RUBY THUMBPRINT VALUES – See above.

No. 1628 – FANCY KING'S CROWN – Contemporary of King's Crown, made by Canton Glass Co., in Marion, Indiana, in the 90s. K. Bk. 5-77 shows a sketch of it, calling it FRAMED JEWEL. In book 6 plate 27 she shows what she says is the same pattern in the original ad of the firm; it is however very unlike the sketch. As can be seen from this photo, the pattern is very similar to King's Crown; note in this the large thumbprints are oval and they alternate with a smaller one. Non-flint, clear only. Wine $20.00; goblet $25.00. Found with ruby and in other pieces.

1680
Nailhead

1683
Nail

1686
Plume

1689
Interlocking Crescents

1692
Lightning

1695
Snake Drape

1698
Hawaiian Lei

1701
Mascotte

No. 1680 – NAILHEAD – L. 108, 158 – M. 48 – K. Bk. 4-41. Clear, non-flint of the 80s. Some of it was made in the last days of the Sandwich factory as fragments were found there; it's of the late 70s or early 80s. Flat sauce $10.00; spooner $25.00; goblet, tumbler $30.00; celery $35.00; creamer $30.00; covered butter $45.00; water pitcher $45.00; wine $20.00; cordial $35.00; square & round plate $15.00; covered sugar $40.00; covered compote $45.00. *OMN Gem. Bryce, Higbee, 1885.*

No. 1683 – NAIL – K. Bk. 2-87 and Bk. 6-plate 7 – M. Bk. 2-34 calls it RECESSED PILLARD – RED TOP and on p. 63 same book shows the same and calls it RECESSED PILLAR – THUMBPRINT BAND. Made in Pittsburgh in 1892. Non-flint in clear and red flashing. The recessed pillar is really a nail and the thumbprint is its large head. Bodies of erect pieces have squarish squat bowl with deep collar. Bowls $25.00; footed sauce $15.00; spooner $35.00; open sugar $30.00; creamer $40.00; butter $65.00; covered sugar $50.00; goblet $55.00; water tray $40.00; water pitcher $75.00; pair salt and peppers $75.00. With red flashing 100% more. *Ripley & Co., 1892.*

No. 1686 – PLUME – L.V. 26 – M. 30 – K. Bk. 2-64. Made by Adams & Co. of Pittsburgh in the late 80s and in the early 90s. Comes in clear, and with top flashed in red; non-flint. In some pieces the plumes can be found in vertical position. Not to be confused with the old flint plume pattern, made in earlier days of the Sandwich factory. Flat sauce $10.00; footed sauces $15.00; spooner $30.00; creamer $35.00; covered butter $55.00; cakestand $70.00; water pitcher $65.00; covered sugar $45.00; covered compote $65.00; tumbler $30.00. In this pattern, red flashing adds 100% to the value. *U.S. Glass, 1892.*

No. 1689 – INTERLOCKING CRESCENTS – M. 113 – K. Bk. 5-73 calls it DOUBLE ARCH. Rather heavy, well designed, non flint goblet of the early 90s. Four piece set is mediocre. Goblet $20.00; covered butter $30.00; creamer $25.00; covered sugar $30.00. *King, Son & Co., 1880, U.S. Glass, 1893.*

No. 1692 – LIGHTNING – M. 108 – K. Bk. 3-100. Clear, non-flint of the late 90s. Flat sauce $20.00; wines $95.00; many bowls $45.00; spooner $70.00; open sugar $45.00; goblet $85.00; tankard or round creamer $90.00; celery $75.00; open compote $75.00; covered butter $100.00; covered sugar $95.00; tankard water pitcher $100.00; round water pitcher $100.00; covered compote $125.00; cakestand $90.00. *U.S. Glass, 1893.*

No. 1695 – SNAKE DRAPE – M. 137. Clear, non-flint of the 80s. Goblet $35.00.

No. 1698 – HAWAIIAN LEI – M. 46. Clear, non-flint. Wine $20.00; goblet $50.00; *bowl $15.00; open sugar $15.00; creamer $20.00; compote $20.00 – 40.00; plate $18.00. Higbee, circa 1900, some marked with bee.*

No. 1701 – MASCOTTE – L.V. 42, 43 – M. Bk. 2-132 calls it MINOR BLOCK. Clear, non-flint of the 80s. Flat sauce $8.00; footed sauce $15.00; salt shaker $25.00; spooner $30.00; many sizes open bowls $15.00 – 35.00; tumbler $20.00; open sugar $20.00; open compote $20.00 – 30.00; celery $35.00; pair of salt shakers $50.00; covered butter $50.00; goblet $45.00; water pitcher $75.00; platter $45.00; covered sugar $40.00; covered bowls $35.00 – 40.00; covered compote $55.00 – 75.00; covered cheese dish $75.00. *Ripley & Co., 1874, U.S. Glass, 1891, aka Dominion. Etched 20% more, ruby stain 50% more. Very rare in color.*

1704
Cottage

1707
Angora

1710
Crochet Band

1713
Crystal Band

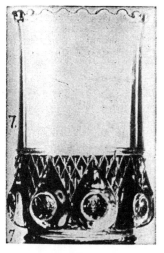

1716
Reverse Torpedo

1719
Torpedo

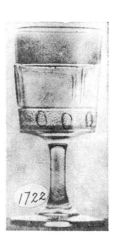

1722
Snakeskin and Dot

1725
Button Band

No. 1704 – COTTAGE – L.V. 64 – M. 171 calls it DIN-NER BELL – K. Bk. 1-39 calls it FINE CUT BAND. Three authors – three names, isn't it about time we got together? Made by Adams of Pittsburgh in the late 70s. Pitchers have interesting handles formed by cuffed hands holding a horizontal bar. Non-flint, a few colored pieces in dark green are scarce. Flat sauce $10.00; footed sauce $12.00; salt $35.00; tumbler $35.00; spooner $20.00; mug $25.00; cup $15.00; bowls $25.00 – 40.00; cruet $65.00; 6", 7", 8", 9", 10" plates $15.00 – 35.00; wine $30.00; champagne $35.00; goblet $35.00; tray for water set $40.00; creamer $40.00; water pitcher $50.00; covered butter $45.00; cakestand $45.00; *butter with flange $125.00. Goblet reproduced, clear & colors.*

No. 1707 – ANGORA – M. Bk. 2-27. Clear, non-flint of the late 80s. Goblet $15.00; creamer $18.00; covered sugar $20.00; covered butter $35.00.

No. 1710 – CROCHET BAND – M. Bk. 2-70. Millard shows a thin goblet with the same pattern. I've seen a complete setting in the same design in the thin which was made in the late 90s. Evidently this was a reissue of the heavy type shown here which dates from the 80s. Only goblet in this $15.00. Many variations on this "needle etching." *The glass is blown, not pressed, which would eliminate it from early American pattern glass. Bryce Bros. made many of these in a multitude of forms from about 1890 – 1920.*

No. 1713 – CRYSTAL BAND – M. Bk. 2. Clear, non-flint of the 80s. Only goblet $15.00.

No. 1716 – REVERSE TORPEDO – K. Bk. 3-100 lists this as Bull's Eye with Diamond Point a name already well known for a fine old flint pattern described here earlier. M. Bk.

2-50 lists this as DIAMONDS AND BULL'S EYE BAND and on p. 76 of the same book lists the etched goblet of the same pattern as BULL'S EYE BAND. Because it definitely needs a new name and is the reverse of design unit in Torpedo I'm so naming it Reverse Torpedo. Clear, non-flint of the early 90s. Sauce $20.00; bowls $40.00; spooner $35.00; tumbler $45.00; wine $90.00; goblet, scarce $125.00; water pitcher $135.00; covered butter $75.00; covered sugar $45.00; covered compote $100.00; *jelly compote $65.00. Dalzell, Gilmore & Leighton.*

No. 1719 – TORPEDO – K. Bk. 2-107 – M. 46 calls it PIGMY. Clear, non-flint made in Pennsylvania in the 80s. In demand and hard to find. There is a slight variation in the decoration of the large drops as used in different pieces. Flat sauce $15.00; footed sauces $18.00; individual salts $12.00; several sizes of bowls $25.00 – 40.00; spooner $35.00; open sugar $20.00; goblet $55.00; covered butter $85.00; syrup $90.00; cruet $90.00; creamer $45.00; lamp $75.00; water pitcher $85.00; covered sugar $45.00; covered compote $85.00 – 125.00; wine $85.00; tumbler $35.00; *milk pitcher $75.00. Thompson Glass, circa 1889.*

No. 1722 – SNAKESKIN AND DOT – L. 74 – M. 62. Clear, non-flint combined with textured band, or on flat pieces, all-over texturing. Non-flint of the late 70s. Not well known. Goblet $25.00; celery $30.00; creamer $20.00; covered sugar $30.00; plates 4½" to 7" $15.00. *Bakewell & Pears. Two types of hand holding base, male & female.*

No. 1725 – BUTTON BAND – K. Bk. 3-111. Clear, non-flint, of the late 80s. Creamer on legged base, tankard type. Goblet $25.00; creamer $30.00; covered butter $40.00; covered sugar $35.00; *water pitcher $50.00.*

1728
Wigwam

1731
Block and Fan

1734
Oregon

1737
Fans with Diamonds

1740
Draped Fan

1743
Ribbon Candy

1746
Loops with Fans

1749
Barred Ovals

No. 1728 – WIGWAM – K. Bk. 8-11 – M. 23 calls it TEEPEE but K. Bk. 2-78 uses this term for one of the late imitation cut glass patterns. Non-flint, made by the Iowa Glass Co., Iowa City, in the late 80s. Clear only. Goblet $55.00; spooner $45.00; covered butter $80.00; covered sugar $65.00.

No. 1731 – BLOCK AND FAN – L.V. 41, 85 – M. Non-flint, clear and clear with red flashing, made by Richards and Hartley in Tarentum, Pa., in the late 80s. Flat sauce $8.00; footed sauce $12.00; large oblong relish $25.00; bowls $15.00 – 45.00; open sugar $20.00; celery vase $35.00; goblet $45.00; large plate $25.00; sugar shaker $45.00; water pitcher $50.00; cruet $65.00; open scalloped edge compote $40.00; butter covered $50.00; pair salt and pepper shakers $30.00; sugar $50.00; large cakestand $55.00. Red flashing 125% more.

No. 1734 – OREGON – *Oregon is the preferred name of another pattern, aka "Beaded Loops" by U.S. Glass, part of the "States" series.* L.V. 44 – M. Bk. 2-59 calls it SKILTON (preferred). Non-flint, clear or clear, flashed with ruby blocks, made in the late 80s or early 90s. Spooner, creamer, celery are flat. Footed sauce $10.00; salt shaker $25.00; spooner $35.00; celery $25.00; goblet $45.00; water pitcher $55.00; covered butter $40.00; covered sugar $35.00; covered compote $45.00; with red blocks 100% more. *Richards & Hartley, 1890, U.S. Glass, 1891.*

No. 1737 – FANS WITH DIAMOND – L. 76 – M. 64 – K. Bk. 3-18. Clear, non-flint of the late 70s. Creamer comes in two forms, one type has one fan extending up to handle joining, the other has fan continuing around body of piece in straight line. Sugar is not as large as many of the old ones and therefore is more practical; finial is ovoid, and half of it is stippled. Flat sauce $10.00; spooner $20.00; large oval vegetable dish $20.00; egg cup $35.00; goblet $25.00; wine $35.00 (scarce); covered butter $40.00; water pitcher $65.00; creamer $35.00; covered sugar $35.00; open sugar $20.00; open compote $20.00; covered compote $45.00.

No. 1740 – DRAPED FAN – M. Bk. 2 – K. Bk. 3-82 uses the old trade name Comet which is now used for fine old flint. Clear, non-flint, made by Doyle & Co. of Pittsburgh, in the 80s and reissued by the U.S. Glass Co., when they merged in the 90s. Spooner $18.00; wine $15.00; creamer $20.00; butter $25.00; water pitcher $35.00; cakestand $35.00; covered sugar $25.00; goblet $20.00; open compote $20.00; covered compote $35.00.

No. 1743 – RIBBON CANDY – K. Bk. 1-33 – Bryce – L.V. 32 – M. Bk. 2-76 calls it DOUBLE LOOP, the same name given to another entirely different pattern. Non-flint first made by Bryce Bros. of Pittsburgh in the 80s. Clear only, saucer $20.00; sauce $10.00; footed sauce $12.00; cup $20.00; spooner $30.00; oval, relish $20.00; tumbler $25.00; cruet $65.00; bowls $10.00 – 25.00; goblet $65.00; celery $25.00; compote $30.00; 6", 7", 8" plates $8.00 – 30.00; small cakestand $35.00; pitcher $45.00; creamer $25.00; 10" cakestand $50.00; covered butter $55.00; syrup $90.00; pitcher (milk), scarce $55.00; square, covered honey dish $75.00; covered sugar $40.00; covered bowls, covered compotes $30.00 – 45.00. *Rarely found in emerald green, 125% more.*

No. 1746 – LOOPS AND FANS – L.V. 24 – M. 139 calls it INVERTED LOOPS AND FANS – K. Bk. 1-60 calls it LOOP AND DIAMOND. Loops are plain, design showing in them in the picture is a reflection. Contemporary of Ribbon Candy. Same values.

No. 1747 – MARYLAND – *#1746 & 1747 are the same pattern, most commonly called Maryland. Prices are approximately 50% more than Ribbon Candy.* L.V. 37. (Not pictured.) Contemporary of Loops and Fans above. The same, only in this the diamond, made of little diamonds, between the loops is missing. *Often found with gold, add 25%.*

No. 1749 – BARRED OVALS – L.V. 41 – K. Bk. 6-25 and plate 26 – M. Bk. 2-35 shows it frosted calling it Frosted Banded Portland and on p. 11 of the same book shows it with purple calling it Purple Block Portland. One can see this is an entirely different family than Portland treated elsewhere in these pages. Made in factory of George Duncan under U.S. Glass Co., of Pittsburgh in 1892. This same factory probably produced it in the 80s and this was reissue. Sauce $10.00; spooner $35.00; open sugar $20.00; water bottle $45.00; open compote $50.00; celery $35.00; goblet $40.00; creamer $45.00; butter $50.00; water pitcher $100.00; covered sugar $60.00; covered compote $85.00; small plate $25.00. Finial carries the frosted oval motif; frosted or color flashed 100% more.

1752
Three Stories

1755
Block with Stars

1758
Bungalo

1761
Panel and Star

1764
Diamond Prisms

1767
King's Curtain

1770
Diamonds with
Double Fan

1773
Boling

No. 1752 – THREE STORIES – M. 24 – K. Bk. 5-36 and Bk. 8-18 and plates 22, 23, 24. Clear, non-flint, made by *Bryce Higbee* of Pittsburgh in the mid 80s. Flat sauce $8.00; footed sauce $10.00; relish $12.00; spooner $25.00; handled mug $20.00; bowls $22.00; celery $30.00; goblet $25.00; platter $20.00; tumbler $30.00; covered butter $45.00; water pitcher $50.00; covered sugar $35.00; wine $20.00; Kamm calls this BLOCK AND PLEAT. *Aka Persian. Rare in amber & blue.*

No. 1755 – BLOCK WITH STARS – K. Bk. 1-110 – L. 164 No. 19 – L.V. 54 calls it HANOVER (preferred) – M. 133 calls it BLOCKHOUSE. Non-flint, made in Pennsylvania in the late 80s. Comes in clear, canary, amber, and blue. Many forms. Spooner $25.00; many sizes of bowls $10.00 – 20.00; tumbler $25.00; wine $25.00; open compote $40.00; celery $25.00; water pitcher $55.00; creamer $30.00; butter $40.00; cakestand $45.00; sugar $45.00; covered compote $50.00. Canary 100% more, amber 25% more, blue 50% more.

No. 1758 – BUNGALO – M. 24 – K. Bk. 4-101. Clear, non-flint, contemporary of Block with Stars, above. Same values. *U.S. Glass, 1891.*

No. 1761 – PANEL AND STAR – L.V. 61 – K. Bk. 3-75 calls it COLUMN BLOCK. Clear, non-flint of the late 80s, made by O'Hara Glass Co. of Pittsburgh. Flat sauce $7.00; footed sauce $10.00; salt shaker $12.00; open sugar $15.00; spooner $20.00; tumbler $15.00; celery $30.00; pickle jar $40.00; open compote $25.00; cruet $40.00; covered butter $50.00; creamer $25.00; covered sugar $35.00; pair cologne bottles $50.00; tall covered compote $55.00; goblet $25.00.

No. 1764 – DIAMOND PRISMS – M. Bk. 2-58. Non-flint, geometric of the mid-80s. Wine $95.00; goblet $110.00; large plate $75.00. *Indiana Tumbler & Goblet (Greentown). Pitcher $150.00; tumbler in chocolate $600.00;*

No. 1767 – KING'S CURTAIN – M. 90. Clear, non-flint of the early 80s. Many forms. Flat sauce $10.00; spooner $35.00; slat shaker $25.00; open sugar $20.00; goblets $35.00; 7" plate $20.00; covered butter $55.00; water pitcher $90.00; wine $25.00; cakestand $45.00; covered sugar $50.00. *Amber 200% more.*

No. 1770 – DIAMONDS WITH DOUBLE FAN – M. Bk. 2-88. Clear, non-flint of the late 1900s. Goblet $45.00. *Indiana Tumbler & Goblet (Greentown). Cup $15.00; pitcher $95.00.*

No. 1773 – BOLING – M. Bk. 2-138. Clear, non-flint of the late 80s. Comes with gilt top, removal of which is improvement. Wine $30.00; goblet $35.00. *Good gold now 50% more.*

1776
Cane

1779
Panelled Cane

1782
Crazy Patch

1785
Currier and Ives

1788
Two Panel

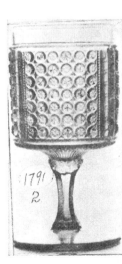

1791
Three Panel

1794
Cathedral

1797
Beaded Oval Window

No. 1776 – CANE – L. 132, 160 – M. 122 – K. Bk. 3-39. Non-flint, made over several years from the mid 80s by different firms so one should expect slightly differing details. Found frequently in color, apple green being the most common, which is a reversal of the general order. Flat sauce $7.00; spooner $20.00; relish $15.00; open sugar $20.00; goblet $25.00; wine $30.00; "toddy" $15.00; tumbler $20.00; berry bowls $20.00; finger bowls with plain margin $15.00; water pitcher $40.00; covered butter $45.00; sugar, covered $35.00; large tray for water set $35.00. Green & canary 100% more, amber 25% more, blue 50% more. Reproduced. *Gillinder & Sons, 1885, McKee, 1894.*

No. 1779 – PANELLED CANE – M. 32 – K. Bk. 4-11 calls it CANE COLUMN. Non-flint of the mid 80s made in clear, canary, amber and blue. Flat sauce $5.00; spooner $20.00; open sugar $20.00; wine $20.00; covered butter $35.00; creamer $25.00; covered sugar $35.00; goblet $20.00. Creamer very interesting in line. Canary 100% more, amber 25% more, blue 50% more.

No. 1780 – CANE AND ROSETTE – L.V. 61 – M. Bk. 2-162 calls it FLOWER PANELLED CANE. (Not pictured.) Same as panelled Cane above only there is a rosette in the center of each plain panel and the finials have the rosette on each of their six sides. Contemporary of the other Canes, though I've never seen this one in color. Flat sauce $12.00; footed or collared base sauce $15.00; wine $20.00; open sugar $20.00; footed salt $25.00; champagne $65.00; goblet $55.00; open octagonal flat dishes $20.00; celery $25.00; cordial $35.00; flat butter $55.00; small cakestand $45.00; water pitcher $100.00; large cakestand $75.00; footed butter $50.00; creamer $40.00; covered sugar $55.00; covered compote $90.00; covered octagonal dishes $30.00. If color does exist in this form of Cane, it is scarce and would be worth 100% more. *Geo Duncan & Sons, 1885.*

No. 1782 – CRAZY PATCH – M. Bk. 2-71. Clear, non-flint of the late 80s. Only goblet $35.00. *King Son & Co., 1880s; U.S. Glass, 1891.*

No. 1785 – CURRIER AND IVES – L. 110 – L.V. 86 – K. Bk. 3-117. Non-flint of the 80s, made by Bellaire Glass Co., Findlay, Ohio. Rare in color. Scenic tray, balky mule on railroad tracks, small with one row of pattern $65.00; same scene, larger tray with two rows of geometric pattern $75.00; goblet, plain stem $35.00; knob stem goblet $35.00. The four piece set is interesting; butter is rectangular, but unevenly so; syrup has square lines. Covered butter $50.00; covered sugar $45.00; decanter $60.00; wine $25.00; spooner $35.00; oval sauce $15.00; syrup $75.00; oval relish $12.00; flat sauce $10.00; 7" plate $35.00; milk pitcher $65.00; water pitcher $75.00; master salt $40.00; open compote $50.00; covered compote $95.00; large plate $35.00; cup and saucer $40.00. *Blue, amber, canary. Amber 30% more, blue 65% more.*

No. 1788 – TWO PANEL – L. 159, 160 – M. 53 – K. Bk. 3-45. Non-flint, made by Richards & Hartley Glass Co., of Tarentum, Pa., in the early 80s. Comes in many colors, canary, 2 shades of blue and amber; interesting oval shapes. Individual salt dips $10.00; flat sauce $10.00; collared sauce $15.00; master salt $15.00; spooner $25.00; mugs $20.00 – 30.00; flat relish $15.00; many bowls $15.00 – 45.00; wine $20.00; goblets $30.00; creamer $35.00; butter $40.00; flat lamp $45.00; celery $25.00; lamp on standard $75.00; covered sugar $40.00; covered compote $45.00; water pitcher $55.00. Apple green 80% more, canary 100% more, amber 30% more, blue 75% more. Goblets now copiously reproduced, especially in color.

No. 1791 – THREE PANEL – L. 96, 159 – M. 133 – K. Bk. 3-115. Non-flint, made by Hartley & Co. of Tarentum, Pa.., in 1888. Comes in clear, canary, amber and blue. The celery is most interesting, shaped more like a vase, with a ruffly top; it's not easy to find $35.00; footed sauce $12.00; spooner $30.00; open sugar $20.00; handled mugs $20.00; tumbler $25.00; open compote $45.00; creamer $35.00; butter $45.00; milk pitcher $55.00; water pitcher $75.00; covered sugar $40.00. Canary 75% more, amber 20% more, blue 50% more. Clear goblet $30.00; wine $25.00.

No. 1794 – CATHEDRAL – L. 58, 146 – M. 18 – K. Bk. 1-21. Non-flint of the 80s; made in Pittsburgh. Comes in clear, canary, amber, blue, ruby, and a much sought-after amethyst. Flat sauce $12.00; footed sauce $15.00; various sizes of bowls, spooner, open sugar, tumbler $35.00; open compote $60.00; water pitcher $200.00 (scarce); goblet $45.00; wine $35.00; covered sugar $45.00; covered compote $95.00. Canary 100% more, amber 30% more, blue 75% more, amethyst 150% more, *ruby 50% more. Fish relish $30.00; boat salt $20.00.*

No. 1797 – BEADED OVAL WINDOW – M. 91 – K. Bk. 2-39 calls it OVAL MEDALLION. A contemporary of Cathedral and made in the same colors. I believe I'm asked to identify this more than any other pattern; people like it but do not recognize it. Interesting oval shaped pieces; finials have Maltese cross in relief on oval. Flat sauces, several sizes, spooner $30.00; open sugar $20.00; wine $30.00; goblet $25.00; covered butter $50.00; tray $35.00; creamer $30.00; covered sugar $40.00; covered compote $60.00. Colors 40% more with the exception of amethyst which is 150% more.

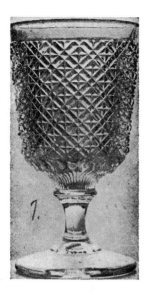

1800
Fine Cut

1801
Diamond Cut
with Leaf

1804
Fine Cut and Block

1807
Sequoia

1810
Fine Cut and Panel

1813
Romeo

1816
Lattice

1819
Graduated Diamonds

No. 1800 – FINE CUT – L. 138, 160 – M. 110. Made in Pittsburgh in the 80s; comes in clear, canary, blue, and amber. Loses value when old soap residue fills the crevices. *Scrubbing with toothbrush and detergent will remove some residue.* Sauce $15.00; spooner $30.00; open sugar $20.00; covered butter $65.00; covered sugar $45.00; creamer $35.00; 6", 7", 10" plates $12.00 – 20.00. Canary 50% more, amber 25% more, blue 50% more. *Bryce Bros.*

No. 1801 – DIAMOND CUT WITH LEAF – L. 108, 144 – M. 89. Interesting, non-flint of the early 80s. Clear and very scarce amber, canary, and blue. Wine $35.00; spooner $25.00; creamer $35.00; butter $60.00; covered sugar, open sugar, 7" plate, 9½" plate $25.00. Any color 40% more. *Reproduced.*

No. 1804 – FINE CUT AND BLOCK – L. 161 – M. 28 – K. Bk. 1-43. Made by Crystal Glass Co., of Wheeling, W. Va., prior to 1892, and by McKee Glass Co., of Pittsburgh, of Jeanette, Pa., in 1894. There are two shapes, one has extremely large footed sugar, creamer, and a real large (true buttermilk) goblet; the other is the type with normal size of goblet, flat spooner, creamer, covered sugar, and butter. It's non-flint, made in all clear, all yellow, all amber, all blue; then there is that most popular clear with block of these colors and pink. Plates are pointed stars. Glass is thin and rather mediocre in quality but is serrated edges give it charm. The demand for pieces with colored blocks is tremendous. I've seen a charming dresser arrangement using the ice cream tray for dresser tray, the cologne bottles, and the flat butter for powder puffs. For all over clear; individual salt dips $10.00; footed sauces (large) $15.00; rectangular relish $12.00; mug $25.00; spooner $30.00; cologne bottle $65.00; covered sugar $45.00; covered butter $65.00; ice cream tray $65.00; plate $10.00 – 12.00; goblet $35.00; regular size, large goblet $55.00; small cakestand $45.00; large cakestand $75.00; jelly compote $20.00; wine $30.00; salt shaker $15.00; flat lamp $85.00; rare large combination dish, listed as orange bowl and tray $40.00. Solid color 40 – 50% more; with colored blocks of yellow, amber, blue, pink 100 – 150% more.

No. 1807 – SEQUOIA – M. Bk. 2-140. Really heavy fine-cut and a good goblet to use with all the miscellaneous patterns in heavy fine cut and heavy flattened fine cut, many of which have no goblet. Clear, non-flint of the late 80s. Goblet $25.00.

No. 1810 – FINE CUT AND PANEL – *OMN Russian* – L. 61, 160 – M. 89 – K. Bk. 7-82. Made by several of the Pittsburgh area factories in the 80s and reissued by the U.S. Glass Co. in the early 90s. Non-flint in clear and color. Footed sauce $15.00; spooner, open sugar $20.00; cup $15.00; creamer $35.00; butter $55.00; wine $30.00; goblet $25.00; waste bowl $30.00; other bowls $25.00; 6", 7" plates $15.00 – 30.00; water pitcher $85.00; platter, tray for water set $40.00. Canary 50% more, amber 25% more, other blue 50% more. *Rare emerald green wine $95.00.*

No. 1813 – ROMEO – M. 90 – On p. 66, Millard shows this in milk white and erroneously lists it as BLOCK AND FAN. Clear goblet $25.00; milk glass $45.00.

No. 1816 – LATTICE – L. 78 – M. 97 – K. Bk. 4-40 calls it DIAMOND BAR. Dainty, medium weight, well designed pattern of the 80s. Flat sauce $6.00; footed sauce $8.00; spooner $20.00; open sugar $12.00; egg cup $20.00; goblet $20.00; open compote $20.00; 6", 7" plate $10.00; 10" plate $15.00; bread tray "Give us, etc." $25.00; covered butter $30.00; water pitcher $75.00; covered sugar $40.00; covered compote $45.00.

No. 1819 – GRADUATED DIAMONDS – M. Bk. 2-80. Clear, rather light weight, non-flint of the late 80s. Only goblet $25.00.

No. 1817 – BLOCK AND TRIPLE BARS – M. Bk. 2-88. (Not pictured.) Same as its contemporary, Romeo, only this has bars on foot. Goblet $20.00.

1822
Hand

1825
Open Plaid

1828
Basket Weave

1831
Pressed Diamond

1834
Shovel

1837
Opposing Pyramids

1840
Scalloped Prisms

1843
Pillared Crystal

No. 1822 – HAND – L. 107 – M. 120 – K. Bk. 3-9. Clear, non-flint, made by O'Hara Glass Co., in Pittsburgh in the late 70s or early 80s. There are several patterns which use a hand, such as Cottage, which uses a hand on the handle, and Tree of Life which has hand holding a ball for a stem. The true pattern by this name has a clenched fist, holding a bar, as finial on covered pieces, otherwise it is the plain geometric shown. Frequently, the platter is not recognized as belonging to the set; it can be used as service plate as there are no other plates and it is not too large to be so used. Erect pieces are tall, slender and well proportioned. Flat sauce $10.00; footed sauce $12.00; spooner, open sugar $20.00; pickle $15.00; bowls, 7", 10" $25.00 – 45.00; goblet $50.00; cakestand $55.00; pitcher $75.00; open compote $35.00; platter $55.00; covered jam jar $65.00; covered sugar $75.00; covered compote $95.00; very scarce wine $65.00; *flat butter $120.00; footed butter $75.00.*

No. 1825 – OPEN PLAID – M. 127 calls this Plaid, but as that term has been used for another pattern I'm adding word. Non-flint, of the 80s. Goblet $25.00, *complete table set and pitcher known. Beaver Falls.*

No. 1826 – PLAID – L. 76. (Not pictured.) Little known, non-flint of the 80s. Few pieces have ever been found. The surface is divided into inch squares, and each of these is again divided into tiny squares. Creamer $25.00; open sugar $20.00; celery $28.00.

No. 1828 – BASKETWEAVE – L. 104 – M. 127. Non-flint of the 80s. Clear with other colors, canary, amber, and blue being fairly common. This is not the same basketweave we find in milk glass, that was an earlier pattern, some of which we find dated 1868; its design is slightly different. Flat sauce $10.00; tumbler $25.00; cup and saucer $30.00; egg cup $15.00; open sugar $20.00; water pitcher $45.00; plate $20.00; open compote $40.00; syrup pitcher $45.00; scenic tray for water set $35.00; goblet $25.00; creamer $30.00; butter $40.00; covered sugar $35.00. Goblets, trays, water pitcher now reproduced in colors. Canary 50% more, amber 25% more, blue 50% more, *apple green 50% more.*

No. 1831 – PRESSED DIAMOND – L.V. 70 – M. Bk. 2-113 calls it ZEPHYR – K. Bk. 8-33. Non-flint of the 80s, made in Wheeling, W. Va., in clear, yellow (fairly plentiful) and scarce amber and blue. Flat sauce $7.00; spooner $25.00; celery $30.00; erect, but not footed cup $12.00; salt shaker $20.00; open sugar $20.00; bowls, including finger bowls $15.00 – 25.00; wine $25.00; goblet $30.00; 11" plate $15.00; open compote $30.00; water pitcher $45.00; creamer $25.00; butter $40.00; covered sugar $35.00. I've seen a huge covered compote 11" in diameter $75.00. Canary 50% more, amber 25% more, or blue 50% more. *Central Glass.*

No. 1834 – SHOVEL – M. 68. Clear, non-flint of the 80s; goblet pleasing and it and its contemporary, Opposing Pyramids, below, make two suitable goblets to use with printed Staffordshire china. Pieces other than goblets and wines are mediocre. Goblet $30.00; wine $22.00; tumbler $18.00; creamer $20.00; butter $45.00; water pitcher $75.00; covered sugar $45.00.

No. 1837 – OPPOSING PYRAMIDS – M. Bk. 2 – K. Bk. 8-31 and plates 48, 49. Made in Pittsburgh in 1889 and called Flora, a strange name for a geometric. Values same as for its contemporary, Shovel, listed above. *Bryce, Higbee & Co.*

No. 1840 – SCALLOPED PRISM – M. 55 – L.V. calls it TRIPLE BAR – K. Bk. 8-plate 5. Made by Doyle of Pittsburgh in the late 80s and continued by U.S. Glass Co. in reissue in 1891. Clear, non-flint. Tumbler $20.00; spooner $22.00; goblet $25.00; covered butter $35.00; covered sugar $35.00.

No. 1841 – STAGGERED PRISM – M. 55. (Not pictured.) Contemporary of Scalloped Prism, above; same values. This is very like the other prism above, only in this the prisms go almost to the top of the goblet and are all plain; there is no row divided into squares as in the other.

No. 1843 – PILLARED CRYSTAL – M. 55. Clear, medium heavy and I've seen a flint wine and one non-flint. Possibly of the early 70s. Non-flint, wine $15.00; goblet $25.00; flint, wine $50.00; goblet $55.00.

1846
Diamond Block
with Fan

1849
Clear Block

1852
Akron Block

1855
Bars and Buttons

1858
Milton

1861
Valencia Waffle

1864
Ashman

1867
Daisy and Block

No. 1846 – DIAMOND BLOCK WITH FANS – M. 136 – L.V. 65 calls it BLOCKADE – K. Bk. 4-25 calls it Challinor 309, the firm by whom it was made in Tarentum, Pa., in the 80s. Clear, non-flint, with distinguishing heavy patterned knob at bottom of stem. Finials carry the pattern. Footed sauces $15.00; spooner $25.00; 7" square plate $15.00; goblet $25.00; waste bowl $15.00; tumbler $20.00; relish dish $15.00; open sugar $20.00; bowls $15.00; open compote $20.00; water pitcher $55.00; covered butter $55.00; wine $24.00; sugar $45.00; covered compote $50.00; cakestand $55.00.

No. 1849 – CLEAR BLOCK – M. Bk. 2-61 – K. Bk. 2-83 calls it BARRELLED BLOCK. It's the same as Red Block with no red flashing. Non-flint of the early 90s; erect pieces are squat and handled on either sides. Made in Pittsburgh. Flat sauce $7.00; mug $25.00; individual creamer $20.00; cup $15.00; spooner $25.00; open sugar $15.00; relish $15.00; wine $20.00; tumbler $20.00; goblet $25.00; bowls $15.00; celery $30.00; open compote $30.00; creamer $30.00; butter $45.00; covered sugar $35.00.

No. 1849 – RED BLOCK – L. 162 – M. 57. Same as Clear Block above only top band and hexagons are red. Flat sauce $20.00; spooner $40.00; individual creamer $30.00; mug $35.00; open sugar $30.00; relish $25.00; wine $35.00; goblet $45.00; creamer $55.00; covered butter $65.00; covered sugar $60.00. Now reproduced.

No. 1850 – HEXAGON BLOCK – M. 136. (Not pictured.) Same as Clear Block above, only double row of hexagons. Same values as Clear Block.

No. 1851 – DOUBLE RED BLOCK – M. Bk. 2-93. (Not pictured.) Same as Hexagon Block above, only this has red flashing. Values same as for Red Block.

No. 1852 – AKRON BLOCK – *Aka Richmond* – M. Bk. 2-11. Contemporary of Clear Block; same values.

No. 1855 – BARS AND BUTTONS – K. Bk. 1-76. Another of the same family as Clear Block. *Same pattern as above. On pitchers & tumbler, bars are on angle. Values about 25% more.*

No. 1856 – BLOCK AND DOUBLE BAR – M. 136. (Not pictured.) Same as Bars and Buttons only instead of hexagon in the design unit there is a diamond; fancy stem with knob formed by band of short vertical prisms. Same values as other clear members of this block family. *Nickle Plate Glass & U.S. Glass.*

No. 1857 – BLOCK WITH SAWTOOTH BAND – M. 136. (Not pictured.) Another of the Clear Block family. This has the row of hexagons, row of elongated hexagons below and below that, around the lower edge of goblet bowl, a row of very large sawteeth; facetted knob stem. Same values as other members of the family.

No. 1858 – MILTON – M. 67 – L.V. 48 terms what seems to be the same according to drawings 2 and 3 in row 4 CUBE AND DIAMOND. In the drawing of the goblet, the units are placed underneath each other, while in this pattern, as in drawings 2 and 3 they alternate as they do in this pattern. Clear, non-flint of the late 80s. 4 sizes of mugs $10.00 – 25.00; cruet $45.00; covered mustard $35.00; claret $20.00; goblet $25.00; wine $20.00; salt shaker $20.00; condiment set on tray, glass with stand with cruet, salt and pepper shaker $65.00; glass container with castor bottles $95.00. *Occasionally found in blue and amber, 50% more than clear. Bellaire Goblet, 1889. Dalzell, Gilmore, 1890.*

No. 1859 – BLOCK AND JEWEL – M. 105. (Not pictured.) Same as Milton, only this has a round jewel in the squares instead of the diamonds. Only goblet $25.00. In identifying and checking these block patterns it is wise to analyze the design unit and then check up on their placing, be it parallel or alternate.

No. 1861 – VALENCIA WAFFLE – M. 71 – L. 153 No. 17 – K. Bk. 1 calls it BLOCK AND STAR – M. Bk. 2-23 shows it with ROUND BASE. Non-flint of the late 80s; comes in clear, canary, amber and blue; canary is most plentiful color. Pieces are square; flat sauce $10.00; footed sauce $12.00; spooner $25.00; open sugar $20.00; relish $12.00; water pitcher $45.00; compote $30.00; celery $35.00; wine $35.00; goblet $30.00; covered butter $45.00; covered sugar $35.00; covered compote $65.00. Round base 10% less; canary 100% more; blue 50% more, amber 25% more. *Apple green 100% more. Adams & Co., 1885.*

No. 1864 – ASHMAN – M. 119 – K. Bk. 1-89 calls it ETCHED FERN which does not describe as it comes without etching also. Also known as CROSS ROADS. Clear, non-flint of the mid 80s, made in many forms. Pieces are rectangular in shape and there are frequent variations in the form of the same piece; butter dish comes with conventional finial and in the form in which the finial is a huge, hollow ball. I've found this type with a small bouquet of artificial flowers within the ball. Sauce dish $10.00; relish dish $15.00; spooner $40.00; open sugar $20.00; celery $30.00; many sizes of bowls $30.00; wine, open compote $25.00; goblet $25.00; large water tray $40.00; creamer $35.00; covered sugar $45.00; many sizes of compotes from 6" to a huge 12", covered $95.00; cakestand $50.00. *Riverside Glass, 1885.*

No. 1867 – DAISY AND BLOCK – M. 27. Clear, non-flint of the late 80s. Only goblet $20.00. *Usually gray glass, probably a jelly container.*

1870
Banded Cube

1873
Cube

1876
Oswego Waffle

1879
Square Waffle

1882
Waffle with
Spear Point

1885
Latticed Block

1888
Kalbach

1891
Six Row Kalbach

No. 1870 – BANDED CUBE – M. 135. Clear, non-flint of the mid 80s. Many of these cube and block patterns of the mid 80s had the four piece table set but most of them were mediocre in line. A comparative value would be creamer $20.00; butter $30.00; covered sugar $25.00; spooner $20.00.

No. 1873 – CUBE – M. 135 – L.V. 41 calls it BLOCK. Same as Banded Cube above only here dividing line between cubes runs to top edge of goblet; stem has knob made of small globules. Same values as above. Four piece set, flat, not footed; small cube finials.

No. 1874 – PULASKI CUBE – M. 90. (Not pictured.) Same as Cube, above, only goblet narrows slightly more and stem widens to center and then narrows to base. Same values.

No. 1876 – OSWEGO WAFFLE – M. 176. Another of the same family. Same values.

No. 1877 – PANELLED WAFFLE – M. Bk. 2-78. (Not pictured.) Same as above only divided into groups by plain panels. Same values.

No. 1879 – SQUARE WAFFLE – M. 81. Another of the same family with same values. *Model Flint Glass, 1889.*

No. 1880 – WAFFLE WITH FAN TOP – M. 81. (Not pictured.) Slightly more slender and slanting in bowl of goblet and row of fan-like prisms around the top. Same values.

No. 1882 – WAFFLE WITH SPEAR POINT – M. 96 – K. Bk. 4-27. Same era but this has more interesting four piece set; here they are footed. Spooner $20.00; wine $25.00; covered butter $35.00; water pitcher $50.00; covered sugar $30.00. *Elson Glass Co., 1887.*

No. 1885 – LATTICED BLOCK – M. Bk. 2-112 – K. Bk. 5-13. This is an earlier form of block pattern, belonging to the 70s. Non-flint, pieces are footed and handles are applied on pitchers which are prettily bulbous in shape. Sauce $7.00; spooner $15.00; open compote $20.00; open sugar $15.00; covered butter $30.00; covered sugar $30.00; covered compote $35.00; water pitcher $40.00.

No. 1888 – KALLBACH – M. 124. Another of the same type and era. Same values.

No. 1891 – SIX ROW KALLBACH – Heretofore unlisted. Relative of Kallbach above; one more row. Same values as others.

THIS IS WHAT I MEAN

When I state, "Clear only," I mean that it is not a pattern in which colors were produced almost as frequently as clear. We find an occasional piece of colored in almost any pattern. Of course, many pieces are reproduced in colors they were never made originally, such as colored Westward Ho, colored Moon and Star, etc.

I do not attempt to list all of the pieces made in any pattern, that would be a physical impossibility. Do not think a piece is fake because you have not seen the piece listed. Remember, the manufacturers of reproductions make these pieces for which there is a demand; or in a rare instance, especially in a late pattern, an old mold may have been found.

1894
Peerless

1896
Hidalgo

1899
Checker with
Rib Band

1902
Loop and Block
with Waffle Band

1905
Siskyou

1908
Three Bar Waffle

1911
Cube—Square Stem

1914
Panelled English Hobnail

No. 1894 – PEERLESS – L.V. 71 – M. 49 – K. Bk. 7-64 and plates 27, 28. Clear, non-flint made by Richards and Harley of Pittsburgh in the 70s and continued for a number of years. Pitchers have applied handles; 5 sizes of cakestands, about 15 types and sizes of open compotes and 8 sizes of covered compotes. 4 sizes flat sauces $8.00 – 10.00; tapered oval relish $15.00; 4 sizes oval bowls $12.00 – 20.00; champagne $30.00; footed salt $12.00; covered footed salt $25.00; egg cup $20.00; open compotes $20.00; goblet $35.00; castor bottles $20.00; celery $25.00; covered butter $40.00; flat, covered pickle jar $40.00; platter $25.00; tumbler $25.00; footed covered butter $50.00; creamers $30.00; covered sugar $40.00; water pitcher $65.00; covered compotes $50.00; 2 sizes small cakestands $35.00; 3 sizes large cakestands $65.00 – 75.00. Here is one pattern that demonstrates how wrong a novice can be by thinking a piece is a fake because it differs in measurements from piece she has seen; the original catalog pages of this catalog show innumerable differences in sizes and shapes and details. They show a goblet with rounded bowl and one with angular bowl; a rounded creamer and an angular one. *Angular piece +10%, mug, applied handle $80.00.*

No. 1896 – HIDALGO – L.V. 49 – M. 176 shows it with frosted top and calls it FROSTED WAFFLE. Clear or clear and frosted, non-flint of the 80s. The lines and proportions of this patterns are so interesting that it is not improved by etching and the etched is of no greater value. Flat sauce $10.00; footed or handled sauce $12.00; salt shaker $15.00; spooner $20.00; open sugar $20.00; goblet $30.00; olive dish $12.00; flat relish $10.00; celery $20.00; sugar shaker $40.00; open compote $40.00; bowls $25.00; creamer $40.00; butter $45.00; water pitcher $40.00; water tray $50.00; covered sugar $40.00; covered tall compote $75.00. Frosted 25% more. *Adams & Co., 1880.*

No. 1899 – CHECKER WITH RIB BAND – M. Bk. 2-107 and on p. 119 shows the same goblet in amber. Only goblet, clear $18.00; amber $30.00.

No. 1902 – LOOP AND BLOCK WITH WAFFLE BAND – M. Bk. 2-83. Contemporary of above; interesting stem. Only goblet $25.00.

No. 1903 – SPECTRE BLOCK – M. Bk. 2-78. (Not pictured.) Contemporary of Loop and Block with Waffle Band which it resembles, only here there are no loops, there is no waffle band; the entire surface, after a small top margin, is covered with these diamonds. Knob on stem, near the top, is made of the diamonds. Only goblet $20.00.

No. 1905 – SISKYOU – M. Bk. 2-140. Another of the Block family; same values.

No. 1908 – THREE BAR WAFFLE – M. 20. And still another of the Blocks. Same values.

No. 1911 – CUBE – SQUARE STEM. Another of the Blocks of the 80s. Interesting stem; goblet. Combinations of these differing cubes and blocks can be made into pleasing sets.

No. 1914 – PANELLED ENGLISH HOBNAIL – M. 26 – L. 86 – L.V. 46 lists this as PANELLED STRAWBERRY CUT but in the reading matter lists it as Panelled Diamonds, a name already in use but in Book 1-86 lists it as Panelled English Hobnail, the name by which it is generally known. Non-flint of the early 90s. Clear: wine $20.00; goblet $25.00; creamer $30.00; butter $55.00; water pitcher $60.00; covered sugar $45.00; spooner $25.00; open sugar $20.00; salt shaker $25.00; flat sauce $5.00. *With red flashing, 50% more. Tarentum Glass Co., 1901.*

1917
Ribbon

1920
Frosted Ribbon

1923
Frosted Ribbon
Double Bars

1926
Double Ribbon

1929
Clear Ribbon

1932
Footed Panelled Rib

1935
Zipper

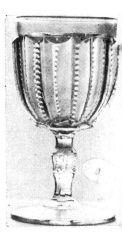

1938
Serrated Prism

No. 1917 – RIBBON – L. 67, 68 – M. 115 shows two goblets, one with straight sides and one which he says has bulging sides, but the difference is so very minor that they would have to be most carefully measured to detect it; there is a slight difference in height which we so often find and which generally means nothing. In an article in *Antiques* in 1927, the date of the compotes was given as in the fifties, or a bit later, but this glass has more of the characteristics of the late 60s. Made by Bakewell, Pears, in Pittsburgh; non-flint, clear and frosted, and though this pattern is frosted we reserve the title Frosted Ribbon for the one with wider frosted panels listed below. I've seen a very few early pieces in which the panels were very rough and I'm told this was done by an abrasive process as opposed to an acid process. I've seen none of this type for 15 years so I know they are not reproductions. The compotes with dolphin stems and scalloped tops are beauties; they come in differing sizes with round or rectangular bowls; values $250.00 – 350.00. Flat sauce $20.00; footed or handled sauce $20.00; spooner $35.00; open bowls $55.00; open sugar $25.00; celery $40.00; covered jam jar (in this the panels on cover are not frosted) $100.00; creamer $40.00; water pitcher $75.00; sugar $65.00; wine, scarce $175.00; covered cheese dish $100.00; very large water tray $125.00; goblet $35.00; waste bowl $45.00; covered compotes $65.00 – 85.00. Bases of sugar, celery, jam jar, etc. matches jam jar lid, and while panelled, is not frosted. Goblet now reproduced. *Rebecca at the Well compote $450.00. Reproduced in clear & color.*

No. 1920 – FROSTED RIBBON – L. 69 – M. 37. Clear and frosted of the 70s. Lighter in weight than the slightly earlier Ribbon, above. Footed sauce $10.00; spooner $35.00; relish $20.00; footed salt $15.00; egg cup $20.00; tumbler $25.00; open compotes $25.00; goblet $30.00; wine $65.00; champagne $55.00; celery $35.00; pitcher $65.00; covered jam jar $85.00; covered butter $55.00; creamer $45.00; covered sugar $50.00; covered compote $95.00. Non-flint as are all the Ribbon patterns. *Duncan, 1889.*

No. 1923 – FROSTED RIBBON, DOUBLE BARS – M. Bk. 2-43. Another form contemporary with Frosted Ribbon above. Goblet $30.00. *King & Sons, 1875.*

No. 1926 – DOUBLE RIBBON – L. 67 – M. 130 – K. Bk. 1-53. Frosted and clear, non-flint ribbon of the 70s. Footed sauces $10.00; spooner $35.00; flat or deep relish $15.00; open sugar $20.00; open compote $25.00; goblet $35.00; egg cup $15.00; creamer $45.00; covered butter $55.00; covered sugar $50.00; covered compote $60.00; *mug $75.00.*

No. 1927 – FLUTED RIBBON – L. 67. (Not pictured.) In this which quite closely resembles Frosted Ribbon, Double Bars, a contemporary, the frosted panel is divided into 4 small frosted sections, alternating with single clear panel. Erect pieces are flat; covered butter is dome resting on plate, with upturned edges. Flat sauce $80.00; spooner $25.00; sugar $20.00; vinegar or oil bottle $20.00; bowls $15.00; handled olive dish $15.00; oblong dishes $25.00; celery $25.00; cup and saucer $25.00; open compote $30.00; water bottle $45.00; 7", 9", 10" plates $20.00 – 30.00; creamer $30.00; covered butter $45.00; water pitcher $65.00; covered sugar $40.00; covered compotes $35.00 – 50.00. This ribbon is slightly later, probably the early 80s; non-flint, clear and frosted.

No. 1928 – DIAGONAL FROSTED RIBBON – M. Bk. 2-23. (Not pictured.) Very like Ribbon, in that while panels are frosted, feet are panelled but not frosted. Slightly rounded ribbons run diagonally, from narrow marginal line. I've seen goblet $30.00; celery $40.00; creamer $40.00; covered butter $45.00; and spooner $25.00. Should be other pieces.

No. 1929 – CLEAR RIBBON – L. 70 – M. 37 shows pattern as generally found with scalloped foot and on p. 79 shows it with round foot which is worth 20% less. Clear, non-flint of the 80s. The etched is in more demand. Prices quoted are for etched, without etching 10% less. Footed sauce $10.00; spooner $25.00; relish $20.00; open sugar $20.00; small cakestand $35.00; bread tray, on feet, with "Give us, etc." $25.00; open compote $25.00; creamer $25.00; covered butter $55.00; large cakestand $50.00; water pitcher $55.00; goblet $25.00; covered sugar $35.00; covered compote $55.00 – 75.00.

No. 1932 – FOOTED PANELLED RIB – L.V. 59. Non-flint of the late 80s. The interesting and identifying feature are the tiny feet. L.V. calls this PANEL AND RIB but it's so similar to another title that I'm adding a descriptive word. Tumbler, spooner, open sugar $12.00; creamer $20.00; covered butter $40.00; covered sugar $30.00.

No. 1935 – ZIPPER – L.V. 36 – M. 105. Clear, non-flint of the 80s, made by Richards and Hartley of Tarentum, Pa. Goblet $35.00; open sugar $25.00; celery $25.00; creamer $35.00; covered butter $55.00; covered sugar $35.00; covered compotes $40.00 – 80.00; many sizes, open compotes $50.00; water pitcher $55.00; covered jam jar $40.00. Finial is flat circle surrounded with row of large beads.

No. 1938 – SERRATED PRISM – M. Bk. 2-17. Late, non-flint of the 90s, but goblet is good simple design. Goblet $18.00.

1941
Clear Diagonal Band

1944
Diagonal Band

1947
Diagonal Band and Fan

1950
Diagonal Block Band

1953
Mitered
Diamond Point

1956
Mitered Prisms

1959
Mitered Frieze

1962
Spiral and Maltese Cross

No. 1941 – CLEAR DIAGONAL BAND – L. 156 – M. 112 – K. BK. 1-45. Clear and stippled, non-flint of the 80s. When I first wrote about this pattern six years ago, I complained that it was a step-child among collectors, who did not appreciate its reasonable prices and good lines. This is no longer true, it is even being used by non-collectors to mellow their modern. Flat sauce $7.00; footed sauce $20.00; spooner $25.00; open sugar $20.00; celery $30.00; wine $25.00; goblet $25.00; open compote $25.00; 7" plate $15.00; water pitcher $65.00; platter with "Eureka" $30.00; creamer $25.00; covered sugar $35.00; covered jam jar $40.00; covered compote $45.00 – 55.00. *OMN California.*

No. 1942 – STIPPLED BAR – L.V. 63. (Not pictured.) This is later, fussier but a few pieces combine well with above. This comes with red flashing which adds nothing to its value. *Not true in present time; red flashing 50% more.* Panels are vertical and are crossed with diagonal, clear panel; covers of butter and sugar are almost pagoda shaped. Values same as Clear Diagonal Band.

No. 1944 – DIAGONAL BAND – L. 140 – K. Bk. 7-8 – M. Bk. 2-71 calls it DIAGONAL BLOCK AND FAN. Clear, non-flint of the 80s, with the occasional colored piece being found. Flat sauce $5.00; spooner $25.00; oval relish $12.00; open sugar $20.00; goblet $30.00; wine $25.00; platter $20.00; creamer $25.00; butter $45.00; covered sugar $40.00; covered compote $50.00. *Amber 50% more, apple green 100% more.*

No. 1947 – DIAGONAL BAND AND FAN – L. 156 – M. 140. Good, clear-cut design of the early 80s. Footed sauce $14.00; wine $35.00; champagne $40.00; goblet $30.00; spooner $20.00; open sugar $20.00; open compote $25.00; celery $35.00; 6", 7", 8" plates $12.00 – 20.00; covered butter $40.00; creamer $35.00; covered sugar $35.00; covered compote $50.00.

No. 1950 – DIAGONAL BLOCK BAND – M. Bk. 2-71. Clear, non-flint of the 80s. Wine $20.00; goblet $25.00. *Other pieces not known.*

No. 1953 – MITERED DIAMOND POINTS – M. 68 – K. Bk. 2-33 calls it MITERED BARS. Clear, non-flint, made in Pittsburgh in the late 80s. Spooner $25.00; wine $30.00; goblet $27.00; open sugar $20.00; creamer $25.00; covered butter $45.00; covered sugar $35.00.

No. 1954 – MITERED DEWDROP – M. 39. (Not pictured.) In this the miters run horizontally instead of vertically as in its contemporary, Mitered Diamond Point, above. Same values.

No. 1956 – MITERED PRISMS – M. 68. Non-flint, of the mid 80s, made in Pittsburgh. Goblet $30.00; blue $45.00. Should be other pieces and other colors, too. *Cake stand $35.00. Aka: Trump, model, 1891.*

No. 1949 – MITERED FRIEZE – M. 50. Dr. Millard lists this as a member of the D. & B. family, but the shapes, the weight of the glass bear little resemblance to that group. Clear, non-flint of the early 80s. Pieces are large. Spooner $20.00; wine $25.00; goblet $20.00; open sugar $15.00; celery $35.00; creamer $25.00; covered butter $35.00; covered sugar $35.00; covered compote $40.00; open compote $20.00; water pitcher $35.00. *Aka: Eldorado, Columbia, 1888 U.S. Glass, 1891.*

No. 1962 – SPIRAL AND MALTESE CROSS – K. Bk. 1-30. Clear, non-flint of the mid 80s. Finials are the Maltese crosses. Creamer $25.00; covered sugar $35.00; covered butter $40.00; spooner $20.00. How do we tell the age of glass when we cannot find a dated catalog? Here is another crutch; in the late 60s and 70s we find acorn finials, often, as we go into the late 70s and 80s we find the Maltese cross common. By no means final, but an aid.

No. 1963 – WEDDING BELLS – K. Bk. 4-113. (Not pictured.) Design unit similar to Spiral and Maltese cross above only here scrolled lines run diagonally in a squat, heavy piece similar to Croesus. This was made in the early 1900s by the Fostoria Glass Co. in Moundsville, Va., and does not belong in Early American Glass lore, but there are those who cannot resist its colors, amethyst and green. I started this page with good, simple patterns and as it went on I included the later forms, hoping collectors will note the difference. Collectors should have more than pieces of glass as a result of their hobby, namely, growth in appreciation.

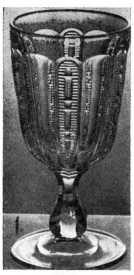

1965
Philadelphia

1968
Panelled Long Jewels

1971
Panelled Jewels

1974
Panelled Sawtooth

1977
Prism and Daisy Bar

1980
Duke

1983
Prism and Panelled
Rosettes

1986
Sedan

No. 1965 – PHILADELPHIA – L. 61. Clear, flint, made by the New England Glass Co. in the 60s. Sauce dish $15.00; spooner $35.00; bowls $25.00; open sugar $20.00; footed oval salt $12.00; egg cup $25.00; wine $50.00; celery $50.00; covered sugar $55.00; goblet $75.00; creamer $40.00; covered bowls $40.00; covered compotes $100.00.

No. 1968 – PANELLED LONG JEWELS – M. 48 calls this pattern by the name of the fine old flint above, so I've rechristened it. This is non-flint of the 80s. Goblet, clear, only $35.00.

No. 1971 – PANELLED JEWELS – M. 48. Non-flint of the 80s. Goblet clear $25.00; canary $50.00; amber $35.00; blue $50.00; *wine same.*

No. 1974 – PANELLED SAWTOOTH – M. 67 – K. Bk. 1-38 calls it FLUTED DIAMOND POINT. Clear, non-flint of the mid 80s. Wine $25.00; spooner $25.00; open sugar $20.00; goblet $40.00; celery $25.00; creamer $20.00; butter $40.00; covered sugar $45.00; large cakestand $45.00.

No. 1977 – PRISM AND DAISY BAR – M. Non-flint of the late 80s or early 90s. Clear, or clear with gilt. Wine $20.00; goblet $25.00.

No. 1978 – GROGAN – M. Bk. 2-98. (Not pictured.) Very like its contemporary Prism & Daisy Bar only this has the rows made up of fine cut instead of D. & B. type pattern; stem here has small ring at top and widens toward bottom. Wine $20.00; goblet $25.00.

No. 1980 – DUKE – M. 115. Non-flint of the late 80s. Clear, only. Collectible in sets but pieces besides goblets and wines are mediocre. Wine $20.00; goblet $25.00; spooner $20.00; open sugar $15.00; creamer $20.00; butter $35.00; covered sugar $35.00.

No. 1981 – TANDEM DIAMONDS AND THUMBPRINTS – M. Bk. 2-4. (Not pictured.) Contemporary of above; this is the same, only there is a row of small thumbprints between the rows of diamonds. Same value as above.

No. 1983 – PRISM AND PANELLED ROSETTES – M. 67. Clear, non-flint, contemporary of above two. Same values.

No. 1986 – SEDAN – M. Bk. 2-119 – K. Bk. 1-17 calls it PANELLED STAR AND BUTTON. Contemporary of above three patterns. Values the same. *Also found in purple slag glass, 200% more, milk glass, 50% more. Challinor & Taylor.*

No. 1987 – PANELLED ROSETTES – M. 163. (Not pictured.) Contemporary of above; this has the panels with rosettes, as above only this has clear panels between and not the little beaded rows. Here the stems are roped which adds about 20% to the value.

1989
Herringbone

1992
Panelled Herringbone

1995
Variance Panels

1998
Banded Variance Panels

2001
Colossus

2004
Diedre

2007
Needles and Pins

2010
Hooks and Eyes

No. 1989 – HERRINGBONE – L. 115, 121 – M. 83 – K. Bk. 7-75. Comparatively light weight, non-flint of the early 80s. Flat sauce $5.00; spooner $15.00; goblet $20.00; open sugar $12.00; covered butter $30.00; water pitcher $50.00; covered sugar $40.00.

No. 1990 – PRISM AND HERRINGBONE – M. Bk. 2-137. (Not pictured.) Herringbone rows run full length, after top clear band, alternating with clear panels. Contemporary of Herringbone; same values.

No. 1992 – PANELLED HERRINGBONE – M. 87 – L. 164 No. 1. Clear, emerald green, rather heavy, non-flint of the early 90s. Clear: goblet $40.00; spooner $30.00; open sugar $20.00; flat sauce $12.00; tumbler $25.00; oval relish $15.00; wine $35.00; bowls $15.00; creamer $25.00; covered butter $50.00; covered sugar $40.00. *OMN Florida. Milk glass is reproduction.*

No. 1992 – EMERALD GREEN HERRINGBONE – K. Bk. 1-47. In very heavy demand, attractive with brass or copper or Bennington pie plates. Flat sauce $18.00; spooner $45.00; 7" square plate $35.00; goblet $50.00; wine $60.00; square berry bowl $25.00; tumbler $40.00; covered sugar $55.00; creamer $50.00. Reproduced.

No. 1995 – VARIANCE PANELS – M. Bk. 2-91. Clear, non-flint of the 80s; found with gilt, red or purple tops. Goblet $25.00. *Red flashed 100% more.*

No. 1998 – BANDED VARIANCE PANELS – M. Bk. 2-148. I generally do not show the banded type of a pattern, but here the banded is not the same pattern as the plain; it's a contemporary of Variance Panels, however, with the same values.

No. 2001 – COLOSSUS – M. 105 – K. Bk. 4-57 calls it LACY SPIRAL. Attractive, non-flint of the mid 80s which should be better known. Spooner $30.00; relish $15.00; open sugar $15.00; flat sauce $7.00; water pitcher $50.00; open compote $25.00; creamer $30.00; butter $45.00; covered sugar $35.00; covered compote $40.00; goblet $35.00.

No. 2004 – DIEDRE – 164. Clear, non-flint of the 80s. Only goblet $35.00.

No. 2007 – NEEDLES AND PINS – M. 69. Another, clear, non-flint of the 80s. Only goblet $35.00.

No. 2010 – HOOKS AND EYES – Bk. 2-60. Clear, non-flint of the 80s; only goblet $40.00. What a nice set could be made by combining the last three patterns on this page.

AUTHENTIC VERSUS OLD

A pattern may be a reproduction and be authentic. That means it will have the details of the design as in the old but it may have been made yesterday and be authentic. I saw an ad in which a dealer quoted "Authentic Imports."

To protect yourself in mail buying specify, "Old and authentic." That means you will get an old piece and as additional protection to be certain you identify your pattern, use pattern numbers given in this book stating listing is from here.

Today collectors and dealers equate old and authentic. If one has an authentic piece, by definition it is old.

2013
Loop and Dart

2016
Loop and Dart with
Diamond Ornaments

2019
Loop and Dart with
Round Ornaments

2022
Leaf and Dart

2025
Loop with Fisheye

2028
Loop and Noose

2031
Double Loop and Dart

2034
Stippled Double Loop

No. 2013 – LOOP AND DART – L. 148, 149 – M. 42 – K. Bk. 8-4. Clear and stippled, non-flint of the late 60s and early 70s. Made in Pennsylvania. Pitchers of this group are attractive in shape and have applied handles. Flat sauce $8.00; footed sauce $15.00; spooner $30.00; relish $12.00; footed salt $25.00; egg cup $20.00; goblet $35.00; celery $35.00; butter $45.00; plate $30.00; creamer $45.00; covered sugar $50.00; pitcher $90.00; covered compote $75.00; footed tumbler $30.00; tumbler $25.00; open sugar $20.00. *Richards & Hartley.*

No. 2016 – LOOP AND DART WITH DIAMOND ORNAMENTS – L. 124, 148 – M. 41. Another of the same family; same values as above. In this the diamond ornaments can vary from an elongated diamond to a squarish one. Combining adds interest and variety.

No. 2019 – LOOP AND DART WITH ROUND ORNAMENT – L. 148, 149 – M. 42. Another of this family. Same values, flint 50% more.

No. 2022 – LEAF AND DART – L. 95, 149 – M. 42. Is sometimes called DOUBLE LEAF AND DART. Another of the same family with the same values.

No. 2025 – LOOP WITH FISHEYE – M. 41. Another of the same family. Same values.

No. 2028 – LOOP AND NOOSE – M. 41. Another of the same family with the same values.

No. 2031 – DOUBLE LOOP AND DART – L. 148 – M. 42 calls it DOUBLE LOOP. Another of the same family; same values.

Note: The seven patterns above are contemporary and one can see how their related shapes and texture would combine to make interesting settings. The pattern below is later, and while the design medium is related, it does not belong with the above.

No. 2034 – STIPPLED DOUBLE LOOP – L. 101 calls it DOUBLE LOOP but there is another pattern by that name. Note how the glass makers of the late 60s handled the seven patterns above; this pattern belongs to the late 80s. The creamer is squat and shapeless; the goblet is brilliant and the redeeming member of the family, it is scarce and in demand $40.00; spooner $20.00; creamer $25.00; covered butter $40.00.

WHAT CONSTITUTES A DEFECT?

Chips, cracks, stains, marked crookedness, faded or scratched color in color flashed glass are defects. Cracks at base of applied handles are a hard to find defect, but if you run your thumbnail along there, you will spot them. They are defects, even though they are heat cracks. In patterns such as Picket, with a serrated edge, roughness is apt to result when they are taken from the mold; this does not materially lower their value. Spots of unfused sand, bubbles, straw lines and very minor crookedness, the type that can only be discovered by minute examination, is not a defect. Reputable dealers specify defects and charge accordingly and are always willing to make good if anything slips by them.

"Heat cracks" or "Heat checks" have nothing to do with the manufacturing process, but are later damage to applied handles caused by a blow or lifting when full with no support.

2037
Egg in Sand

2040
Moose Eye in Sand

2043
Beaded Frog's Eye

2046
Lace

2049
Beaded Mirror

2052
Dewdrops in Points

2055
Arabesque

2058
Drapery

No. 2037 – EGG IN SAND – L.V. 67 – M. 141 – K. Bk. 3-71. Non-flint of the 80s. A few pieces in amber & blue $30.00; have been found, but most of it is clear. Flat sauce $7.00; spooner $20.00; open sugar $15.00; relish $15.00; goblet $30.00; wine $35.00; water pitcher $75.00; deep rectangular platters $20.00; cakestand $70.00; creamer $25.00; butter $60.00; pair of salt and pepper shakers $50.00; covered sugar $35.00; covered compote $40.00. Any color 100% more. *OMN: Bean.*

No. 2040 – MOOSE EYE IN SAND – M. 131. Clear, non-flint of the late 80s. (Why do you suppose Dr. Millard named this moose eye? I'll warrant he had a sense of humor; think of the fun he gave the world.) Only goblet $35.00.

No. 2042 – BEADED FROG'S EYE – M. 141. Clear, non-flint of the late 80s. Only goblet $35.00.

No. 2046 – LACE – L. 24 – M. 113. Clear, non-flint of the 80s. Only goblet $35.00. *Maker unknown.*

No. 2049 – BEADED MIRROR – L.V. 56 – M. Bk. 2-10 calls it BEADED MEDALLION. Attractive, non-flint made by the Boston and Sandwich Glass Co. in the late 60s or early 70s. Pitchers have applied handles, finials are acorns. Clear only. Flat sauce $8.00; spooner $25.00; relish $20.00; footed salt $25.00; goblet $30.00; egg cup $20.00; 6" plate $20.00; covered butter $45.00; covered sugar $40.00; creamer $35.00; covered compote $50.00. *Occasionally in flint.*

No. 2052 – DEWDROPS IN POINTS – L. 87 – M. 130 – L.V. 87 shows how pleasing a setting of this pattern can be. Non-flint of the 70s. Spooner $20.00; oval pickle $12.00; open sugar $15.00; flat sauce $7.00; footed sauce $10.00; open compote $25.00; water pitcher $65.00; creamer $30.00; butter $40.00; covered compote $50.00; covered sugar $35.00; large cakestand (this is most desirable, as it is rimless) $55.00; vine bordered, large plates $25.00; goblets $30.00; wine $20.00. *Plates seemingly most commonly found.*

No. 2053 – BEADED OVAL – M. 47. (Not pictured.) Clear, non-flint of the late 70s. Elongated ovals of stippling, edged with tiny beads, are arranged vertically around the goblet bowl and cover most of it. Only goblet $25.00.

No. 2054 – BEADED CIRCLE – L. V. 34. (Not pictured.) Flint made by Boston and Sandwich Glass Co., in the early 70s. Large circles, formed of dots, go round the center of the piece. Handles are applied. Scarce. Spooner $35.00; goblet $50.00; egg cup $30.00; mug with applied handle $75.00; creamer $100.00; covered sugar $110.00. WARNING – A pattern with a similar design of smaller beaded circles, and which is not ten years out of the dime stores is being offered as this fine, old pattern. In the late, the center of the circle is rounded, that is, the glass is convex. This late glass is very heavy, also.

No. 2055 – ARABESQUE – L. 121, 155 – M. 130 – K. Bk. 1-14. Clear, non-flint of the early 70s. Pitchers have applied handles $75.00; flat sauce $8.00; spooner $20.00; open compote $25.00; open sugar $15.00; goblet $35.00; covered butter $45.00; celery $35.00; creamer $30.00; covered sugar $35.00; covered compote $65.00. Covered compote especially pleasing.

No. 2047 – LACE CHECKERBOARD – (Not pictured.) M. Bk. 2-12 calls it CHECKERBOARD but there is another pattern by that name. Same as Lace above, only instead of ovals the insets in stippled background are diamonds. There are only two rows of diamonds as they are larger and fill the space. Goblet only $35.00.

No. 2058 – DRAPERY – L. 108, 121 – M. 133. Made by Doyle of Pittsburgh and at the Sandwich factory. Clear, non-flint of the 70s. Mrs. Lee shows creamer with molded handle, I've had it with lovely applied handle. In one goblet I've had, the stippling was made of tiny dots; one factory varied it, evidently. Flat sauce $7.00; spooner $20.00; goblet $35.00; egg cup $20.00; creamer, molded handle $25.00; applied handle $40.00; 6" plate $25.00; covered butter $45.00; covered sugar $40.00.

2061
Large Stippled Chain

2064
Stippled Chain

2067
Stippled Bowl

2070
Panelled
Stippled Bowl

2073
Snow Band

2076
Pleat and Panel

2079
Marquisette

2082
Stippled Dart and Balls

182

No. 2061 – LARGE STIPPLED CHAIN – M. Bk. 2-63. Millard calls it Stippled Chain but he has already used that title. Clear, non-flint of the 70s. Creamers have applied handles. Spooner $20.00; goblet $40.00; open sugar $30.00; creamer $40.00; covered sugar $50.00. There were probably other pieces.

No. 2064 – STIPPLED CHAIN – L. 190 No. 4 – L.V. 22 – M. 98. Clear, non-flint of the 70s. Pitchers have applied handles. Flat sauce $7.00; spooner $25.00; relish $15.00; footed salt $25.00; egg cup $20.00; goblet $30.00; covered butter $40.00; covered sugar $35.00; water pitcher $50.00.

No. 2067 – STIPPLED BOWL – M. 154. Clear, non-flint and flint of the 70s. Goblet $20.00; *egg cup $25.00.*

No. 2068 – ORANGE PEEL – M. 64. (Not pictured.) Same as its contemporary above, only slightly coarser texture in stippling. This may just have been another lot, with new mold, of above or another factory's interpretation of it. Goblet $20.00.

NOTE: If one fears the reproduction Shell and Tassel goblet or if one's purse won't allow them, these add to the four piece set; in fact the combination of these with the pattern is more pleasing as Shell and Tassel is quite "busy."

No. 2070 – PANELLED STIPPLED BOWL – M. Bk. 2-41 – L. 107 calls it STIPPLED BAND – K. Bk. 3-25. Clear, non-flint of the early 70s. Pitchers have applied handles, finials are acorns. Flat sauce $7.00; tumbler $20.00; footed salt $15.00; relish $12.00; open sugar $15.00; open compote $25.00; goblet $25.00; footed tumbler $25.00; celery $30.00; covered butter $45.00; creamer $30.00; covered sugar $35.00; covered compote $45.00; water pitcher $50.00.

No. 2071 – BANDED PANELLED STIPPLED BOWL – (Not pictured.) M. 72 calls this Stippled Band but it is the same as above, only this has the band of stippling above the pattern. Values the same as its contemporary which does not have the added band.

No. 2073 – SNOW BAND – M. 53 – L. 153 No. 1 – K. Bk. 2-45 calls it PUFFED BANDS. Clear, non-flint of early 80s; pitchers have molded handles. Flat sauce $6.00; spooner $20.00; relish $12.00; open sugar $15.00; wine $25.00; covered butter $35.00; creamer $35.00; goblet $25.00; open compote, covered sugar, covered compote $70.00. I've seen a creamer in this in a rather dark blue; any color rare, 60% more.

No. 2076 – PLEAT AND PANEL – L. 105, 111, 157, 158 – M. 66 – K. calls it Darby, its old trade name. Goblet comes in form pictured and in another slightly differing type, where the long coarse bars do not extend above the shorter row of prisms at the top. This latter type has never been reproduced. Pieces are squared, handles are molded as this is non-flint of the 70s. Flat sauce $12.00; footed or handled sauce $20.00; covered 4" sauce $25.00; spooner $45.00; relish $20.00; open sugar $35.00; rectangular platters, 6", 7" plates $20.00 – 25.00; goblets $45.00; wines, very rare $75.00; water pitcher $85.00; cakestand $90.00; pair salt and pepper shakers $85.00 – 95.00; covered sugar $75.00; covered butter $75.00; covered compote $90.00. One type goblet, 7" plate now copiously reproduced. *Bryce Bros. & U.S. Glass. Colors 200% more, blue, amber, amethyst, canary.*

No. 2079 – MARQUISETTE – L. 159 – M. 130 – K. Bk. 3-70. Clear, non-flint of the early 80s, made by Cooperative Flint Glass Co., of Beaver Falls, Pa. Shapes are that of a lovely chaliced flower, handles are applied and texture is that of the material for which it is so aptly named. Spooner and celery are ideal for vases. Flat sauce $8.00; spooner $20.00; open compote $25.00; celery $30.00; goblet $25.00; wine $30.00; champagne $35.00; open sugar $15.00; covered butter $45.00; creamer $25.00; covered sugar $35.00; covered compote $65.00; water pitcher $75.00.

No. 2082 – STIPPLED DART AND BALLS – M. Bk. 2-33. Clear, non-flint of th early 90s. Creamer, covered butter $45.00; covered sugar $40.00; goblet $35.00.

2085
Raindrop

2088
Burred Hobnail

2091
Thousand Eye

2094
Hundred Eye

2097
Gonterman

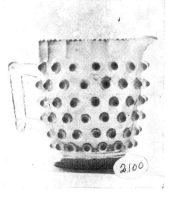

2100
Ruffled Edge Hobnail

No. 2085 – RAINDROP – L. 161. Non-flint of the 80s, comes in canary, clear, amber, blue and light green (scarce). The blue is fairly deep. I've never seen a goblet nor a tumbler, but a tumbler must exist. This pattern is the opposite of the well known Inverted Thumbprint for here the drops protrude and vary in size according to the size of the piece. In Thousand Eye the drops protrude but note the little diamonds between the globules. Bowls, footed, tall open compotes $20.00; flat sauce $5.00; footed sauce, finger bowls $20.00; oval relish $12.00; large handled plate $20.00; cup and saucer $25.00; syrup $45.00; large tray $25.00. Canary 70% more, amber 25% more, blue 50% more, green 70% more. One could combine Inverted Thumbprint goblets with this.

No. 2088 – BURRED HOBNAIL – M. Bk. 2 – 159. Note this is not Barred Hob. Late form of Hobnail, note the little burrs, tiny prisms, around the hobs. Goblet $25.00; covered butter $40.00; creamer $20.00; covered sugar $25.00; mug $20.00. *Canton Glass Co., found in white & blue opaque glass, 70% more.*

No. 2091 – THOUSAND EYE – L. 137, 146, 158 – M. 134 – K. Bk. 1-20. Remember that true Thousand Eye always has the little diamonds between the knobs. Non-flint of the early 80s, made in Pennsylvania, in the 80s. Comes in clear, yellow, light and dark amber, apple green, blue, opalescent and a scarce and very valuable opalescent blue. One type has some of the pieces with three knobs on the finials and on the stems; goblets and wines all come plain, without the knobs. The THREE KNOB THOUSAND EYE is worth approximately 20% more than the plain. Prices for plain stem. Flat sauce $7.00; footed sauce $10.00; toothpick $30.00; spooner $25.00; small mugs $20.00; small hat $30.00; tumbler $30.00; small square plates (all plates have folded corners) $20.00 – 30.00; twine holder $45.00; bowls $25.00; wine $35.00; goblet $30.00; celery in form of larger hat $35.00; platter $30.00; egg cup $20.00; water pitcher $75.00; large round or oval water tray $45.00; cakestand $75.00; syrup $65.00; lamps $95.00; covered honey dish $85.00; covered sugar $40.00; pair cologne bottles $65.00; covered butter $45.00; open compote $25.00; large square plate platter $30.00; round plate $20.00; alphabet edge $25.00; Christmas tree lights $25.00; match holder $25.00; covered compote $50.00; cruet $45.00; canary 50% more, light amber 25% more, blue 50% more. Reproductions in goblets, plates, mugs. *Adams & Co., Richards & Hartley, U.S. Glass.*

No. 2094 – HUNDRED EYE – M. Bk. 2-106. Clear, non-flint of the 90s. Only goblet $25.00.

No. 2097 – GONTERMAN – M. 71. Textured or frosted and amber, non-flint of the 80s; this attractive pattern has been taken for modern. I believe this shown to be a goblet (I've had a differing spooner) but I'm informed by a well-informed glass collector in Maryland that he has a goblet in this with a wide, plain band. Tumbler $45.00; open sugar $40.00; spooner $70.00; celery $85.00; water pitcher $200.00; goblet $350.00; creamer $125.00; covered sugar $150.00; covered butter $200.00; cakestand $125.00; toothpick $95.00. *Goblet rare.*

No. 2098 – KNOTTY ASH – M. 78. (Not pictured.) Contemporary of the late goblet above, only this has very much elongated globules which dwindle to a thick, short stem which is made up of elongated globules. Clear $30.00; dark green $60.00.

No. 2100 – RUFFLED EDGE HOBNAIL – L. 84. Non-flint of the 70s. Creamer $30.00; celery $35.00; finger bowl $25.00; covered butter $50.00; covered sugar (these are squat) $35.00; tumbler $20.00. Comes in amber 25% more; opalescent, shown, 50% more; opalescent blue 125% more, frosted with amber bands 100% more. Frequently found blown.

2103
Hobnail

2109
Fan Top Hobnail

2112
Barred Hobnail

2115
Panelled Hobnail

2118
Flattened Hobnail

2121
Knob Stem
Flattened Hobnail

2124
Printed Hobnail

2127
Umbilicated Hobnail

No. 2103 – HOBNAIL – L. 81 – M. 107 calls this HOB-NAIL – PLAIN STEM. There is a slightly later form of Hobnail goblet on a tall stem which has a ring at the top of the stem which narrows toward the base, but this latter type does not have the character and charm of the earlier type shown here. It is worth 20% less than the one shown here. I'm most proud of my collection of clear hob for it was its charm which won my family into an appreciation of old glass. Goblet shown is type I use. Individual salt dip $5.00; square or round master salt $10.00; toothpick $20.00; mug $15.00; oval relish $15.00; mustard, with either glass or metal top $25.00; deep rectangular relish dish $15.00; pair salt and pepper shakers, flat $40.00; same with thumbprint base $35.00; cakestand $75.00; syrup $75.00; 6", 7" plates $25.00; large water tray $25.00; flat sauce, plain edge, $8.00; collared base sauce with pointed top $15.00; large bowl with pointed top $45.00; finger bowl $20.00; thumbprint base $25.00; goblet $30.00; wine $20.00; 7, 8 row tumbler with hobs beneath base $20.00; 4 sizes of cruets, with hobnail stoppers $30.00 – 50.00; individual creamer $15.00; covered sugar $25.00; child's set: spooner $25.00; covered butter $40.00; covered sugar $35.00; creamer $25.00 each, entire set $150.00. There is a tiny miniature mug, which was used to measure out little red cinnamon candies in the early 1900s, not of old hob quality, but fun to use for cigarettes $5.00. In color, amber 25% more, blue 40% more. I use no color; the sparkle of the hobs is enough but I do combine with other form below. Hobnail now reproduced in clear and color. Those little colored salts seen in shops and those 8 row tumblers, some with fake pontils, are generally fakes. Dark green and that muddy amethyst were never made in the old. *Colors 20% more.*

No. 2104 – HOBNAIL – ORNAMENTED BAND – L. 82. (Not pictured.) With my plain hobnail I use the ornamented band type, which has a small dart band running horizontally around the top margin. Spooner $20.00; covered butter $35.00; creamer $25.00; covered sugar $30.00; celery $25.00; water pitcher $50.00; cup and saucer $35.00. Blue 60% more, *amber 25% more.*

No. 2105 – HOBNAIL – BALL FEET – L. 81. (Not pictured.) In the four piece table set there are more types of hob. This type has four little ball fee and printed top. Values same as for Hob – M. 107, above.

No. 2106 – HOBNAIL WITH SCALLOPED TOP AND FEET – (Not pictured.) In this one the scallops are not as full as in opalescent creamer, shown on previous page; feet are connected by scallops. Same values as Hob – M. 107, above.

No. 2107 – HOBNAIL ON FOUR FEET – L. 84 – (Not pictured.) This is a squared type with four little peg-like feet. Same values as above.

No. 2108 – BLOWN HOBNAIL – (Not pictured.) Generally found in clear or opalescent colors; bases are flat, with hobs and pontil mark (not a faked one). Large square or round flat sauce $10.00; large bowls, matching above $5.00; 10 row water tumbler $25.00; bulbous water pitcher $50.00; celery $30.00; clear yellow 75% more, opalescent yellow 100% more, opalescent 50% more, clear cranberry 200% more, opalescent cranberry 300 – 500% more, amber 50% more. NOW REPRODUCED, at times with fake pontils or with simulated pontil marks.

No. 2109 – FAN TOP HOBNAIL – L. 71, 83 – M. 18. Goblet in this is frequently found in jelly container type $20.00; in fine quality $30.00; rectangular platter $30.00; fine heavy, deep bowl $35.00. *Bowl reproduced, blue, amber, clear.*

No. 2112 – BARRED HOBNAIL – L.V. 56 – M. Bk. 2-83 – K. Bk. 1-110. A later type of hobnail, this belongs to the 90s and sometimes comes with frosted finish which does not alter value. Also found in goblet with thin stem, covered with hobs. Goblet $30.00; flat sauce $8.00; spooner $30.00; bowls $15.00; water pitcher $75.00; creamer $25.00; butter $45.00; covered sugar $40.00. *Amber frosted mustard $40.00. Two different forms in creamers, sugar, goblet.*

No. 2115 – PANELLED HOBNAIL – L. 84 – M. 33 – K. Bk. 1-67. Another of the later hobnail forms, late 80s or early 90s. Comes in clear, canary, amber, blue, and green. Hobs not as large or as brilliant as in the earlier types. Flat sauce $5.00; bowl $12.00; spooner $20.00; open sugar $20.00; small plate (erroneously called Toddy plates; these were found as bottom of wire basket used for calling cards) $12.00; wine $20.00; open compote $25.00; goblet $25.00; creamer $20.00; butter $35.00; covered sugar $30.00; covered compote $40.00. Amber 25% more, canary 50% more, blue or green 50% more.

No. 2118 – FLATTENED HOBNAIL – L. 71 – M. 33. Another of the later hobnail forms. Values same as Panelled Hob, above.

No. 2121 – KNOB STEM FLATTENED HOB – M. 33 calls this Printed Hob but that's an error, see below. Another of the late members of the family; values same as for Panelled Hobnail.

No. 2124 – PRINTED HOBNAIL – M. 33. Another of the late members of the family; values same as for Panelled Hobnail. *Covered mug in blue $50.00.*

No. 2127 – UMBILICATED HOBNAIL – M. Bk. 2-9. Really not a hob at all; here they are indentations like an umbilical. Prices same as for Panelled Hobnail.

2130
Dew and Raindrop

2133
Coin and Dewdrop

2137
Candlewick

2140
Popcorn

2143
Beaded Dewdrop

2146
Loop with Dewdrop

2149
One Hundred One

2152
Beaded
Oval and Scroll

No. 2130 – DEW AND RAINDROP – L. 57, 69 – M. 78 – K Bk. 4-113. Clear, non-flint made in the 1900s in Indiana in a cheaper grayed quality; the cheaper quality does not have the row of tiny dewdrops on the stem as the better one has. Prices given are for the good quality. Flat sauce $7.00; spooner $15.00; open sugar $15.00; berry bowl $20.00; creamer $20.00; tiny cordial $18.00; goblet $25.00; pair salt and pepper shakers $30.00; covered butter $35.00; water pitcher $40.00; wine $20.00; covered sugar $25.00. Goblets now reproduced in good type. *Federal Glass, Indiana Glass, Kokomo Glass. Stemware reproduced: goblet, wine, cordial without dewrop stem.*

No. 2133 – COIN AND DEWDROP – M. Bk. 2-62. Clear, non-flint of the 80s. Only goblet $18.00.

No. 2137 – CANDLEWICK – L.V. 31 – M Bk. 2-9 calls it COLE – K. Bk. 2-31 calls it BANDED RAINDROP. Clear non-flint of the 80s. There are a few rare pieces in milk glass, amber and opalescent blue. Flat sauce $10.00; spooner $30.00; open sugar $20.00; squared relish $15.00; wine $30.00; celery $35.00; bowls $20.00; cup and saucer $30.00; plates, some with turned edges $15.00 – 30.00; goblet $45.00 salt and pepper shakers $45.00; covered butter $50.00; covered sugar $45.00; covered compote $65.00. Colored 90% more, opalescent 100% more. *Milk glass reproduced.*

No. 2140 – POPCORN – L. 15, 71 – M. 73 – K. Bk. 8-19. Sparkling, non-flint of the 70s. Clear only; comes in two forms, one has lines of the ear, the other has the little ear standing out. Spooner $30.00; open sugar $25.00; wine $60.00; goblet $50.00; covered butter $65.00; covered sugar $50.00; with ears 30% more. *Pitcher $100.00.*

No. 2143 – BEADED DEWDROP – L. 57 – M. 119 – K. Bk. 7-46 uses its trade name, Wisconsin *(the preferred name today)*. Clear, non-flint with one form being made in Pittsburgh in the 80s and again, poorer quality made in Indiana in 1898. Sauce $10.00; toothpick $80.00; spooner $30.00; open sugar $20.00; handled relish $15.00; mustard $25.00; celery tray $30.00; wine $85.00; tumbler $30.00; sugar shaker $45.00; individual creamer or sugar $25.00; large bowls $20.00; vegetable or relish dish $15.00; large mug $30.00; oil or vinegar bottles $40.00; sizes of plates $25.00 – 35.00; cup and saucer $50.00; syrup $120.00; little covered bowls $30.00; goblet $75.00; covered sugar $85.00; large cakestand $65.00; pair salt and pepper shakers $45.00; condiment set $75.00; tall salt and pepper $50.00; horseradish, mustard $100.00; erect celery $40.00. *Banana stand $75.00; butter $95.00. U.S. Glass.*

No. 2146 – LOOP WITH DEWDROPS – L. 79 – M. 89 – K. Bk. 1-72. Plentiful, non-flint of the 90s; clear only. Flat sauce $5.00; footed sauce $7.00; spooner $25.00; 4 sizes of bowls $10.00 – 15.00; mug $18.00; relish $12.00; celery $30.00; cup and saucer $25.00; pickle jar $25.00; water pitcher $45.00; pair salt and pepper shakers $35.00; tumbler $20.00; wine $18.00; goblet $25.00; oval vegetable dishes $10.00 – 15.00; tall jelly compote $15.00; covered sugar $30.00; covered jelly compote $20.00; covered butter $30.00; covered compotes $35.00 – 45.00; creamer $20.00; syrup $45.00; condiment set on tray $50.00; cakestand small $35.00; large $45.00.

No. 2149 – ONE HUNDRED ONE – L. 72, 74-141 – M. 82 – K. Bk. 1-71. Clear non-flint of the late 70s. Goblets and wines now hard to find. Flat sauce $8.00; footed sauce $10.00; flat relish $15.00; spooner $25.00; open sugar $20.00; open compote $25.00; water pitcher $75.00; 7", 8", 9", plates $20.00 – 30.00; 11" plate, agriculture center $40.00; covered butter $50.00; goblet $65.00; celery $45.00; covered sugar $45.00; covered compote $65.00. *Goblet reproduced in clear and amber.*

No. 2152 – BEADED OVAL AND SCROLL – L. 77 – M. 119 – K. Bk. 1-61. Clear, non-flint of the mid 80s. Flat sauce $7.00; spooner $20.00; open sugar $15.00; bowls, relish $12.00; goblet $30.00; wine $20.00; open compote $25.00; pitcher, water $45.00; covered butter $40.00; covered sugar $35.00; covered compote $55.00.

2155
Dewdrop

2158
Panelled Dewdrop

2161
Beaded Panels

2164
Beaded Arch Panels

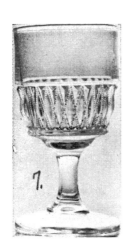

2167
Duquesne

2170
Beaded Dart Band

2173
Dewdrop Band

2176
Jewelled Drapery

No. 2155 – DEWDROP – L. 71 – M. 77. Non-flint of the 80s, made in clear, amber, canary and blue. Flat sauce dishes, 2 sizes $7.00; oval dish $10.00; spooner $20.00; double relish dish, has leaf between the two shallow sections $20.00; creamer $20.00; covered butter dish $35.00; open compote $20.00; open sugar $15.00; covered sugar $35.00; water pitcher $40.00; wine $20.00; goblet with plain base $25.00; with dewdrops on base $30.00. Canary 100% more; amber 25% more; blue 75% more.

No. 2156 – DEWDROPS WITH INVERTED THUMBPRINT – M. 70. (Not pictured.) Same as above only there is a row of inverted thumbprints above the dewdrops. Values same as plain goblet.

No. 2157 – DEWDROP WITH DIAMOND QUILTED TOP – M. Bk. 2-36. (Not pictured.) Another goblet, just the same as Dewdrop only this has a top of diamond quilted. These two contemporaries come in the colors, too. Values same as Dewdrop.

No. 2158 – PANELLED DEWDROP – L. 72, 75 – M. 123 – K. Bk. 5-31 – Bk. 7-11. Clear, non-flint of the late 70s; two types, with plain base and with rows of dewdrops on the base. Flat sauce $6.00; footed sauce $8.00; spooner $20.00; oval relish $12.00; open sugar $15.00; goblet $30.00; tumbler $25.00; small creamer $20.00; wine $25.00; celery $30.00; jam jar $35.00; platter "Give us etc.," $25.00; champagne $30.00; large tumbler with applied handle (lemonade) $40.00; large creamer $30.00; covered sugar $35.00; covered butter $40.00; goblet with dewdrops on base $35.00; covered cheese dish $60.00.

No. 2161 – BEADED PANELS – M. Bk. 2-96. Clear, non-flint of the 80s. Interesting stem. Only goblet $30.00.

No. 2164 – BEADED ARCHED PANELS – Hitherto unlisted. Goblet $35.00; *large and small mug $25.00. Dark blue 100% more.*

No. 2167 – DUQUESNE – M. Bk. 2-56. Rather light weight, non-flint geometric of the 80s. Only goblet $30.00. *Not to be confused with another Duquesne (Wheat & Barley).*

No. 2170 – BEADED DART BAND – M. Bk. 2-27. Clear, non-flint of the 80s. Goblet $35.00; ruby stained $75.00.

No. 2173 – DEWDROP BAND – M. 138. Another non-flint of the 80s. Goblet $25.00; *champagne $25.00.*

No. 2176 – JEWELLED DRAPERY – M. 138. Clear, non-flint of the 80s. Only goblet $35.00. Some of these non-flint geometrics may seem unimportant but if you will look at these last four you will note what an interesting service a collection of related ones could make.

2179
Loop and Jewel

2182
Lacy Dewdrop

2185
Jewel Band

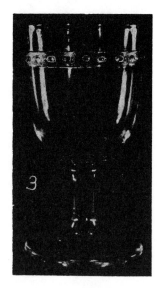

2188
Dot Band

2191
Sunburst

2194
Diamond and
Sunburst

2197
Plain
Sunburst

2200
Prism and
Diamond Band

No. 2179 – LOOP AND JEWEL – L.V. 27, 28 – M. Bk. 2-134 – K. Bk. 1-66 calls it JEWEL AND FESTOON. Non-flint, made in Ohio in the late 80s. Flat sauce $4.00; several sizes of bowls $10.00 – 18.00; spooner $20.00; sherbert cups $10.00; relish $12.00; goblet $25.00; water pitcher $45.00; plate $12.00; pair salt and pepper shakers $25.00; covered butter $30.00; covered sugar $25.00.

No. 2182 – LACY DEWDROP – L. 154 No. 1 – M. 93 – K. Bk. 3-108. Clear and milk white of the late 80s, made in Pennsylvania and then in Indiana in the *1900s*. Production has been almost continuous and seldom do we see a piece of the old, especially in the milk glass goblet, water pitcher and tumblers. Flat sauce $5.00; spooner $25.00; open sugar $20.00; mug $15.00; bowls $15.00; creamer $20.00; covered sugar $25.00; goblet $30.00. In milk glass 25% more. *Kansas preferred name today. Reproduced by Kemple in colors & milk glass.*

No. 2185 – JEWEL BAND – L.V. 30 – M. 24 – K. Bk. 2-29 calls it SCALLOPED TAPE. In 1951, I listed this as a little known, bargain patterns; it certainly has made friends. Medium weight, non-flint of the 80s of excellent design. Flat sauce $6.00; footed sauce $8.00; spooner $20.00; open sugar $15.00; relish $12.00; goblet $25.00; egg cup $15.00; wine $15.00; bread plate $18.00; covered butter $35.00; covered sugar $30.00; cakestand $45.00; water pitcher $50.00.

No. 2188 – DOT BAND – Hitherto unlisted. Clear, non-flint of the 80s. Good, simple chaste design, excellent choice for flowered or scenic china. Only goblet $20.00.

No. 2191 – SUNBURST – L. 12 – M. 77. Clear, non-flint of the 70s, rare pieces in color, the goblet shown is one of them, being amber. Handled sauce $8.00; spooner $15.00; open sugar $15.00; goblet $25.00; egg cup $20.00; double relish dish $20.00; celery $20.00; cakestand $35.00; 11" bread plate, "Give us etc.," $20.00; 6", 7", 11" plates $12.00 – 20.00. *OMN Peerless, Albany Glass.*

No. 2194 – DIAMOND AND SUNBURST – L. 78 – K. Bk. 1-15. Clear, non-flint of the late 60s. Flat sauce $6.00; spooner $25.00; footed salt $20.00; relish dish $12.00; individual butter pat $10.00; tumbler $25.00; goblet $30.00; egg cup $20.00; wine $25.00; open compote 25.00; celery $30.00; open sugar $15.00; syrup $45.00; covered butter $35.00; cakestand $40.00; creamer $25.00; applied handle, decanter $40.00; covered sugar $45.00; covered compote 40.00.

No. 2197 – PLAIN SUNBURST – M. 176 calls this one Diamond Sunburst – L.V. 33 calls this DIAMOND SUNBURST VARIANT. Clear, non-flint of the late 80s. Wine $15.00; goblet $20.00; creamer $15.00; covered butter $35.00; celery $18.00; spooner $18.00; flat sauce $5.00; platter $20.00. *Cruder than #2194.*

No. 2200 – PRISM AND DIAMOND BAND – M. 100. Clear, non-flint of the 80s. Pitchers have applied handles. Spooner $15.00; wine $12.00; goblet $20.00; creamer $20.00; butter $25.00; covered sugar $35.00; covered compote $40.00; celery $20.00; water pitcher $45.00.

2221
Loop and Pillar

2209
Beadle

2218
Celtic

2215
Diamond Horseshoe

2206
Radiant

2212
Pequot

2203
Pinwheel

2204
Coachman's Cape

No. 2203 – PINWHEEL – M. 100 – K. Bk. 4-140. Clear, non-flint, of the 90s. Kamm calls it CANNON BALL PINWHEEL. Pieces other than goblet of little value; imitation cut glass type.

No. 2206 – RADIANT – L.V. 70 – M. Bk. 2-50 calls it DYNAST. Non-flint, made in Ohio in the late 80s. Flat sauce $6.00; collared sauce $7.00; spooner $25.00; wine, tumbler $15.00 – 20.00; bowls $12.00; goblet $40.00; creamer $30.00; celery $35.00; open compote $25.00; covered butter $50.00; covered sugar $35.00; cake plate $40.00; pair salt and pepper shakers $35.00; syrup pitcher $40.00; covered compote $45.00. This pattern is so busy that etched is not as effective as the plain.

No. 2209 – BEADLE – M. 83 – K. Bk. 4-48 calls it SNOWSHOE. Contemporary of Radiant, above, same values.

No. 2212 – PEQUOT – M. Bk. 2-127. Non-flint of the late 1870s. Comes with gilt and colored tops. Colored top goblet $75.00; other values the same as Radiant. *Portland Glass, more value than Metz lists, 25 – 30% more.*

No. 2215 – DIAMOND HORSE SHOE – K. Bk. 2-110 – K. 8-59 and plates 61, 62, 63, 64. Clear, non-flint of the mid 90s made in Pennsylvania by the Greensburg Glass Co. & Brilliant. Many pieces; much better without etching. Flat sauce $10.00; footed sauce $15.00; oval olive $15.00; wine $25.00; tumbler $30.00; handled mug $25.00; spooner $25.00; open sugar $20.00; goblet $40.00; open compote $30.00; 10" bread tray, large star in the center with row of prisms and diamond $30.00; tray for wine set with rim of diamonds $40.00; water pitcher $50.00; covered butter $60.00; covered sugar $45.00; covered compote $65.00. *Ruby stain 100% more, cakestand $50.00; decanter $50.00; water tray $30.00. OMN Aurora.*

No. 2218 – CELTIC – M. Bk. 2-15. Clear, non-flint of the late 80s. Values same as Loop and Pillar below.

No. 221 – LOOP AND PILLAR – M. Bk. 2-44 – K. Bk. 1-104 calls it Panelled Jewel, a name which has been well know for years for another pattern. Attractive, though late, being non-flint of the 1900s. Comes with all kinds of enamel and colored decorations. Many pieces. Toothpick $55.00; flat sauce $10.00; footed sauce $15.00; punch cup, pretty flared cup with saucer $30.00; spooner $35.00; open sugar $25.00; relish, bowls $15.00; goblet $40.00; celery $45.00; covered butter $50.00 – 70.00; covered sugar $50.00. There is no difference in value between the large and small creamers and sugars. Candlestick $100.00; *with rose stain 100% more. Pitcher $50.00; children's items 100% more. OMN Michigan, preferred. U.S. Glass.*

No. 2204 – COACHMAN'S CAPE – M. Bk. 2-106. Clear, non-flint of the mid 80s. Comes in a very fine, clear quality but is frequently found in grayed, dull glass. For fine quality wine $20.00; goblet $30.00; grayed glass 40% of this. *Red flashed 50% more.*

PRIMITIVE WORK VS. CRUDITY

There are those who find it difficult to appreciate the primitive type of expression and distinguish it from the crudity of mass production. The primitive is an honest attempt at expression of ideas within one; that person may be a child or an unsophisticated, untutored adult. It is a direct outpouring of feeling an attempt to put an emotion into a concrete form, expecting no reward but their individual pleasure in the finished product. On the contrary, the poorly designed mass produced article is made the other way around — the profit motif is the first consideration and the maker tries to anticipate what the buyer would like; he tries to figure out something that can be produced quickly and cheaply and generally ends up with nothing but an expression of poor taste.

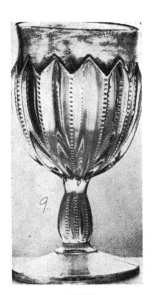

2227
Portland

2230
Banded Portland

2233
Beaded Coarse Bars

2236
Tulip Petals

2239
Diamond Shield

2241
Notched Bar

2244
Tapered Prisms

2247
Rounded Prisms

No. 227 – PORTLAND – M. 96 – K. Bk. 1-105. Non-flint of the 1900s, made in Pittsburgh, Ohio and Indiana. Could not have been made by Portland Glass Co., which operated only from 1867 to 1873; this is later glass which came with gilt, a characteristic of late 90s and early 1990s (remove this and one has a simple, well designed pattern) easily found and one which is at home in modern, traditional or casual surroundings. Comes in several sizes of pieces, is easily found, is relatively inexpensive and has not been reproduced. It is a bargain in the pattern glass field. Tray for boudoir set $12.00; candlesticks, candlesticks, pair $100.00; pair of pomade jars $40.00; powder box $30.00; ring stand are the only pieces not found too often $40.00. Flat sauce $8.00; oval flat sauce $12.00; oval or round, small or large spooner $20.00 – 30.00; individual creamers $15.00; open sugars $15.00; handled relish $12.00; oval pickle $12.00; long celeries $20.00; tall celeries $25.00; innumerable sizes of bowls $12.00 – 20.00; cups $12.00; cruets $35.00; pair salt and peppers $50.00; sardine dish $30.00; goblets $25.00; wine $25.00; sugar shaker $40.00; vases from tiny to 15" tall $25.00; glass lamps, tall $190.00 or flat 90.00; handled decanter $65.00; tankard water pitcher $100.00; covered butter $65.00; covered sugar $90.00; covered jam jar $65.00; covered jelly compote $35.00; footed punch bowl $200.00; covered compotes $45.00. Colored candle sticks $250.00 – 300.00 a pair.

In the words of the radio announcer: "What do you want to buy? What do you want to pay? Portland has it, everyday."

A misattribution to Portland Glass. Actually made by U.S. Glass in early 1900s. The gilding covers the entire body and seldom found in good condition, but good is highly collectibe, contrary to Mrs. Metz thoughts. Rarely found in canary or cobalt.

No. 2230 – BANDED PORTLAND – M. Bk. 2-9 – K. Bk. 2-89 calls it PORTLAND WITH DIAMOND POINT BAND. Contemporary of above, comes in almost as many pieces, but its values in everything but wine and goblet (which remain the same) are 10% higher. This comes with colors of not too clear a variety flashed on, either just below the banding, just above it or above and below it. For blue, yellow or gold flashing the values are 100% higher than Portland in every- :hing. *Aka Virginia, U.S. Glass.*

No. 2230 – MAIDEN BLUSH – L.V. 35. What won't a little color do. Imagine the boudoir set, pieces listed under Portland, brings $350.00 for the set and other pieces bring 100% – 200% of the price of plain Portland. *This is a color, rather than a different pattern.*

No. 2233 – BEADED COARSE BARS – M. Bk. 2-15. Contemporary of Portland; *slightly less value than Portland.*

No. 2236 – TULIP PETAL – M. Bk. 2-16 – K. Bk 4-115 and Bk. 6 pl. 28 – CHURCH WINDOWS. Clear, non-flint of 1903. Values less than Portland. *Also came the Maiden Blush 100% more.*

No. 2239 – DIAMOND SHIELD – M. 55. Clear, non-flint late 80s. Wine $20.00; goblet $25.00.

No. 2241 – NOTCHED BAR – M. Bk. 2-160 – K. Bk. 5-62 calls it BALL. This pattern was listed in McKee's catalog of 1894 which is probably the date when most of it was made; but in their catalog of 1917, 23 years later, they listed the cruet. It is possible that they found the old mold at the later date and reissued it, but is is also probable that old stock was found in a warehouse and marketed. In 1925, I knew of a case where old warehouses in Indiana divulged large stocks of glass, made 25 years previously. Goblet and wine are similar to earlier patterns; finial is a maltese cross, erect pieces are squatty and round, hence the name "Ball." Non-flint: wine $30.00; castor bottler $35.00; goblet $145.00; cruet $45.00; creamer $45.00; covered butter $95.00; covered sugar $95.00. Jam jar has wide ground stopper like candy jar $75.00; spooner $50.00; mug $70.00; *syrup $145.00; covered cheese dish $150.00. Canadian; "Nova Scotia Crown."*

No. 2244 – TAPERED PRISM – Clear, non-flint goblet of the 90s but has fine lines. Wine $20.00; goblet $25.00.

No. 2247 – ROUNDED PRISMS – Heretofore unlisted, non-flint of the late 80s. Only goblet $25.00.

2250
Flat Diamond

2253
Panelled Diamonds

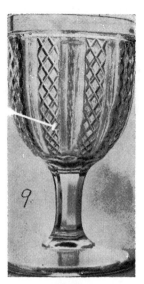

2256
Clear and
Diamond Panels

2259
Stars and Stripes

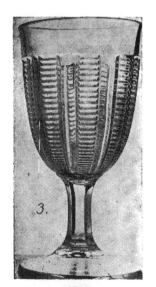

2262
Panelled Pleat

2265
Flame

2268
Panelled Zipper

2271
Zipper Slash

No. 2250 – FLAT DIAMOND – L.V. 32 – M. 59 calls it LIPPMAN. Clear, non-flint of the 70s; pitchers have applied handles. Flat sauce $4.00; goblet $20.00; celery $20.00; spooner $15.00; open sugar $10.00; covered butter $35.00; covered sugar, $30.00; creamer $20.00; wine $20.00.

No. 2251 – PANELLED DIAMOND POINT – L. 104. (Not pictured.) This could easily be confused with pattern above; only this is flint of the 60s and the panels of diamonds run to the top of pieces where they end in little fans which form scalloped edges. Goblet $13.50; wine $10.00. Scarce, not well known.

No. 2253 – PANELLED DIAMONDS – L. 164 No. 10 – M. 89. Clear, non-flint of the 80s. Only goblet.

No. 2256 – CLEAR AND DIAMOND PANELS – Heretofore unlisted. Non-flint of the 80s. Goblet $15.00; *wine $10.00. Quality is often poor, container glass.*

No. 2259 – STARS AND STRIPES – K. Bk. 2-70. Non-flint of the early 1900s. Goblet $12.50; other pieces mediocre. Creamer, covered butter, covered sugar. *Aka Mardi Gras (more common), U.S. Glass, 1898, also ruby flashed, 100% more.*

No. 2262 – PANELLED PLEAT – M. Bk. 2-42. Made by Robinson Glass Co., in Zanesville, Ohio, in 1894. Another of the late, non-flints which has the design of earlier glass. Spooner $15.00; goblet $20.00; creamer $20.00; covered butter $35.00; covered sugar $30.00.

No. 2265 – FLAME – M. 88. Another non-flint of the mind 80s. Wine $25.00; goblet $30.00.

No. 2268 – PANELLED ZIPPER – M. Bk. 2-139 and on 136 shows it in amber, so there are probably other colors. Clear goblet $30.00; amber goblet $45.00.

No. 2271 – ZIPPER SLASH – K. Bk. 3-83. Non-flint of the late 80s, clear and with top in yellow, sometimes found with souvenir markings. Wine $12.00; spooner $25.00; creamer $25.00; covered butter $45.00; covered sugar $35.00. Yellow 30% more.

THE OLD AND THE NEW LIVE TOGETHER

In the early days of our country, life was, by necessity, simple; products were functional; as a result, much that was good was produced in an unhurried, painstaking atmosphere. Later in our history, prosperity brought our adolescent "show-off" stage, the last of the Victorian period with its gaudy over ornamentation. We've grown up now, and our designers, young in years, at times, are mature in knowledge. Thoughtfully they seek the good of the old and combine it with the better of the new. New design in all fields is keyed to the old, frank, direct approach; the period approach is recognized as unnatural. The casual of one era blends with the casual of another; the formal of one age is at home with the formal of another time. There is good in all periods if we know how to find and use it.

2274
Banded Swirl

2277
Short Swirl

2280
Charleston Swirl

2283
Greenfield Swirl

2286
Jersey Swirl

2289
Panelled Swirl

2292
Left Swirl

2295
Swirl with
Beaded Band

200

No. 2274 – BANDED SWIRL – M. Bk. 2-105. Clear, non-flint of the 80s. Only goblet $25.00.

No. 2277 – SHORT SWIRL – M. 92. Non-flint of the 80s. In my edition of *Millard's Goblets,* there is a typographical error and the title of this and Short Teasel are interchanged. Only goblet $20.00.

No. 2280 – CHARLESTON SWIRL – M. 160. Clear and colored non-flint of the 80s. Amber goblet shown $25.00; clear $20.00; canary $35.00; blue $30.00.

No. 2283 – CHARLESTON SWIRL – M. 160. Clear and colored goblet of the 80s. Canary shown clear $20.00; amber $25.00; blue $35.00.

No. 2286 – JERSEY SWIRL – M. 28 – L. 69, 163 calls it SWIRL. Clear and colored, non-flint of the 80s. Salt dips $10.00; collared base sauce $10.00; cup $12.00; spooner, open sugar $20.00; wine $20.00; tumbler $15.00; open compote $20.00; celery, buttermilk (large) goblet $35.00; 6", 8", 10" plates $15.00 – 30.00; creamer, regular sized goblet, covered compote, cakestand $30.00; covered sugar $30.00; covered butter $35.00; canary 100% more, blue 75% or amber 25% more. Many, many reproductions in the colored, and in the clear goblets. *Windsor Glass.*

No. 2289 – PANELLED SWIRL – Hitherto unlisted. Non-flint of the 80s. I've seen a huge cakestand in this $55.00; goblet also large $35.00.

No. 2292 – LEFT SWIRL – M. Bk. 2-134. Clear, non-flint of the 80s. Goblet $20.00; *pitcher $35.00. Aka Cyclone.*

No. 2295 – SWIRL WITH BEADED BAND – M. Bk. 2-147. Clear, non-flint of the 80s. Only goblet $10.00.

No. 2296 – BEADED SWIRL – L.V. 41 – M. Bk. 2-79. (Not pictured.) The number of Swirl patterns is endless. This is a most interesting one in which the swirled bands are separated by strips of beads which go to top of most pieces except goblet and celery. Of the late 90s. The stem is prettily swirled its full length. Wine $15.00; spooner $20.00; open sugar $15.00; relish $12.00; tumbler $15.00; finger bowls $15.00; pair salt and pepper shakers $25.00; cruet $20.00; bowls $15.00; goblet $20.00; water pitcher $35.00; creamer $25.00; covered butter $35.00; syrup $40.00; cup and saucer $20.00; covered sugar $25.00; covered compote $35.00; cakestand $30.00.

No. 2297 – BEADED SWIRL WITH DISC BAND – M. Bk. 2-107. (Not pictured.) Contemporary of above. This is not quite as heavy and band of beads is more delicate; around the top of goblets and at top and bottom of erect pieces is a band of discs with a dot center. I have a salt shaker in this, stamped on bottom, "Hartman Furniture Co., Chicago, 1903." It was a Christmas advertising novelty given to customers. I've seen this combined with amber; the discs were amber, and in some cases the beads were amber. Values same as for Beaded Swirl above; with color 50% more.

2298
Grand Inverted
Thumbprint

2301
Stanley Inverted
Thumbprint

2304
Tegman Inverted
Thumbprint

2307
Ohio Inverted
Thumbprint

2316
Orion Inverted
Thumbprint

2319
Inverted Thumbprint
with Daisy Band

2313
Waterford Inverted
Thumbprint

2310
Ferguson Inverted
Thumbprint

No. 2307 – OHIO INVERTED THUMBPRINT – M. 169 – L. 161 No. 5. Clear and colored of the 80s. In this thumbprint the colors are fainter than in the others. Shape is lovely. Clear: wine $10.00; goblet $15.00. Canary 100% more; amber 25%, blue 75%, green 75% more.

No. 2304 – TEGMAN INVERTED THUMBPRINT – M. 170. Note this has stars between the thumbprints just as Inverted Thumbprint and Star does (shown with star patterns) but this latter pattern has angular bowl while this is rounded. Goblet: clear $15.00; canary $35.00; amber $25.00; blue $30.00.

No. 2301 – STANLEY INVERTED THUMBPRINT – M. 151 – L. 161 No. 3 – K. Bk. 1-87. Sugar, creamers, bowls, etc., are on little feet. Flat sauce $5.00; footed sauce $7.00; bowls $7.00; spooner $15.00; open sugar $12.00; creamer $20.00; covered butter $30.00; covered sugar $25.00; covered compote $35.00; open compote $20.00. Canary 100% more, amber $25.00; blue 75% more. Wine $12.00; goblet $18.00.

No. 2298 – GRAND INVERTED THUMBPRINT – M. 21. Clear and colored of the 80s. Goblet: clear $15.00; canary $30.00; amber $20.00; blue $25.00; *apple green $25.00.*

No. 2310 – FERGUSON INVERTED THUMBPRINT – M. 170 – L. 161 No. 2. Clear and colored goblet of the 80s. Clear, canary, amber, blue. This type of inverted thumbprint is copiously reproduced in colors. *Made by many factories, including Greentown.*

No. 2311 – BENNINTON INVERTED THUMBPRINT – M. 169. (Not pictured.) Same as Ferguson Inverted Thumbprint above with thumbprints going all the way to the edge, only here they are smaller. Same shape; same values.

No. 2313 – WATERFORD INVERTED THUMBPRINT – M. 151. Another clear and colored goblet of the 80s. Clear $15.00; canary $30.00; amber $20.00; blue $25.00.

No. 2305 – BLAZE INVERTED THUMBPRINT – M. 170. (Not pictured.) Same as Stanley Inverted Thumbprint, only in this the bowl is more flaring and the thumbprints are slightly farther apart. Same values as for Stanley.

No. 2316 – ORION INVERTED THUMBPRINT – L.V. 24 – M. 151. This type is slightly later, made in Indiana, 1893. The later we get, the more trimming we find. Many pieces; creamers, etc., have fancy fluted bases. Spooner $30.00; footed sauce $12.00; wine $15.00; open sugar $15.00; bowls $15.00; celery $30.00; goblet $30.00; round plate $15.00; platter $20.00; creamer $20.00; covered butter $35.00; open compote $30.00; covered sugar $35.00; covered compote $40.00. Yellow or opalescent 100% more; milk white, black 50% more; amber 20% more; blue 50% more; green 60% more.

No. 2319 – INVERTED THUMBPRINT WITH DAISY BAND – M. Bk. 2-57. Contemporary of above, and like it, comes in many pieces and colors. Dark green goblet pictured. Prices same as for its contemporary, Orion Thumbprint. K. Bk. 2-117 calls this HONEYCOMB WITH FLOWER RIM. *Aka (preferred) Vermont, U.S. Glass, 1890s. Toothpick widely reproduced. Goblet $45.00; covered sugar $65.00; creamer $40.00; toothpick $65.00. Pieces other than stemware have 3 feet. Emerald green 100% more.*

2322
Janssen

2325
Six Panel

2328
Long Bowl

2331
Very Tall

2334
Anheuser Busch "A"

2337
Inverted Prism

2340
Clear Amberino

2343
Tailored

No. 2322 – JANSSEN – M. Bk. 2-125. Clear, non-flint of the 80s. Only goblet $20.00.

No. 2325 – SIX PANEL – Hitherto unlisted. This and the three following are not collectors' items in but one sense of the word and that is to use them in the summer cottage or family room to collect compliments when tall, cold liquids are indicated. Of the the 80s or 90s, clear and non-flint $20.00.

No. 2328 – LONG BOWL – Hitherto unlisted. Yes, they could be used for flowers. $18.00.

No. 2331 – VERY TALL – Hitherto unlisted. There are more types of these; some have thumbprints. *Is identical in form to the Centennial Ale listed in book 2.* $25.00.

No. 2334 – ANHEUSER BUSCH "A" – M. 120. This has contemporary, Anheuser Busch, "Faust." Then there is the one with the dancing goat. Ale $100.00.

No. 2337 – INVERTED PRISM – M. 23. Clear and colored, non-flint of the 80s. Amber goblet shown $22.00; clear $18.00; yellow $30.00; blue $25.00.

No. 2340 – CLEAR AMBERINO – M. 75 calls this Amberino but because that is the name of a type of glass, clarification is needed. Only goblet, clear $15.00.

No. 2343 – TAILORED – Hitherto unlisted. Non-flint, clear, of the 80s. This and one above have good lines and could prevent table setting from becoming too busy if china, etc., had much pattern. Goblet $18.00; wine $10.00.

NOTE: All of the above are utility barware and various sizes of goblets are usually the only forms. Most factories made such glass ware, often indistinguishable from factory to factory.

ETCHED OR NON-ETCHED

Most patterns were made plain and with etching. I have tried to give no name to patterns in which the etching figured in the title; it is not wise to call a pattern by the etching because etching comes in so many forms; we find the bird or swamp life etched on patterns, at another time the same pattern will have the fern and berry etching, at another the maple leaf etching and then again a variety we have not seen before. Most patterns are as important non-etched but there are a few such as Dakota and Pineapple Stem where it adds to the value. I've made the discrimination in values where it applies; otherwise there is no difference.

We find many patterns frosted; again the same situation exists; for instance Art when frosted has no more value than the plain because there are more collectors for the plain, whereas in Blocked Arches the value is increased. I've noted these in the text.

2346
Prism and Clear
Panels

2349
Short Ribs

2352
Triple
Beaded Band

2355
Rib and Block

2358
Coarse Rib

2361
Lined Ribs

2364
Mioton Plain Stem

2367
Dodged Prisms

This is a page of simple, ribbed, non-flint patterns of the 80s. With scenic or flowered dishes, in a country cottage, or for the family room, these are practical. They can fit in with lovely period furnishings, happily; it's much better to combine sets. Most of these have other pieces and sample values would be: Sauces $6.00; spooner $15.00; open sugar $12.00; creamer $15.00; covered butter $20.00; covered sugar $15.00; wine $14.00; open compote $15.00; covered compote $25.00; goblet $20.00.

No. 2346 – PRISM AND CLEAR PANELS – M. 24.

No. 2349 – SHORT RIBS – M. 76.

No. 2352 – TRIPLE BEADED BAND – M. Bk. 2-139. This pattern 50% more than above listing in everything but goblets.

No. 2355 – RIB AND BLOCK – M. 2-128. This pattern 50% more than top listing in everything but goblets.

No. 2358 – COARSE RIB – M. 76. Note narrow lines between prisms.

No. 2361 – LINED RIBS – Hitherto unlisted. Another pattern with little lines between the ribs.

No. 2364 – MIOTION, PLAIN STEM. This has scalloped top at prism endings. M. Bk. 2-54 shows this with ringed stem.

No. 2367 – DODGED PRISMS – M. Bk. 2-125.

STUDY GROUPS

Many of the so-called "study groups" of our clubs are not study groups at all. They meet, listen to a lecturer (frequently selected for his fee or lack of fee) who tries to cover a subject in 60 minutes. Another week, another subject. I'd like to suggest another approach especially valuable for the group whose exchequer is small. Take a dreary day and use it preparing for an antique jaunt. Select an article from a magazine which pays recognized writers to write on their specialized field. Have a member read aloud a paragraph at a time and discuss it. Look up what standard texts have to say on the subject. Limit the discussion to a single pattern or a very few related patterns or topics, such as "mold marks." Then when you go out and buy an article from your trusted dealer ask him to answer a question or two or guide your reading. Remember, a dealer can't educate the entire community but we will be willing to help his customers.

2370
Bull's Eye
and Spearhead

2373
Spearhead

2376
Texas Bull's Eye

2379
Prism and
Bull's Eye

2382
Panelled "S"

2385
Oval Loop

2388
Haley's Comet

2391
Block and Circle

208

No. 2370 – BULL'S EYE AND SPEARHEAD – M. 45 – L.V. 47 calls it BULL'S EYE VARIATION. Clear, non-flint, made 1880 – 1890s. Spooner $25.00; wine $30.00; tumbler $25.00; castor bottle $30.00; egg cup $20.00; creamer $25.00; celery $30.00; night lamp $125.00; covered butter $40.00; decanter $45.00; covered sugar $60.00; open compote $40.00; covered compote $75.00; goblet $35.00. *Bellaire & Model, and U.S. Glass.*

No. 2373 – SPEARHEAD – M. 45. Clear, non-flint of the mid 80s. Values same as Bull's Eye and Spearhead. *Lookalike reproduced celery vase in clear and colors.*

No. 2376 – TEXAS BULL'S EYE – M. 156 – L. 50 calls it BULL'S EYE VARIANT. Has been known as Eyewinker, but another well known pattern has that name. Values the same as Bull's Eye and Spearhead. *Aka Filley.*

No. 2379 – PRISM AND BULL'S EYE – M. 63. Clear, non-flint of the mid 80s. Wine $20.00; spooner $30.00; open sugar $15.00; creamer $20.00; butter $30.00; covered sugar $25.00; goblet $25.00.

No. 2382 – PANELLED "S" – M. 88. Another good geometric of the 80s. Only goblet $25.00.

No. 2385 – OVAL LOOP – L.V. 44 – M. 14 calls it QUESTION MARK – K. Bk. 4-135. Clear, non-flint, made in Pennsylvania in the 80s. Footed sauce $7.00; many round and oval bowls $8.00 – 15.00; spooner $20.00; tumbler $25.00; wine $20.00; salt shaker $10.00; sugar shaker $35.00; celery $25.00; goblet $35.00; water pitcher $125.00; covered butter $35.00; creamer $20.00; covered sugar $25.00; covered compote $45.00.

No. 2388 – HALEY'S COMET – M. 164. Clear, non-flint; same values as its contemporary below.

No. 2389 – SNAIL – K. Bk. 2-69 and Bk. 7-123 or plate 23. L.V. 46 calls it COMPACT. (Not pictured.) Same as Haley's Comet above, only in Snail, all of the comet's tails run in the same direction, whereas in the comet one, they form a continuous line. In the Snail this continuous line is missing, each one is a separate unit. Individual salt $20.00; flat sauce $20.00; salt shaker $40.00; tumbler $40.00; cup $25.00; waste bowl $30.00; rose bowl $40.00 – 60.00; spooner $35.00; individual creamer $20.00; individual covered sugar $30.00; toothpick $40.00; bowls $20.00 – 35.00; sugar shaker $40.00; celery $35.00; cruet $100.00; 6", 7" plates $12.00 – 20.00; covered jelly compote, water pitcher, creamer, butter $65.00; syrup $125.00; covered sugar $70.00; covered cheese dish $120.00; wine $75.00; goblet $85.00; covered compote $60.00 – 120.00; *banana stand $160.00. George Duncan & Sons, later U.S. Glass, 100% – 200% more for ruby stain.*

No. 2390 – DOUBLE SNAIL – K. Bk. 5-93. (Not pictured.) *Two patterns are questionable, although Duncan & Sons lists a "Double Snail" as their pattern No. 2389.* Two rows of snails, meet in the middle of the piece; one set of tails goes to upper edge, the other set goes to the base. Same values as Snail, its contemporary.

No. 2391 – BLOCK AND CIRCLE – M. 113. Another one of the 80s. Only goblet $30.00.

No. 2392 – CIRCLE AND DOT – M. 101. (Not pictured.) Same as Block and Circle only the background space between top loop and center diamond is filled with little dots; stem has round knob, near top. Goblet $25.00.

2394
Jewelled Moon and Star

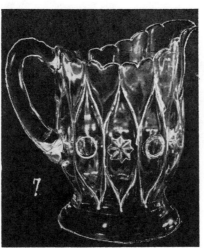

2406
Hearts of Loch Laven

2397
Moon and Star

2400
Art

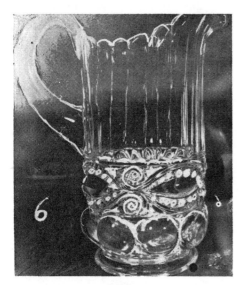

2412
Eyewinker

2409
Priscilla

2415
Big Block

No. 2394 – JEWELED MOON AND STAR – L.V. calls it MOON AND STAR VARIATION – M. Bk. 2-62 calls it MOON AND STAR WITH WAFFLE STEM. Comes with moons frosted as shown here and with clear moons; with the triangles and dots in blue or red or amber and blue or amber and red. Heavy, non-flint made in Ohio in the 90s. Prices quoted are for the amber and blue, with red and amber 50% more; all clear, with no color 30% less. Much in demand. Flat sauce $15.00; oval relish bowls $35.00; bowls, tumbler $35.00; open compotes $40.00; syrup $100.00; covered butter $65.00; covered sugar, covered jelly compote $60.00; pair salt and pepper shakers $70.00; celery $35.00; creamer $40.00; large water tray $85.00; water pitcher $75.00; cruet $60.00; covered large compote $85.00; wine or goblet $50.00; *cakestand $60.00. Cooperative Flint Glass Co.*

No. 2397 – MOON AND STAR – L. 69, 103 – M. 109 and 134 shows it again, with frosted moons – K. Bk. 1-80. Clear, or clear and frosted, non-flint, made in Pittsburgh in the 90s. The all-over colored and opalescent which are seen, are fakes. Kate Smith chose this as one of her patterns, because of her theme song, "When the moon comes over the mountain," word got around, prices skyrocketed and out came the fakes. After the rush of fad buying passed, the pattern returned to normal prices. Type with moons frosted is worth 30% more than these listed for all clear. Flat sauce, individual salt dips $10.00; many sizes of bowls, open sugar $25.00; oval pickle $20.00; spooner $35.00; footed sauce $15.00; covered butter $75.00; large rectangular tray $60.00; goblet $45.00; footed tumbler $35.00; covered bowl $40.00; large tray for water set $60.00; pair salt and pepper $50.00; claret $40.00; syrup $60.00; cheese dish $65.00; scarce cruet $75.00; covered compotes $50.00 – 100.00; cakestand $85.00; wine $45.00; creamer $45.00; covered sugar, covered bowls $60.00; egg cup $30.00; lamp, tall $150.00; many, many reproductions. *All solid colors are reproductions, amberina, avocado, opalescent, blue. Adams, Cooperative Flint, later, U.S. Glass . Ruby stain 100% more.*

No. 2400 – ART – L.V. 45 – M. 108 – K. Bk. 3-77. Heavy, clear, non-flint, made by Adams & Co., of Pittsburgh in the 80s and reissued by the U.S. Glass Co., in the early 90s. Flat sauce $10.00; footed sauce $15.00; relish $20.00; spooner $25.00; open sugar $20.00; open compote $45.00; celery, cruet $20.00; covered butter $65.00; creamer $40.00; covered sugar $65.00; covered compote $70.00; cakestand $60.00; wine $80.00; goblet $60.00; banana dish $90.00; *frosted diamonds 20% more.*

No. 2406 – HEARTS OF LOCH LAVEN – M. 30 – K. Bk. 8-24 calls it SHUTTLE (preferred). Made in two distinct qualities; we find many grayed wines and punch cups, values $10.00; but goblet and other pieces come only in fine clear glass or a few pieces of chocolate glass such as mug or tankard type creamer $75.00. Brilliant glass, wine $15.00; straight mug $25.00; spooner $35.00; open sugar $30.00; covered butter $150.00; pretty heart shaped edge, bulbous creamer $45.00; covered sugar $75.00; goblet (rare) $95.00. Made in Indiana in the late 90s. Chocolate 250% more. *Indiana Tumbler and Goblet (Greentown), rarely found in blue and chocolate. Rare wine in chocolate has sold for $1,200.00+.*

No. 2409 – PRISCILLA – L.V. 72 – M. 141 – K. Bk. 4-92. Late, brilliant, clear, non-flint, made by Dalzell, Gilmore and Leighton Co. in Findlay, Ohio, in the late 80s. There were other factories which made it, too, some was put out without the little lines around the moons. This was not the reproduction; there are MANY REPRODUCTIONS IN CLEAR, OPALESCENT AND SUCH COLORS AS WERE NEVER MADE ORIGINALLY. The fakes too have the moons with the little lines. Some forms of this were in Montgomery Ward's catalog of 1894. Has been known as STEELE and LATE MOON AND STAR. Flat sauce $8.00; toothpick $40.00; syrup $75.00; cup and saucer $25.00; mug $30.00; several types of relish dishes $20.00; spooner $30.00; bowls $25.00; open sugar $20.00; creamer $25.00; covered butter $45.00; covered jelly compote $40.00; cruet $40.00; cakestand $65.00; wine $30.00; goblet $40.00; open compote $40.00; rose bowl $35.00; celery $40.00; covered cracker jar, covered compote $60.00 – 75.00. With red dots 100% more.

No. 2412 – EYEWINKER – K. Bk. 5-76 and plate 39. Heavy, popular pattern, made in Findlay, Ohio, in the 90s. No goblet, but Cannon Ball or Atlas combine well. Finials are trimmed with balls. Many of the dishes have edges which turn in. Flat sauce $15.00; scalloped edge open compotes $50.00; plates $35.00 – 60.00; spooner $60.00; open sugar $45.00; syrup $125.00; tall lamp $200.00; bowls $35.00; covered sugar $125.00; covered butter $90.00; creamer $55.00; covered compote $60.00 – 150.00; banana dish $120.00; *pitcher $120.00. Reproduced in colors. Dalzell, Gilmore & Leighton.*

No. 2413 – BOW TIE – M. Bk. 2-5 – K. Bk. 6-plate 17. (Not pictured.) Non-flint made by Thompson Glass Co., Uniontown, Pa., in 1886. The goblet is covered with bow ties, or as has been said, airplane propellers arranged vertically so one has to turn the piece sideways to see what the pattern is; in the bowls, etc., there are two panels, plain at top, and two rosettes at bottom. The bowls in this are the heaviest pieces of glass I've ever seen. This pattern has been confused with Eyewinker, above; goblet $75.00; bowls $45.00; compotes $65.00 – 80.00. There should be other pieces, *spooner $45.00; large fruit bowl $150.00; cakestand $110.00; pitcher $80.00; covered butter $75.00.*

(Continued on Page 213)

2418
Diamond **Band**

2421
Fancy Diamonds

2424
Curved Brooch Bands

2427
Rabbit Tracks

2430
Ionia

2433
Swirl and Diamond

2437
Bar and Diamond

2440
Loop with
Stippled Panels

No. 2418 – DIAMOND BAND – M. 49. The first five goblets shown on this page are clear, non-flints of the late 80s and early 90s. The wine $20.00 and the goblet $30.00 are the desirable pieces in these patterns. The following pieces are mediocre in them and are not recommended: spooner $20.00; open sugar $15.00; bowls $10.00 – 15.00; creamer $15.00; covered butter $35.00; covered sugar $25.00. A setting of the differing goblets or wines can be very interesting.

No. 2421 – FANCY DIAMONDS – K. Bk. 4-74 calls it THREE-IN-ONE. See above. I've just noted a cracker jar, reproduced, in this in the gift shops. I wonder if the old mold were not found. *Reproductions also in vaseline.*

No. 2424 – CURVED BROOCH BANDS – Contemporary of BROOCH BANDS – M. Bk. 2-120 in which the design goes up beyond middle of the goblet bowl and is straight, not curved as this is. *Only goblet.*

No. 2421 – RABBIT TRACKS – M. 103. See its contemporary, Diamond Band above.

No. 2430 – IONIA – M. 137. See Diamond Band, at top.

No. 2431 – BELFAST – M. Bk. 2-60. (Not pictured.) Same as Ionia, above, only in this the little row of diamonds between arches is absent. Same values.

No. 2433 – SWIRL AND DIAMOND – K. Bk. 2-106 and Bk. 6, plate 11. Clear, non-flint, made in 1890 by Riverside Glass Co., at Wellsburg, W. Va. More interesting than many of the era. Flat sauce $8.00; bowl $20.00; relish $15.00; tumbler $30.00; open sugar $20.00; covered butter $40.00; footed, tankard water pitcher $40.00; creamer $25.00; covered sugar $30.00.

No. 2437 – BAR AND DIAMOND – L.V. 62 – M. 142 calls it KOKOMO by which name it has been well known – K. Bk. 3-84 calls it R. and H. SWIRL BAND. Made by Richards and Hartley in Tarentum, Pa., in the late 80s. Non-flint, clear, or clear with red flashed top. 2 sizes flat sauces $7.00; footed sauce $8.00; salt $12.00; spooner $20.00; tumbler $20.00; 4 sizes of dishes $6.00 – 12.00; sugar shaker $20.00; wine $15.00; goblet $30.00; salt $15.00; cruet $25.00; decanter $20.00; celery $15.00; hand lamp $85.00; condiment set $60.00; open compotes $25.00; bread plate $15.00; flat butter $20.00; water pitcher $45.00; footed covered butter $40.00; covered sugar $25.00; covered compote $40.00; ruby flashed 100% more.

No. 2440 – LOOP WITH STIPPLED PANEL – M. Bk. 2-44 – L.V. 27 calls it TEXAS. Comes in clear, or with red or gilt edge as many of its contemporary non-flint patterns of the early 1900s do. Toothpick $35.00; individual open sugar $15.00; sauce $10.00; large spooner $45.00; open sugar $20.00; bowls $15.00 – 30.00; footed salt $50.00; goblet $100.00; creamer $30.00; water pitcher $200.00; covered butter $75.00; covered sugar $75.00; cakestand $75.00; syrup $150.00. Color adds 100%. *Reproduced in small sugar and creamer, and others. Texas preferred name. Rose stain 60% more.*

No. 2441 – STIPPLED LOOP – M. Bk. 2-27. (Not pictured.) Same as its contemporary, Loop with Stippled Panels, above, only in this the stippled panels go up to within an inch of the rim. The goblet in this is narrower, with straighter sides. Values the same as for its contemporary. *U.S. Glass.*

(Continued from Page 211)
No. 2415 – BIG BLOCK – L.V. 70 calls it HENRIETTA. Another of the very heavy patterns, in non-flint of the 90s. A piece or two can make effective decor, more would be overpowering. Comes with blocks flashed in red and green also. Clear: sauce $10.00; cup and saucer $20.00; salt shaker $15.00; individual sugar $20.00; creamer $20.00; gas globe $15.00; spooner $15.00; tumbler $15.00; master salt $12.00; handled olive dish $15.00; open sugar $10.00; celery tray $20.00; covered mustard $25.00; rose jars $10.00 – 20.00; bowls $15.00; covered pickle $25.00; covered rose jar $30.00; sugar shaker $35.00; tankard water pitcher $45.00; covered sugar $30.00; covered butter $35.00; salt and pepper shaker in holder $35.00; large cakestand $40.00; platter $20.00. With red flashing 60% more. *U.S. Glass.*

2443
Bull's Eye
and Daisy

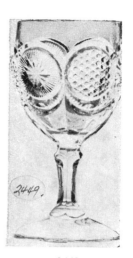

2446
Knobby
Bull's Eye

2449
Cane and Star
Medallion

2452
Bull's Eye and
Diamond Panels

2453
Bull's Eye
and Fan

2458
Paisley

2461
Cornucopia

2464
Hickman

2403
Heart with
Thumbprint

No. 2443 – BULL'S EYE AND DAISY – M. 166. A typographical error in Millard's GOBLETS caused endless confusion between this and goblet below; I hope this nomenclature will straighten it out. The goblets on this page are all members of the fussy families of the 1900s. The goblets and wines can be used to advantage in plain surroundings, but most of the other pieces are hopeless. For all clear; wine $15.00; goblet $20.00. *U.S. Glass. Colors of ruby, green and purple 100% more.*

No. 2446 – KNOBBY BULL'S EYE – M. 166. clear, and clear with gold, rose, green or amethyst eyes. See first on page for values.

No. 2449 – CANE AND STAR MEDALLION – M. Bk. 2-69. See first on page.

No. 2452 – BULL'S EYE AND DIAMOND PANELS – M. 109. See first on page.

No. 2459 – BULL'S EYE AND FAN – M. Bk. 2-141. See first on page; one shown is emerald green $40.00.

No. 2458 – PAISLEY – M. Bk. 2-83 and on plate 102 shows it with purple dots. See first on page.

No. 2461 – CORNUCOPIA – M. Bk. 2-69 – K. Bk. 4-72 calls it LIBERTY. See first on page.

No. 2464 – HICKMAN – M. 57 and on 112 calls the same patterns LA CLEDE. See first one on page. Pictured, emerald green goblet $70.00; relish $20.00.

No. 2403 – HEART WITH THUMBPRINT – L.V. 23 – K. Bk. 2-102 – M. 63 calls it BULL'S EYE IN HEART. For me, this is a much too busy pattern to be good design, but it is very popular because of heart motif. I have no right to try to change the feeling of the romantically inclined members of the collecting fraternity, so here goes: Flat sauce $15.00; heart shaped relish $25.00; handled olive dish $20.00; individual open sugar $15.00; toothpick, individual creamer $35.00; bowls $40.00; wine, goblet $65.00; med. plate $25.00; large plate $55.00; creamer $65.00; covered butter $85.00; covered sugar $85.00; *cakestand $125.00; cruet $90.00; syrup $80.00; ice bucket $65.00; banana boat $85.00; cordial $150.00; pitcher $200.00.* Ruby stained 200% more 1890. Rare in dark green, or cobalt blue, 100% more for these. *Tarentum Glass Co.*

UNIMPORTANT BUYS FROM
IMPORTANT DEALERS

Don't hesitate to go to the important dealer (that is, if there is such a thing as an important person) for a small purchase; you will probably find it there at a better price than in the shop where a good piece is a rare occurrence. If you respect the dealer's time, he will be glad to help with even a small purchase; in all probability, he is no economic royalist and will surely match your honesty and sincerity with the same. The novice shouldn't be afraid of those "at the top"; he needs the help of a seasoned dealer; and the right kind of dealer likes to teach his customers and watch them grow into informed collectors. Do you remember the story of the private, who in the darkness of the camp asked a passing buddy for a light. As General Pershing snapped on his lighter and saw the consternation and fright in the private's face, the general smiled and said, "Here, son, but watch out, I might have been the sergeant."

2467
Daisies in Oval Panels

2470
Blocked Arches

2473
Recessed Ovals

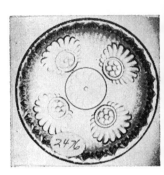

2476
Shell and Jewel

2479
Pointed Jewels

2482
Mitered Diamonds

2485
Dart

2488
Pannier

No. 2467 – DAISIES IN OVAL PANELS – M. Bk. 2-115 and same book, plate 92 shows the same thing, only with purple dots. K. Bk. 1-58 calls it BULL'S EYE AND FAN. Clear, sometimes combined with color, non-flint of the mid-90s. Flat sauce $8.00; spooner $15.00; bowls $12.00; open sugar $12.00; wine $20.00; goblet $25.00; creamer $25.00; butter $45.00; covered sugar $35.00. With colored dots in eyes 20% more. *Blue pitcher with gold $120.00; tumbler $50.00.*

No. 2470 – BLOCKED ARCHES – K. Bk. 6-24 and plate 32 – L.V. 45 calls it BERKELEY. Flat sauce $7.00; spooner $25.00; salt shaker $20.00; cup $20.00; tumbler $25.00; finger bowl $20.00; pair salt and pepper shakers $40.00; cup and saucer $40.00; cruet $40.00; bowl $15.00; goblet $35.00; wine $20.00; syrup jug $65.00; cracker jar (shown) $65.00; creamer $30.00; covered butter $40.00; covered sugar $35.00. Non-flint, clear, or clear and frosted made by U.S. Glass Co. in 1894. Though late, design is good, and with frosting, 25% more in value, it's most attractive.

No. 2473 – RECESSED OVALS – M. Bk. 2-65 – and shows the same thing on plate 91 and calls it RECESSED OVAL WITH BLOCK BAND – L.V. 38 calls it MELTON. Non-flint of the 70s; pitchers have applied handles. Flat sauce $60.00; spooner $18.00; wine $20.00; covered butter $35.00; covered sugar $30.00; creamer $20.00; goblet $25.00.

No. 2476 – SHELL AND JEWEL – L.V. 73, 75 – K. Bk. 1-68. Flat sauce shown and shells seem shortened in the picture, most pieces show a row of balls between the fans on the edge. Non-flint of the 90s, which comes in clear, stippled background, blue and a most peculiar luster-like blue green. Blue is worth 100% more than clear, other shade 50% – 100% more: 2 sizes flat sauces $10.00; tumbler $22.00; spooner $25.00; open sugar $15.00; creamer $35.00; small covered butter, open compote $20.00; covered sugar $35.00; covered butter $60.00; water tray $50.00; banana dish $85.00; water pitcher $45.00; no goblet. *Colors: sapphire blue, cobalt blue, light amber, emerald green. Two forms: round and pointed shells made by several companies: Westmoreland, Fostoria and Jefferson.*

No. 2479 – POINTED JEWEL – K. Bk. 1-95. Clear non-flint of the late 80s. Wine $25.00; goblet $35.00; *cup and saucer $25.00.* Other pieces mediocre. *Columbia Glass.*

No. 2482 – MITERED DIAMONDS – L.V. 31 – M. Bk. 2-35 calls it PYRAMID – K. Bk. 4-129 calls it SUNKEN BUTTONS. Four of the pyramids, such as shown on this platter, extend up the sides of the goblet and wine. Clear, canary, amber and blue, non-flint made in Ohio, in the late 80s. Flat sauce $7.00; footed sauce $10.00; salt shaker $15.00; relish $15.00; spooner $20.00; open sugar $15.00; creamer $25.00; pair salt and pepper shakers $70.00; platter $25.00; covered butter $35.00; goblet $25.00; wine $20.00; covered sugar $35.00; covered compote $40.00. Canary 100% more, amber $25% more, blue $75% more.

No. 2485 – DART – K. Bk. 3-4. Clear, non-flint, made in Ohio, in the 80s. Footed sauce $10.00; covered butter $35.00; creamer $25.00; covered sugar $30.00; goblet $25.00; spooner $20.00.

No. 2488 – PANNIER – M. Bk. 2-103. Clear, non-flint of the 80s. Only goblet $30.00.

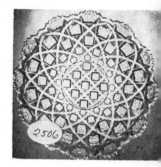

2491
Broughton

2494
Tobin

2512
Chain Thumbprints

2506
Bridle Rosettes

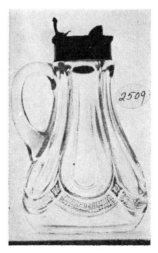

2503
Sawtoothed Honeycomb

2500
Thumbprint Pillows

2509
Galloway

2497
Pillow and Sunburst

No. 2491 – BROUGHTON – M. Bk. 2-79 – K. Bk. 2-121 calls it PATEE CROSS. Very late, non-flint. Goblet, clear $20.00; green $40.00. Other pieces mediocre, not worth collecting. *Toy pitcher $40.00; toy tumbler $15.00.*

No. 2494 – TOBIN – M. Bk. 2-136. Very late, the 90s. Goblet $25.00; wine $15.00.

No. 2497 – PILLOW AND SUNBURST – K. Bk. 1-100. Of the early 1900s, covered sugar.

No. 2500 – *Pictured is old flint pattern Four Petal.*

No. 2503 – SAWTOOTHED HONEYCOMB – K. Bk. 1-112. Another very late, late 90s. M. Bk. 2-94 calls it SERRATED BLOCK AND LOOP. Comes with red top, also. *Goblet $20.00; footed orange bowl $100.00; pitcher $50.00; syrup $50.00; toothpick $25.00; ruby stain 100% more; ruby toothpick $150.00.*

No. 2506 – BRIDLE ROSETTES – M. Bk. 2-15. Made in 1915 and now being put out in MANY FORMS IN NEW MILK GLASS. Goblet $30.00 or plate $20.00; in case you want to use glass mother (not even grandmother) had. *Celery $25.00.*

No. 2509 – GALLOWAY – M. 7 – K. Bk. 3-89 calls it VIRGINIA. Clear, non-flint of the 1900s. Flat sauce $8.00; toothpick $25.00; relish $12.00; spooner $20.00; bowls $15.00; wine $40.00; tumbler $30.00; individual creamer $25.00; individual covered sugar $45.00; goblet $75.00; creamer $30.00; syrup jug $70.00; covered butter $60.00; covered sugar $40.00; *punch bowl $175.00; under tray $100.00. U.S. Glass and Jefferson Glass. Rose stain 100% more, also in children's dishes, Galloway Aka Woodrow in Canada.*

No. 2512 – CHAIN THUMBPRINTS – K. Bk. 3-55 – M. Bk. 2-115 calls it THUMBPRINT WITH SERRATED BAR. Clear, non-flint of the the late 90s. Footed sauce $8.00; spooner $15.00; creamer $15.00; covered butter $30.00; covered sugar $30.00; water pitcher $35.00; goblet $20.00.

HOW OLD IS IT?

Old folks like to tell stories of "the good old days" and nostalgia rather than fact, dictates the details. We get many false stories of age of family heirlooms from old folks who think they are telling the truth. The old woman of 80 says, "That's 150 years old, it belonged to my grandmother who had it all her life." Let's check. The woman of 75 or 80 was born when her mother was 20 years old, and that would make the mother 95 if she were alive today; if she were born when her mother was 20 years old the grandmother of the old lady might be 115 or 120 years old now. But she acquired this piece when she was 40 years old that would have to be subtracted leaving the approximate age of the piece at 75 years. Give it the benefit of a few years difference in birth date or date of acquisition and one can see that in all probability the piece would date no later than 85 years earlier — a far cry from the 150 years claimed.

2515
Short Panelled
Diamonds

2519
Triple Triangle

2536
Fine Cut Bar

2524
Peacock Feather

2527
Esther

2530
Flower Flange

2521
Arched Ovals

2533
Flowered Scroll

No. 2115 – SHORT PANELLED DIAMONDS – M. 57 shows this with red top and calls it Panelled Diamonds – Red top but this is not the same as Panelled Diamonds hence the change. Clear goblet $25.00; with red top 50.00.

No. 2519 – TRIPLE TRIANGLE – L.V. 56 – M. Bk. 165 – K. Bk. 8-73. Medium weight, non-flint in the early 90s. Flat sauce $12.00; spooner $20.00; punch cup $10.00; mug $20.00; tumbler $25.00; creamer $20.00; wine $25.00; goblet $30.00; butter covered $35.00; covered sugar $40.00; pitcher $65.00. *Doyle, U.S. Glass. Ruby stain 100% more.*

No. 2521 – ARCHED OVALS – M. Bk. 2-80. Clear and clear, flashed with red. Clear: wine $15.00; goblet $20.00; wine $30.00; goblet $50.00; cakestand $35.00. *U.S. Glass, 1900.*

No. 2524 – PEACOCK FEATHER – L. 106. Clear, non-flint, late 90s. Not to be confused with old flint Sandwich product of same and similar names. Flat sauce $8.00; spooner $30.00; relish dish $15.00; tumbler $30.00; bowls $20.00; jelly compote, extremely rare $250.00; tall cruet $55.00; flat handled lamp $65.00; syrup $250.00; pair salt and pepper shaker, rare $150.00; open compote $35.00; covered sugar $45.00; tall lamp $150.00; water pitcher $75.00; large cakestand $75.00; cruet $40.00; covered compote $95.00; Lamps available in 5 sizes of lamps; *blue and amber lamps, $500.00.* No goblet. Extremely rare in color. *Miniature creamer $125.00; 18" shade $300.00. Aka Georgia, Richards and Hartly, 1890.*

No. 2527 – ESTHER – K. Bk. 5-54 and plates 12 and 36 – M. Bk. 2-114 calls it TOOTH AND CLAW. Made by riverside Glass Co., in Wellsburgh, W. Va., in 1896. Clear and a very popular emerald green, amber stain. Berry bowls have little feet and the design is inside, on the bottom of the bowl. Because of the importance of the green I'm quoting prices on it: sauce dish, little feet $20.00; toothpick $75.00; oval relish $25.00; open, scalloped edge compotes $65.00; cruets $150.00; syrup $175.00; tumbler $60.00; water pitcher $175.00; covered compote $125.00; spooner, open sugar $50.00; creamer $70.00; covered sugar $90.00. Clear 50% of this. *Celery $90.00; condiment set $350.00; amber stain same.*

No. 2528 – CROESUS – K. Bk. 4-112. (Not pictured.) I'll never know what started this pattern up the ladder, it's heavy, gaudy, awkward, and was made by the Riverside Glass Works in Wheeling, W. Va., in 1897. *Very limited supply, much in demand.* Prices are for green; toothpick, individual creamer, sauce dishes $75.00; tumbler $65.00; spooner $95.00; pair salt and pepper shakers $95.00; creamer $100.00; cruet $350.00; covered sugar $175.00, covered butter $195.00; water pitcher $400.00; celery $300.00. Amethyst 50% more and clear 25% of this. *Covered butter reproduced.*

No. 2530 – FLOWER FLANGE – K. Bk. 1-83. In *Thumbnail Sketches*, Mr. Brothers calls it DEWEY *(now preferred)* in whose honor it was named. Made at Greentown, Indiana, in the late 90s. Green, amber, or canary. Clear prices: flat sauces $40.00; spooner $70.00; open sugar $40.00; tumbler $75.00; creamer $50.00; covered sugar $100.00; pair of salt and pepper shakers $45.00. *Chocolate glass more, occasionally found in cobalt, milk glass, Nile green, large covered butter reproduced. Chocolate 150% more, green 20% more, canary 40% more, Nile green 100% more.*

No. 2533 – FLOWERED SCROLL – K. Bk. 6-plate 55 calls it Duncan 2000 as it was made by Duncan Glass Factory at Washington, Pa., in 1893. It is much sought after in the form in which the flowered scroll is colored, generally amber and I'm quoting for this type: tumbler $45.00; spooner $40.00; covered sugar $80.00; creamer $55.00; water pitcher $120.00; milk pitcher $100.00; covered butter $90.00. Clear, 50% of this.

No. 2536 – FINE CUT BAR – K. Bk 2-49. This is a late piece and I show it here because it is the pattern listed M. 142 as Viking and this has caused confusion, for of course, it is nothing like the older pattern known by that name. Creamer $20.00; goblet $30.00; wine $20.00.

2539
Daisy and Button
with Thumbprint

2542
Daisy and Button
with Crossbar

2545
Daisy and Button
with Flat Stem

2548
Double Panel
Daisy and Button

2551
Square
Daisy and Button

2554
Daisy and Button
Almond Band

2557
Daisy and Button
with Rimmed Oval Panel

2560
Hartley

DAISY AND BUTTON – L. Pages 167 to 171. Non-flint, made in many colors and forms from the early 80s to the first part of the 1900s. I've seen a stamp moistener with the patent date of 1882. Pieces with patent dates or "Patent pending" are not reproduced. REPRODUCTIONS ARE LEGION. THE WORST OF THE PITFALLS. Fakes are in all colors, including a horrible amberino and a muddy amethyst. We find REPRODUCTIONS IN TUMBLERS, CREAMERS, COVERED SUGARS, COMPOTES, ROUND AND SQUARE PLATES, SQUARE PLATE-LIKE DESSERT DISHES, CANOES, FANS, COAL HODS, GOBLETS, MATCH HOLDERS, SLIPPERS, SHOES, WHISK BROOMS, CUPS, SAUCERS, ETC., WITH BUTTER-FLY HANDLES. No pattern for a novice to collect; if you can't resist it, get it at a gift shop. There are many types; plain, cross-bar, V ornament, thumbprint or plain panels, and with heavy wide panels. There were many novelty and differing shapes such as butter tubs, the Sitz bath tubs shown here; there are those with inverted buttons with panels of darts or fine-cut, these later types never having been reproduced.

No. 2539 – DAISY & BUTTON WITH THUMBPRINT – M. 129. Comes all-over clear, amber, canary, blue, apple green and with thumbprint panels in amber, deep blue and red, the latter two very scarce. Flat sauces $10.00; footed sauce (square in this type, as are compotes, etc.) $15.00; spooner $25.00; mugs $20.00; celery $30.00; tumbler $25.00; goblet $30.00; creamer $25.00; butter $40.00; covered sugar $35.00; water pitcher $80.00. These prices for all clear; for all canary 100% more; for all blue 50% more, with amber thumbprint stripe 100% more; with deep blue or red stripe 150% more. *Adams & Co., pitcher & goblet reproduced.*

No. 2540 – AMBERETTE – This is the name used for the D. & B., when it is like above but has no thumbprint, just a plain stripe. In demand, *goblet $165.00; compote $350.00. Amberette is not identical to Daisy & Button with Thumbprint. The dividing panels are smaller, more convex and rise to top of large pieces. Clear panels are worth 50% more of amber stained ones.*

No. 2543 – PLAIN DAISY AND BUTTON VALUES – Flat sauces, round, square, clover leaf shape $12.00 – 15.00 depending on size and depth; spooner $30.00; open sugar $20.00; celery, flat $25.00; covered butter $75.00; water pitcher $125.00; covered sugar $45.00; open compote $35.00; covered compote $60.00; small round or square plate $15.00; fan relish

$20.00; whiskbroom relish $35.00; slipper $35.00; hat, small $40.00; dated hat, slipper, whiskbroom ("Patent Pending" counts as dating) $50.00; crescent shaped bone dishes $20.00; ice cream trays $70.00; large bulbous water pitchers, brilliant; unusual shapes in large bowls as shown, are considered rarities and have not been reproduced. Canary 100% more, amber 25% more, blue 50% more. *Ale $20.00; caster bottle $20.00; condiment set $125.00; toothpick $25.00; goblet $40.00; lamp $150.00; tumbler $25.00; wine $20.00.*

No. 2542 – DAISY AND BUTTON WITH CROSSBAR – M. Bk. 2-62. See plain D. & B. values 10% more.

No. 2542 – DAISY AND BUTTON WITH V ORNAMENT – (Not pictured.) Same as above, has V where above has crossbar. Value 10% more.

No. 2545 – DAISY AND BUTTON WITH FLAT STEM – M. 142. A later form, not a reproduction, demand for which keeps its values up to plain. Only goblet.

No. 2548 – DOUBLE PANEL DAISY AND BUTTON. Another of the later forms. Only goblet, Value same as plain. HERETOFORE unlisted.

No. 2551 – SQUARE DAISY AND BUTTON – M. 171. Of the later family.

No. 2554 – DAISY AND BUTTON, ALMOND BAND – M. 142. Member of the later family. Only goblet; same value as plain.

No. 2557 – DAISY AND BUTTON WITH RIMMED OVAL PANELS – L.V. 79 No. 12. Late member of the family. Value 10% less than Plain D. & B.

No. 2560 – HARTLEY – L. V. 42-M. 34 calls it D. & B. with Oval Panels but the design is that of Fine Cut – K. Bk. 1-69 calls it PANELLED DIAMOND CUT AND FAN. Non-flint of the 80s. Flat sauce $12.00; wine $40.00; open sugar $30.00; goblet $45.00; butter covered $50.00; creamer $40.00; open compote $35.00; water pitcher $90.00; covered sugar $50.00; covered compote $60.00; large cakestand $75.00. This is not reproduced. *Richards & Hartley, U.S. Glass. Hartley found in clear, yellow, amber and blue.*

2563
Daisy and Button Huge Oval Bowl

2566
Daisy and Button Large Octagonal Bowl

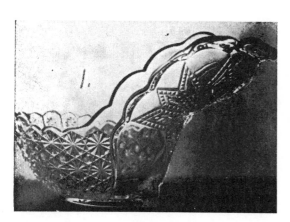

2569
Daisy and Button Sietz Bath Tub

2572
Pointed Panel
Daisy and Button

2590
Daisy and Button with Finecut Panels

No. 2563 – D. & B. HUGE OVAL BOWL – Here is a most unusual piece of this pattern, in a piece never reproduced. Canary yellow, it measures 9" x 12" by 6" deep, would be considered a rarity. In clear $75.00; in canary $140.00; in amber $100.00; in blue $120.00.

No. 2566 – D. & B. LARGE OCTAGONAL BOWL – Another, rare piece in this well known pattern, design deep and very brilliant; one shown is in a vibrant amber. Clear $60.00; canary $120.00; amber $75.00; blue $100.00. Dimensions 10" diameter, 5" deep.

No. 2569 – D. & B. SIETZ BATH TUB – A very rare novelty piece, which has never been reproduced. Bath tub $100.00; *blue $200.00; yellow $200.00; amber $150.00.*

No. 2572 – POINTED PANEL DAISY & BUTTON – L. 154 No. 15 – M. 34 calls it PANELLED DAISY AND BUTTON – K. Bk. 3-38 calls it QUEEN *(now preferred).* Clear and colored, made in 1894 by McKee Glass Co. of Jeannette, Pa. Inverted buttons. Sauce dish $10.00; spooner $30.00; open sugar $25.00; wine $25.00; goblet $35.00; creamer $30.00; covered butter $50.00; water pitcher $65.00; covered sugar $35.00; covered compote $45.00. Yellow 100% more, amber 25%, apple green 100% more; blue 75% more. *Cakestand and butter reproduced, by Mosser in vaseline.*

No. 2590 – D. & B. with FINECUT PANELS – Heretofore unlisted. Inverted buttons. Sauces and bowls are rectangular in shape. Never reproduced. I've not seen goblet or tumbler and would like to hear of them. Footed sauce $10.00; water pitcher $50.00; creamer $30.00; covered butter $40.00; covered sugar $35.00.

No. 2591 – D. & B. with PRISMS – K. Bk. 7-22. (Not pictured.) Contemporary of above; same shape, same values. Where the D. & B. with Finecut Panels has the finecut, this has a fancy, prism-like ornament extending down the panel. This has not been reproduced.

BEWARE OF THESE STATEMENTS

"I got it in an old home" or "I buy all my things from old homes." The old person may just have bought that D. & B. hat at the dime store as it reminded her of a childhood possession. Things may have been late gifts.

"This came from the Such and Such collection." Documentary evidence is necessary. If the owner were Mr. Beef Baron, he may have had more money than knowledge of antiques or taste in art.

"Very valuable because only five were made." In only very rare instances do we know how many were made or how many are now in existence.

"I'm going to let you have this at a bargain because I know you love it so." Dealers are sympathetic but how long could they stay in business if they operated on this basis. A winning smile has covered many a faulty transaction.

"There's a story attached to that piece, etc., etc." A dealer handling quantities of stock has little time to tell or collect stories; most of her merchandise comes from scouts and she knows not from where... she knows the article.

2599
Mephistopheles

2602
German Ale

2605
King

2608
Queen

2611
Sable Arche

2614
German Goblet

2617
French Goblet

2620
Waterford Goblet

FOREIGN GOBLETS – I think it very wise for a goblet collection to have a few foreign goblets as a basis of comparison.

No. 2599 – METHISTOPHELES – Millard's use of this as frontispiece sent collectors scurrying and prices soaring. Then it was publicized that this was a German ale glass and that they were plentiful on the continent. *In demand: goblet $65.00; pitcher $150.00; tall tumbler $60.00.*

No. 2602 – ALE GLASS – German, contemporary of above, non-flint $40.00.

No. 2605 – KING – Another German Ale; value $75.00; *pitcher $150.00; less frequently found than Queen.*

No. 2608 – QUEEN – Another German Ale, value $75.00; *pitcher $150.00. A prince and princess form is reported.*

No. 2611 – SABLE ARCHE – McKerin 138. McKerin shows this on the catalog page of the firm which was the representative of the Baccarat factory. It is dated 1840. Value $100.00. *Look-alike flint reproduction in clear and cobalt.*

No. 2614 – GERMAN GOBLET – Note coat of arms. Value only as specimen.

No. 2617 – FRENCH GOBLET – Later than the lacy Sable Arche.

No. 2620 – WATERFORD – This is the type our well-to-do neighbors of the British Isles used, while we used patterns ones which we pressed.

IT IS A MISTAKE TO THINK THAT:

Glass is fake because the dealer has a complete set of a pattern; fakers put them out one, three, five at a time. An established dealer frequently buys entire collections.

That a piece is a fake because your "pet" author has not listed it.

That a piece is old because it is chipped. Some fakes have been out years.

That everything displayed in a museum is valuable or is correctly labeled. A museum reflects life — our own museum has glass pieces which sell for less than $5.00. I recently saw a piece of glass which was in Montgomery Ward's catalog of 1915 listed as "Lacy Sandwich." They have no expert on glass and the woman who donated it had been victimized.

That a dealer's stock is valuable because she has such wonderful things in her own collection. Some very few make the trash bring in the cash, and fine pieces go into their own chests.

That a piece is valuable because you saw a similar one priced high. The slight difference may make the valuation difference or I've seen a dealer put a price of $125.00 on a pair of candlesticks to protect them till he found out what they were. They were worth less than $5.00.

BULK OR BEAUTY

Years ago, at the Chicago show, I saw a rare, choice piece of glass in the booth of one of our foremost authorities on blown glass. It was just the piece needed to give character to the collection of a doctor whose collection I was striving to improve. As soon as the doctor came in I led him to the piece, which incidentally, was reasonable priced. To my surprise and chagrin, he did not buy it. The other dealer, who at this time had more experience with the public than I, said, "Don't be surprised, he is just one of those people who likes to buy bulk." Since then I've learned how wise he was; it's so hard to explain why the tiny cordial may be worth more than the goblet and why the milk pitcher can be worth more than the creamer.

2575
Fans with Crossbar

2578
Atlanta

2581
Many Diamonds

2584
Balder

2587
Georgia Belle

2590
Medallion Sunburst

2593
Rexford

2596
Star Whorl

IMITATION CUT GLASS GROUP – This type of non-flint was made from the early 90s through the first part of the 1900s. Many came with colored or gilt tops; removal of gilt helps. Most had four piece table set plus many novelties. Neither in age nor character are they early American. Wines and goblets can be used in some situations, but other pieces are beyond the pale. Wines $12.50; goblets $12.50 – 15.00. In allover dark blue or green the color gives them 100% more value. When I look at this page, I'm reminded of an experience as a beginning teacher. I was bending over a child's desk, in an art class, trying to inspire a little lad and show him the possibilities in his design. In walked the principal, Mr. McGinty, a dear old soul who was noted for other things besides his art appreciation. His sense of duty told him he should get into the act and show the young teacher how to do it. Over to the desk he came and started to make meaningless scrolls as additions to the design. Then with a beaming smile, "Make it fancy, son, that's the way; trim it up," says he. How the workman of this type of late Victorian product loved to "make it fancy and trim it up."

No. 2575 – *CHAMPION* FANS WITH CROSSBARS – M. Bk. 2-90. *Goblet $35.00; compote $30.00; celery $35.00.* Not as bad as some, slight semblance of meaningful motif. *McKee.*

No. 2578 – ATLANTA – M. Bk. 2-63. *Goblet $25.00; wine $15.00.*

No. 2581 – MANY DIAMONDS – Another one.

No. 2584 – BALDER – M. 14. and in Bk. 2-67 the same is called KAMONI. *Preferred PENNSYLVANIA. U.S. Glass. Rare in emerald green or ruby stain.*

No. 2587 – GEORGIA BELLE – M. 56. Some semblance of design.

No. 2590 – MEDALLION SUNBURST – M. Bk. 2-114. *Bryce, Higbee, 1895. OMN: Banquet.*

No. 2593 – REXFORD – M. Bk. 2-63. Just another. *J.B. Higbee, full line of items, currently in demand. OMN: Alfa.*

No. 2596 – STAR WHORL – M. Bk. 2-90. I could go on indefinitely if I needed these to fill a book, but I don't. This ought to be a warning. *Aka JUNO, DOUBLE PINWHEEL, goblet $30.00; wine $20.00.*

Imitation cut patterns have a following and have increased in value since Metz's day. Prices are generally about the same for any pattern. Clear, non-gray glass preferred without sun-turned purple tint. General values are goblet $20.00 – 30.00; wine $15.00 – 20.00; butter $30.00; celery tray $15.00; sauce $5.00 – 10.00; cakestand $35.00; spooner $20.00; creamer $20.00; sugar $20.00 – 25.00.

2629
"Would Be" Sandwich

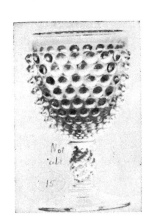

2632
New Hobnail

2626
Frosted Block

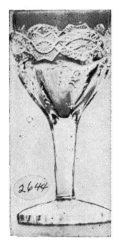

2644
Panelled Iris

2638
Iris

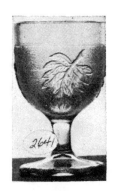

2641
Leaf Egg Cup

2635
Catawba Grape

NO! NO! A THOUSAND TIMES NO!

No. 2626 – FROSTED BLOCK – K. Bk. 3-26. Not old. First made for the dime stores about 30 years ago; comes in sticky pink, bilious green and clear in many pieces.

No. 2629 – "WOULD BE" Sandwich, still in the stores in the backwoods. Saw some in a recent small show labeled, "45 years old." Wonder how one could tell them from those out ten years ago. I can recall them 20 years ago, but not 45.

No. 2632 – NEW HOBNAIL GOBLET – Never was an old one like this. Improving on the fine, old ones, they put hobs on the stem.

No. 2635 – CATAWBA GRAPE – M. Bk. 2-89. In listing this, M. 89 states it is modern, yet I've seen more people victimized by this than by any other clear or milk glass. It was in the dime stores not too long ago and came in clear, all-over frosted tumblers, wines and water pitcher. Some gift shops still have it.

No. 2638 – IRIS & *HERRINGBONE* – Background has all-over rows of Herringbone and it takes a beautiful picture. In the dime stores in many pieces, goblets, wines, plates, pitchers of all sizes, covered sugars and covered butters, plates, etc. How is it that dealers don't see it there. Recently at a small show, a lovely person who has had a shop for about 15 years, displayed a set in which two were pink, two were blue, and two were yellow; all were a frosted glass. I can only say that evidently some are like the old lady who "had no use for book learning." *Not in current production, but in great demand.*

No. 2641 – LEAF EGG CUP – These are as thick as dandelions around here. Never was an old one like them. Again, they take a good picture. Many times, novice dealers have brought them to me to identify. I've told them and at times I've seen them continued in the shop or at the show at a price of $10.00. *Some made by Greentown, container ware.*

No. 2644 – PANELLED IRIS – M. Bk. 2-48. I know some patterns of the 80s were continued at later dates, namely after U.S. Glass Co. was formed by a merger; I know that Ashburton was made for 30 years but when one sees a pattern listed in a 1915 catalog listing, especially when it has no characteristics of the 80s, it's difficult to accept that as the date.

If you still like these No! No!'s you should have them, but please don't pay the prices of early glass for them. when you protest to the dealer who offers them to you, you will probably hear, "That Metz woman doesn't know everything about old glass." The dealer is telling the stark truth; so agree and smile sweetly. You know one can't teach, without learning, and can't learn without teaching. What happened when Americans, especially scholars and leaders became too cocky? Sputnik appeared in the skies. What are we Americans doing about it? Polishing up our sense of humility, honesty and humor and resolving to do better. That goes for all Americans, antique collectors, dealers and writers — and it's fun! *What was current with Metz is now collectible with many, but still is not considered EAPG.*

SIZE GROUPS FOR COMPARISON

GROUP 1. No. 1—LADY'S GOBLET in Squared Ashburton. No. 2—REGULAR GOBLET in Excelsior. No. 3—REGULAR GOBLET in Finecut and Block. No. 4—BUTTERMILK GOBLET in Finecut and Block. No. 5—SO-CALLED BUTTERMILK GOBLET in Stippled Panel is really an OPEN SUGAR.

GROUP 2. No. 1—FOOTED MASTER SALT in Barberry. No. 2—FOOTED MASTER SALT in Tulip and Sawtooth. No. 3—FOOTED MASTER SALT in Eureka. No. 4—EGG CUP in Sunburst. No. 5—DOUBLE EGG CUP in Hercules Pillar.

GROUP 3. No. 1—REGULAR SIZED WINE in Ashburton. No. 2—LARGE WINE in Ashburton. No. 3—CLARET in Pillar. No. 4—HANDLED WHISKEY in Belted Worcester.

GROUP 5. No. 1—Tiny CORDIAL in Panelled Nightshade. No. 2—Regular sized WINE in Popcorn. No. 3—CHAMPAGNE in Stippled Peppers. No. 4—FOOTED TUMBLER in Stippled Peppers. No. 5—Regular TUMBLER in Pineapple Stem.

INDEX

INDEX (Cont)

INDEX (Cont)

INDEX (Cont)

INDEX (Cont)

INDEX (Cont)